The Potsdam Tradition

W. Charles Lahey

THE POTSDAM
TRADITION

A History and a Challenge

Appleton-Century-Crofts

Division of Meredith Publishing Company, New York

Contents

Illustrations

Foreword

The Potsdam Tradition—A History and a Challenge is the sesquicentennial history of a college that has played an important role in American education. It pioneered in the preparation of "common" (public) school teachers in New York State and public school music teachers in the United States.

The story is based on the assumption that the history of a college is an integral part of the history of a society that is being continually altered. These same forces exist on the college campus and challenge education. A college is molded by the tests it meets and its record becomes its living tradition. Such is the story of the Potsdam tradition. Emphasis is placed on individuals and programs that are relevant to this theme.

This story could not have been written had it not been for the help of many persons. Special credit is due Thomas P. North, Jr., who edited the entire manuscript; Dr. William D. Claudson for his collaboration on Chapters Six, Seven and Eight; Professor Earl G. Houston for checking authenticity of the manuscript; Dr. Thomas M. Barrington for his critical comments and suggestions on the manuscript. Special thanks is due to Dr. Roger C. Greer and his staff at the college library and to the staff of the Potsdam Museum, who put at my disposal all relevant materials.

W. Charles Lahey

Potsdam, New York
1965

The Potsdam Tradition

Chapter One

THE FORMATIVE YEARS

Smoke from a burning foller drifted over the hamlet of Potsdam, New York. Eight men sauntered into a frame building on Union Place. It was past midday on September 17, 1816. In a few minutes they emerged and walked over to Benjamin Raymond's land office on the banks of the Racquette River. It was late in the afternoon when they departed.

St. Lawrence Academy, eventually to become the State University College at Potsdam, New York, was officially launched by this meeting of the Board of Trustees. This was the first in a series of almost daily meetings. They got down to business immediately. Benjamin Raymond was elected chairman; Sewall Raymond, clerk; and Liberty Knowles, treasurer. Other board members in attendance were: Pierce Shepard, Azel Lyman, Joseph Reynolds, Robert McChesney and Russell Atwater. Absent were David Parish, Nathan Ford, Louis Hasbrouck, Roswell Hopkins and Ebenezer Hulburd.[1]

Time was short. Many problems had to be solved if school was to be opened on September 30. Finances, staff, curriculum, student recruitment and regulations and numerous other problems faced the board. The state did not require any community to establish an academy, therefore the local board had to rely on local initiative and resources.

The Board of Regents had invested the Board of Trustees with adequate powers to cope with these problems. As a corporate unit, the trustees were a self-perpetuating body. They had charge of the property and revenue of the Academy and could fix tuition rates, appoint and discharge teachers and other personnel. They could prescribe the courses of instruction, establish admission requirements and promulgate student regulations.[2]

Much was accomplished in those September meetings. Financial support for the Academy was the first order of business. A four-man committee was appointed to handle the literature lot granted to the Academy for partial support.[3] Members were instructed to survey lots and the necessary roads. As soon as possible, they were to lease the lots, not to exceed 60 acres for more than 14 years. Annual rent was fixed at one peck of wheat per acre, but the first one or two years were rent free.[4]

The most immediate source of income would be the tuition fees. At their first meeting the trustees fixed the following fees for each quarter:

Reading and Writing $2.50
English grammar, cyphering, mathematics
   and bookkeeping 3.00
Dead languages 3.50
Logic, rhetoric, composition, moral
   philosophy, natural philosophy and
   French .... 4.00[5]

Two other financial decisions were made. A value of $500 was placed on the Academy lot and building. A more perplexing problem was the collection of subscriptions pledged at an earlier date. Now that the school was an actuality the money could be used. The trustees passed a resolution making subscriptions payable on September 25, 1816. If payment could not be made interest was payable semiannually.[6]

Bylaws were adopted by the board on September 30, 1816.

They included the following:

1. Candidates for admission into this Academy shall apply to the preceptor who shall admit none but such as can stand in a class and read in plain English readings.
3. Every member of this institution shall regularly and seasonably attend public worship on the Sabbath Day and shall abstain from all diversions, business, visiting and walking and all disorderly and unbecoming behaviour on that day.
4. All students shall on the evening next preceding and succeeding the Sabbath Day abstain from all such diversions as may tend to disturb those who religiously observe either of those evenings.
5. Any student who shall propose to attend steadily on the service of any other regular Christian society than that where the preceptor attends shall (if above the age of 21 years) signify such desire in writing to the preceptor and, if under the age of 21 years, shall procure such writing from his or her parent or guardian.
6. No scholar shall be guilty of indecent or immoral conduct, drunkenness, blasphemy, profane swearing, lying, stealing, playing at games for hazard or making tumultuous noises to the dishonor or disturbance of the Academy or to the disturbance of the village.
8. No student shall be absent from his or her boarding house after nine o'clock at night.
10. There shall be annually four public examinations before the preceptor and trustees and such other persons as may please to attend. The examinations shall be on Tuesday next preceding the expiration of each quarter.
12. All damage done to buildings or other property belonging to the Academy shall be paid by the scholar who shall have done it if he can be found; if not each scholar shall pay an equal proportion.
15. The preceptor shall be charged with the execution of the foregoing laws and may adopt and use such rules and regulations for the internal government of the Academy as he shall from time to time think proper and consider to the improvement of the students and for enforcing such laws and regulations he may,

when milder measures fail, proceed to suspension or dismission, provided however if any student shall think himself aggrieved by the decision of the preceptor he may appeal to the standing committee.[7]

Trustees of St. Lawrence Academy had authority to prescribe courses of study. The state law of 1787, Magna Carta of academies, had invested all local boards with this power. Even though the Board of Regents was placed in control of all academies by this 1787 law, the law did not prescribe a curriculum or designate any required subjects. It was clear in this law, however, that the Regents had power over the curriculum and could exercise it at their discretion. Once the local trustees had adopted a curriculum, they had to submit it to the Regents for ratification and revision. The Regents were also required to visit and inspect the academies.[8]

In 1816 there was still no prescribed curriculum nor designated subjects. The trustees formulated the following curriculum, and it was approved by the Regents. The curriculum was organized into two divisions: the classical, or Latin, and the English. It was the traditional course of study in early academies.

Classical	*English*
Dead languages (Latin-Greek)	Reading
Mathematics	Writing
Logic	English grammar
Rhetoric	Cyphering
Moral philosophy	Bookkeeping
Natural philosophy	French
Geography	Composition [9]

On September 30, 1816, Nahum Nixon, preceptor and only teacher, opened the St. Lawrence Academy to a class of 42 students. Twelve studied reading and writing, seventeen English grammar and cyphering, ten mathematics, geography and composition, and three dead languages. In addition to tuition, the students paid an average of $2.50 per week for board and room in local homes.[10]

To explain the founding of St. Lawrence Academy by the mere coincidence of men, local initiative and state supervision is like explaining whiskey in terms of corn, copper and coopers. A cultural terrain lay beneath this educational phenomenon and provided the inner dynamisms for the establishment of the school.

The initiative for the Academy rested with men in a frontier environment. Frederick Jackson Turner has labeled this phenomenon a rebirth of American institutions. The need for the school rested on an emerging capitalistic, industrial mobility that would utilize science and technology to produce the necessities of life for all Americans. The demand for the Academy depended upon a democratic mobility that had caught sight of the fulfillment of democratic vistas, made possible by this science and technology. Access to this fulfillment depended, in part, on an adequate education.

The times were challenging and anything but auspicious for the founding of St. Lawrence Academy. Potsdam was a frontier region and the movement for incorporation coincided with the War of 1812. The formative years, 1816–1826, were marked by financial problems brought on by a depression, by problems of staff and equipment, by problems of a society in transition from one historical period to another, and by the early stirrings of the Jacksonian revolution.

How these tests were met depended not only upon the times but upon the character of the people in the town and on the Board of Trustees. Both the inhabitants and the tests were products of the same historical forces. Consequently, these people were both the products and the molders of these forces. And they came personally to represent a twofold purpose of education, which became the dual function of the Academy.

Through the medium of the school, these persons assumed for themselves and society both a conservative and innovating function. They assumed the obligation of transmitting the cultural heritage to the new generation but at the same time attempted to provide the new generation with the intellectual and moral tools to assess the forces confronting it, and to make necessary changes. The times would make this twofold task formidable.

This dual function was strikingly revealed in the people on the Potsdam frontier. The conservative role was played by Federalist landlords who opened up the area. The innovating function was played by the yeoman farmers who were seeking the fulfillment of the democratic promise.

Federalist families of New York City had fortunes to invest and the wild, unoccupied lands of the northern frontier beckoned. In 1802, David M. Clarkson, Garret van Horne and their partners purchased land in Potsdam from William Constable. By 1821 this purchase had been subdivided into smaller parcels, and separate deeds were granted to Levinius Clarkson, Herman LeRoy, Nichols Fish, John C. Clarkson, Garret van Horne, William Bayard and Thomas S. Clarkson.

The Clarksons, especially, were more than just speculators. They settled in Potsdam and played a prominent role in the institutional growth of the town. In 1803 these landlords dispatched Benjamin Raymond, their land agent, to initiate the development of their investments.

Potsdam's landlords were not unaware of the problems of a frontier region. Unlike the pre-Revolutionary War frontier, which had advanced at about a mile per year, the postwar frontier had advanced about thirty miles per year. This increased rate had important social implications, creating a broad subfrontier area behind the advancing frontier line. This was the "backwoods" region where Americans and American institutions began all over again. Probably the greatest effect of this subfrontier was in its intensification of individualism.

Federalist landlords had a basic philosophy for the development of their holdings. "The first object is, therefore, to open such roads as shall bring the lands within the reach of persons desirous to explore them. The expense is trifling, and consists in felling a line of trees, and laying a log causeway where the ground renders this precaution necessary. As the settlement progresses, these roads are generally improved by the overseers of highways. . . . To this simple outline may be added, that it will, perhaps devolve upon the proprietor, to erect a grist mill and sawmill. The former is indispensable, the latter a public convenience. . . . A country thus prepared has but few attractions for real farmers." [11]

Landlords knew that settlers must be attracted to Potsdam and the land brought "into a train of settlement. It is the actual settlement which gives superior value, not the quality alone of soil or local situation." [12]

Federalists planned to provide the initial momentum by providing the absolute essentials. Once the opportunity for land became available they were sure that the pioneer himself was enough of a speculator to continue the development.

This philosophy had two important facets for future institutional development in Potsdam. It meant that landlords probably would not make any further financial commitment to the development of the area. This would be left to local initiative. Also, it meant that Potsdam soon would be tied into the more settled area. This transportation revolution would hasten economic, political and social development. And significantly, it would expose Potsdam to the new forces of democracy and a capitalistic, industrial economy.

Raymond and his working parties developed these minimal improvements in 1803–1804.[13] A sawmill was in operation in the fall and the gristmill was started and completed in 1804. Roads were surveyed in different directions from Potsdam. By the fall of 1803, the road from Stockholm through Potsdam to Canton was sufficiently cleared of underbrush to permit the passage of a team of horses. Both Canton and Stockholm already had been opened to settlement and a similar developmental program was under way.

There were two main access roads to the Potsdam area. The

Chateaugay Road had been underbrushed through from Plattsburgh to the St. Regis River by 1800. Nathan Ford had
cleared the Oswegatchie Road from Ogdensburg to Carthage
where it made connections with the road to Utica. Otherwise
people would use the natural network of rivers of northern
New York—the St. Lawrence, Racquette and others.

Even while Raymond was at work settlers began to arrive
from New England. This bore out another assumption of the
Federalist policy. "The principal land speculations were in no
small degree influenced by the prospect of receiving . . . the
surplus population of New England; an expectation founded
on reasonable ground, considering that our lands adjoined,
and combined with this natural course many local advantages. . . . Could it be supposed that a farmer would search for
lands in the states of Ohio or Indiana, when nearly two
millions of acres were lying at his door and offered for sale and
settlement? The idea was preposterous!" [14]

During 1803, approximately twenty-eight settlers signed
land contracts with Raymond and started the backbreaking
work of pioneer farming. This was at best a desperate adven-
ture. Farms had to be cut out of the forest and land prepared
for tilling. Claiming a farm from the wilderness was an arduous job and usually took about one generation.

Clearing trees was accomplished either by chopping or
girdling. A confused mass of trees and branches resulted,
referred to as either a slashing or a foller. When the foller
had dried sufficiently the settler applied a firebrand.

The cleared fields presented a grotesque picture of either
stumps or girdled trees. Some of the fields were sown with
wheat, above which could be seen numerous ugly stumps of
old trees surrounded by girdled trees. The march of the
frontier in Potsdam was marked by billowing clouds of smoke
as the frontiersman either cleared his land initially or increased his acreage at a later date.

A typical Potsdam pioneer would probably clear three to

four acres the first year. After ten years a family usually had about fifteen acres under cultivation. Each farm generation in Potsdam cleared land down to the post-Civil War period. Actually, there was little need to clear much land the first few years because there were no markets or adequate transportation. Also, at this stage of history, it was necessary to leave a portion of one's timber standing. Here the pioneer would find material for his buildings, fences and fuels. Standing timber also provided shelter for cattle as well as a browsing ground for them.[15]

The Town of Potsdam was incorporated February 21, 1806, and by 1810 the town had 928 inhabitants. The nucleus of settlement, the present village, was at the falls of the Racquette River, where Raymond had erected his own home and land office. Clustered around the waterfall were a gristmill, sawmill, fullingmill, carding machine, mechanics shops and fifteen dwellings.[16] The pioneer farmers lived in clearings in the surrounding area.

Each area revealed a typical cleared farm of about fifteen acres. These acres were burned over and stumps dotted the clearings. A log cabin would probably be near the center of the clearing and a small vegetable patch was usually located near the cabin. An infant orchard also could be identified. Largest portion of the cleared area was probably in corn, the great multipurpose crop of the frontier. Livestock, if any, were permitted to roam. This was a typical clearing-in-the-woods civilization, the beginning all over again.

This geographical extension of American society did not bring on social retardation. Even though life in Potsdam was hard and uncertain, the urge for progress prompted an early movement for education.

Parents first taught their own children in Potsdam. Raymond held classes for his children in his house, the Fox and Geese House, on the west side of the Racquette River, around 1804. Friends of the family sent their children and he soon had a large class. Howard Pierce began holding informal classes for youngsters in 1807 on the Canton Road.

In 1807 Raymond requested the Clarksons and Van Hornes to erect a building for religious and educational services. There was no response. This is explained by the Federalist philosophy of making only minimal improvements to their holdings, and improvements did not include education.

Their assumption that settlers in time would handle their own problems was borne out by succeeding events. By 1811 Raymond and others decided that they needed a public building for educational and religious services. Raymond owned part of Lot 29 on Union Lane, near the outer rim of the hamlet, across from the present post office on Union Street. There the men constructed a one-story frame building, 24 by 36 feet, with a small porch and bell, at an estimated cost of $700.[17]

The story of organized religion in Potsdam closely parallels the story of education. Early church services were held in Benjamin Raymond's home. From this group eleven members organized the Presbyterian Church on June 9, 1811, and adopted the Congregational polity. On March 10, 1812, the Reverend James Johnson became the first pastor and the first teacher. Both church and school services were held in the same building that later became the Academy.[18]

This phenomenon was a significant development for education in Potsdam. As long as residents regarded religion as belief in God and in common moral values, they were willing to support a school. But they would expect the school to provide training in the moral and spiritual heritage of America.

While settlement was proceeding and early efforts in education were growing, war came to the North Country.

Residents had foreseen war. As early as 1807, Nathan Ford, land agent for the Ogden family in Ogdensburg, said that threat of war had affected land sales. Joseph Rosseel, the Parish agent in Ogdensburg, complained that the threat of war was hindering commercial expansion.

People of the North Country did not want war for they had no quarrel with Canada. Their area was part of the trading hinterland of Montreal, and British modifications of the Navigation Acts had given a stumulus to North Country economy. Federalist landlords had felt that this would be one of the main factors that would attract settlers.[19]

However, the historical development of the St. Lawrence Valley region depended upon control of the St. Lawrence River. The North Country had been a pawn in the imperialistic rivalries of England and France in the seventeenth and eighteenth centuries. It was one of the main invasion routes to Canada and was destined to be a major theater of war in 1812–1814.[20]

Militia units were called into active service at the outbreak of the war. Citizens of many northern New York communities were drawn into service in the Ogdensburg and Sackets Harbor areas. One company was made up of men from Potsdam, Hopkinton, Madrid and Massena. Bester Pierce of Potsdam was one of the officers.

Although there was no British invasion of Potsdam, the possibility of attack was imminent. The military turnpike from the Carthage area to Malone ran through Parishville and Hopkinton, and American troops in Plattsburgh and Sackets Harbor were shuttled back and forth throughout the war.

Potsdam residents were apprehensive in 1813 when news arrived that General Wilkinson had abandoned his invasion of Canada and had gone into winter camp at French's Mills, Fort Covington. And when Wilkinson abandoned this camp, area residents were sure that the British would attack the undefended frontier. This fear was accentuated when the American army stored 300 barrels of flour in Hopkinton, thirteen miles east of Potsdam.

Late in February, 1814, a British detachment under Major De Heirne raided Hopkinton. They came in six sleighs by way of Moira Corners in the night, and reached Hopkinton before the inhabitants were awake. In addition to the flour they confiscated arms, ammunition, blankets and horses.[21]

Potsdam residents did not panic and leave their homes during the war. One of the unusual features of the times was the continued growth and expansion of the Town of Potsdam. On December 1, 1812, thirty-five people petitioned the Board of Regents for the incorporation of the St. Lawrence Academy. They pledged to raise $5,000. The total sum was divided into 500 shares with each subscriber pledging a certain number of shares. Benjamin Raymond pledged 100 shares.[22] (Only $2,880 was realized from all the pledges.)

The war and some misunderstanding caused a three-year delay in granting the charter. The Regents did not understand that the lot contained a building that would be ready for the school, but Raymond cleared up the misunderstanding in a second petition. He pointed out that he had promised to convey the lot to the Board of St. Lawrence Academy in payment for his 100 shares. In this same note, Raymond, with customary business acumen, pointed out to the Regents that two lots of 640 acres each in Potsdam had been set aside for the support of Gospel and schools. At a town meeting, inhabitants of Potsdam unanimously voted to petition the state to grant the lots as a permanent fund for the Academy. This indicated popular support for the school but also recognized that the state would have to play a role.[23]

The Regents granted the charter for the St. Lawrence Academy on March 25, 1816:

The Regents of the University of the State of New York:
To all to whom these presents shall or may come Greeting: Whereas, Benjamin Raymond, Pierce Shepard, John Burroughs and others, by an instrument in writing under their hands and seals bearing date the twenty-fifth day in January in the year of our Lord one thousand eight hundred and thirteen, after stating that they had contributed more than one-half in value of the real and personal property and estate collected or appropriated for the use

and benefit of the Academy erected at the town of Potsdam, in the County of St. Lawrence, did make application to us the said Regents that the said Academy might be incorporated and become subject to the visitation of us and our successors and that Benjamin Raymond, Liberty Knowles, Pierce Shepard, Azel Lyman, Joseph P. Reynolds, Sewell Raymond, Robert McChesney, David Parish, Nathan Ford, Louis Hasbrouck, Roswell Hopkins, Russell Attwater, and Ebenezer Hulburd might be Trustees of the said Academy by the name of St. Lawrence Academy.

Now Know Ye that We the said Regents having enquired into the allegations contained in the instrument aforesaid and found the same to be true and that a proper building for said Academy hath been erected and finished and paid for and that funds have been obtained and well secured producing an annual net income of at least one hundred dollars and conceiving the said Academy calculated for the promotion of Literature do by these presents pursuant to the statute in such case made and provided signify our approbation of the incorporation of the said Benjamin Raymond, Liberty Knowles, Pierce Shepard, Azel Lyman, Joseph P. Reynolds, Sewall Raymond, Robert McChesney, David Parish, Nathan Ford, Louis Hasbrouck, Roswell Hopkins, Russell Attwater, and Ebenezer Hulburd by the name of "the Trustees of St. Lawrence Academy" being the name mentioned in and by; the said request in writing on condition that the principal or estate producing the said income shall never be diminished or otherwise appropriated and that the said income shall be applied only to the maintenance or salaries of the Professors or Tutors of the Academy.

In Testimony Whereof, We have caused our Common Seal to be hereunto affixed the twenty-fifth day of March in the year of our Lord one thousand eight hundred and sixteen.

Daniel D. Tompkins,
Chancellor of the University of the State of New York.
By order of the Chancellor,
Gideon Hawley, Secretary.[24]

And so, on September 17, 1816, the historic meeting of the Board of Trustees took place in Benjamin Raymond's land office. These same men would soon be called upon to meet new challenges.

Opening of the St. Lawrence Academy on September 30, 1816, was certainly a tribute to local initiative. But new problems arose quickly. Within a short time the trustees were confronted with a paradox: a business depression that lasted to around 1824 and the steady movement of the area into another stage of development.

Trustees soon found that the life of the Academy was threatened by the depression of 1819–1822. Effects of the depression were still felt in Potsdam in 1824. The trustees' first report to the Board of Regents in 1817 clearly indicated basic problems that would dominate their reports for the next seven years.[25]

Tuition money was uncertain and fluctuating. Income from the subscriptions was off and many who had pledged in good faith now found that they could not honor their pledges. The value of the literature lot had declined. The trustees who had placed a value of three dollars per acre on the property later admitted that they couldn't get two dollars. There was so much land for sale that few people wanted to lease. In 1821 five lots of 52 acres each were leased for one peck of wheat per acre—rent free until 1823. In 1822 there were twelve lots cleared and nine were leased. Wheat was selling for 56¢ per bushel. It was obvious that there would not be much income from the lots and in 1823 only two people were able to pay on their leases.[26]

Financial conditions were so bad that trustees had to close the Academy temporarily during the school year 1817–1818 and part of 1818–1819. To make matters worse, they were unable to hire a teacher to replace Mr. Nixon.[27]

The school was operating again during the last part of 1819 and the trustees were very optimistic. "From the ability and zeal of the preceptor [Levi S. Ives] and increased interest of the community," trustees felt they would not be compelled to close down again if they were aided by the distribution of funds set aside for the promotion of literature.[28] It is significant that they recognized and felt a need for some type of government aid. The trustees were hardheaded businessmen and continually pressed for state aid. Frequently they asked that the literature lots in Stockholm and Lisbon be granted to the St. Lawrence Academy.

In spite of this business recession the Potsdam area moved slowly out of the clearing-in-the-woods civilization to that of a town civilization.

The clearing-in-the-woods stage ended when the following developments occurred: the settler's orchard had started bearing fruit; the settler had cleared more acres and his fields bore a variety of crops—hay, wheat, corn and other small grains. He had enclosed his arable land, garden and orchard with a fence, probably either a rail or stone fence. The farmer had also constructed pens and sheds to house his livestock and poultry. A barn held his hay and grain.

The typical Potsdamite had probably enlarged his cabin or replaced it with a frame house. Roads were improved by removing stumps and the farmer had access to the gristmill and other industrial establishments that clustered around falls on the Racquette.

Even though there was no basic change in technology as yet, the farmer did produce a small surplus of grain, primarily the result of increased acreage. The roads offered new avenues of trade.

The hamlet of Potsdam started to grow under the impact of these changes. An eyewitness left us this portrait in 1820: "The village is handsomely laid out, has 65 dwelling houses, 75 families, 4 stores, Methodist and Presbyterian Churches, an academy, a schoolhouse, a printing office, extensive grist and saw mills, carding and fulling mills, a brewery, a furnace, a nail and scythe factory, a spinning and carding machine factory, a sheet iron and tin factory, a blacksmith and distillery." [28]

By 1820 the population of the town increased to 1,911. There were 530 farmers, 44 mechanics, 5 traders, 15 schools, 7,954 improved acres, 3,104 cattle, 440 horses, 4,823 sheep, 20,771 yards of cloth, two gristmills, two carding machines, one brewery, one triphammer and scythe factory, one distillery and five asheries.[29]

The same writer noted that "this town seems to be a kind of focus, for the meeting of roads from all quarters. The Parishville turnpike extends west across it, and the state road north and south. Appropriations have been made for completing the road from Plattsburgh to Malone, which will extend a good road from the former place to Ogdensburg on the St. Lawrence through this town." [30]

Similar changes were wrought in the neighboring towns as the whole area underwent transformation. The basic Federalist philosophy of land development by subsidizing essential improvements bore fruit. It is significant to note here that Federalists were heavily represented on the Board of Trustees of the St. Lawrence Academy.

David Parish, son of a wealthy European banking family, financier of Napoleon and Count Metternich, was one of the great landlords of the North Country. He was the turnpike magnate who more than anyone else brought the whole North Country into a train of settlement with the settled areas. Nathan Ford, land agent of the Ogden family, was instrumental in constructing the Oswegatchie Road into the North Country. Roswell Hopkins, of nearby Hopkinton, was a leader in the same developmental policies. These were men who sensed the times and could provide leadership and capital for a society in transition.

Two perennial problems of the St. Lawrence Academy demanded their attention: a building program and curriculum revision.

The resilience of the Academy upon reopening was amazing. The trustees reported in 1820 that "the high reputation that this institution has obtained in the surrounding country and number of scholars who have attended exceed the most sanguine expectations of the trustees." [31]

Student enrollment started to climb and by 1820 reached 55. A total of 114 had attended at some time during the year. The reputation of the Academy was spreading; students from Oneida and Clinton counties and Montreal and Upper Canada were in attendance. By 1823 there were 75 students in attendance and by 1826 there were 108 in residence and 247 had attended classes at some time during the year.[32]

A twofold problem presented itself. Obviously more classroom space would be necessary, and the school had to assume a dormitory function that only a building program could solve. Earlier students found board and room in the community at a cost ranging from one dollar per week at the bottom of the depression to $2.50 during more normal times.[33]

So the trustees acted, right in the midst of a depression and in a period of historical transition. They reported to the Regents in 1820 that the number of students attending could not be accommodated in the one-room academy. They planned to build a new two-story building of 60 by 36 feet which would be divided into small rooms.[34]

They hoped to have all the building material collected by the winter of 1822–1823, but at that time reported they had the material but lacked the money to proceed. Consequently they petitioned the state for financial assistance. The trustees kept pounding at the State Legislature for assistance to erect a new building. To buttress their demands they purchased a new site, the present site of Snell Hall, Clarkson College of Technology, between Elm and Main Streets.

This transaction evidently impressed the legislature because it appropriated $2,500 to aid in constructing the new building.[35] This sum was raised by the sale of reserved literature lots. The appropriation, more than anything else, reflected the confidence of the state in the Academy as a going institution.

Samuel Partridge, a trustee, was the contractor, and the North Academy Building was erected in 1825. It was constructed of Potsdam sandstone, was 36 by 68 feet and four stories high. The basement was used for the storage of wood. The second floor contained a chapel, a ladies' schoolroom and two students' rooms. The third and fourth floors each contained nine chambers. Space for the library was provided on the fourth floor.[36]

Cornerstone of the North Academy was laid June 1, 1825, with the following inscription:

Town of Potsdam, County of St. Lawrence, State of New York. Settlement of the town commenced by Benjamin Raymond, Esq., from Mass., A.D. 1803. St Lawrence Academy chartered by the State through his influence A.D. 1816. Present Trustees: L. Knowles, P. Shepard, A Lyman, J. P. Reynolds, Sewell Raymond, D. Parish, Roswell Hopkins, Ebenezer Hulburd, Samuel Partridge, J. C. Smith, John Fine, J. N. Vandenheuvel. Rev. Daniel Banks, Principal; Noah Cushman, Assistant. This edifice erected A.D. 1825. Expense $4,000. Alanson Fisher, Mason; Guy C. Noble, Joiner. This village contains 400 inhabitants. The whole town 2700. De Witt Clinton, Governor of The State, June 1, 1825. J. Davison, Engraver.

To which was added by the same engraver, forty-three years later:

The St. Lawrence Academy Building demolished and this plate deposited in the corner stone of the State Normal School on the same site, June 24, 1868. J. Davison, Engraver.[37]

The new Academy opened for classes in 1826. Equipment from the old Academy on Union Street was transferred to it, including the bell, a library of seventy-five volumes and a pair of globes. The old building was purchased by the Presbyterian Church Society. The site of this first academy building is appropriately marked by a plaque, erected in 1916, which reads: [38]

Upon this spot was built in 1810 by Benjamin Raymond
the first school house of Potsdam
First Session 1812
Rev. Jas. Johnson   A.B. Harvard   Teacher
Here from 1816 to 1826 was St. Lawrence Academy
Nahum Nixon   A.B. Middlebury
First Principal

The first curriculum of the St. Lawrence Academy reflected the social goals and ideals of the dominant Federalist class. The values of the patrician class largely shaped the intellectual values of America down to the Jacksonian period. This class felt that it was their function to lead and to set and maintain standards. Not only were they to preserve the knowledge of the past but also to increase its store. By discharging this function they felt that they were giving the younger generation the necessary intellectual and moral tools for social and personal direction. The patrician would admit that a few fine minds were lost for lack of a formal culture, but the average man would not be leading society; rather he was a hewer of wood and drawer of water.

The first curriculum placed an emphasis on mental discipline and emphasized that knowledge was valuable for its own sake and for the cultivation of the mental faculties. The traditional curriculum, dominated by the classics, mathematics and logic, fulfilled these objectives. There were no Regents requirements but this first curriculum was a logical outcome of Federalist influence.

The Academy also provided elementary subjects. Reading, writing, arithmetic, English grammar, cyphering, composition, geography and bookkeeping were offered throughout the period 1816–1826.[39] These were items in the cultural knapsacks of all migrating New Englanders.

To discourage the practice of merely offering elementary subjects and concentrating on them, the Board of Regents passed an ordinance in 1817 requiring all academies receiving state aid to teach the classics and other college entrance subjects. State money was to be distributed according to the number of students in each academy pursuing college entrance subjects. Typical college requirements were Latin (ability to read Virgil), Greek (ability to read Greek Testament) and mathematics. The Regents hoped that academies would thereafter concentrate their instruction on an advanced level.[40]

Effect of this ruling on the curriculum of the Academy was the development of two distinct departments, classical and English. In each annual report the trustees described the classical department and the number of students enrolled. In 1826 there were 36 students in the classical department, and on this basis the Academy received $255.32 from the Regents.[41]

However, an examination of enrollment figures in the 1820's clearly reveals that a majority of students were enrolled in the English department. In 1826 there were 80 students in English compared to 36 in classical, but state aid was based on the latter.[42]

Consequently, there were many protests contending that instruction in the English department suffered because of a lack of financial aid. At this stage of history the purpose of the English department appears to have been to provide an elementary and practical education to those not preparing for college.

Underlying these protests was the fact that Potsdam was in a period of historical transition and was beginning to feel the forces that were transforming America. The social goals and ideals reflected in the original curriculum were being challenged by a strong middle class composed of independent farmers and small businessmen. They insisted on innovation so that they could achieve their democratic aspirations.

It is the essence of a transitional period to find confusion and conflict in practices and ideals. Any attempt at curriculum revision was at best a difficult struggle. The vested interests, the conservatives in this case, were in power.

Benjamin Raymond, founder of St. Lawrence Academy

First St. Lawrence Academy building on Union Street, Potsdam, 1816

North and South buildings of St. Lawrence Academy in the mid-1800's and Presbyterian Church (center)

Asa Brainerd, pioneer in teacher education

Potsdam was on the verge of a revolution in education that would eventually demand wholesale revisions. Stirrings were clear and definite in the early 1820's. As the democratic forces in America slowly mobilized their strength, the St. Lawrence Academy started to innovate and experiment.

By 1826, algebra, geometry and surveying made their appearance, in reply to the growing demand from a utilitarian middle class that education be more practical and useful.[43] These changes were tied to an awareness of the forces that were transforming life in Potsdam and the surrounding area. Drawing and painting were also new additions to the curriculum.

A parallel problem to curriculum revision was faculty recruitment, and both were closely related to the building program of the 1820's.

New staff was added with the increased enrollment and expansion of the curriculum. By the mid 1820's three people were working full-time. Noah Cushman taught arithmetic, geometry and reading; Miss Sally Carpenter was instructor in geography, English grammar, drawing and painting; the Rev. Daniel Banks, principal, taught the other subjects.

By 1827 St. Lawrence Academy was at an educational crossroads. The battle lines were set. Democratic forces were on the move. The aristocratic assumptions behind the Academy's first curriculum were being openly challenged by a set of democratic assumptions.

Schools which had educated for a world of stability were now confronted with the problem of providing an education for a society in transition. Advocates of change were demanding that knowledge now should promote democracy and nationalism. Education should prepare a person for a life in a business and commercial society, as well as an agrarian one. Education for citizenship was now being demanded so that the average person could discharge his civil and social obligations. And above all, education should improve the lot of the common man.

A school is molded by the tests it meets and conquers, and the record of these conquests becomes its living tradition. The test of a living tradition is its ability to sustain an institution in the face of challenge and to inspire quality leadership to effective action.

A number of distinctive elements emerged in Potsdam which established a foundation for the future. This foundation was a combination of ideas with the energy and labor necessary to bring the ideas to fruition in tangible form. The ideas and results became part of Potsdam's living tradition.

Foremost in these elements was the spirit of innovation and experimentation. The initial penetration into the area of curriculum revision was early evidence of this spirit. In the future it would become the source of inspiration and strength as Potsdam encountered a long series of educational problems. It characterized the entire course and development of the institution and provided the impetus for growth and adaptation.

The spirit of the people of Potsdam was an ingredient of primary importance. From the very beginning an unending determination to have the finest possible educative and cultural surroundings impelled the people of the area. They sought out quality leadership and gave these leaders their complete confidence and support. In time the leadership and faculty became infected with the Potsdam spirit.

Directly related to the spirit of the people was their willingness to give financial support to their endeavors. Although the Academy was a self-supporting institution, it was kept alive by the generous purses of the local citizens. This local initiative encouraged the state to lend financial assistance.

The operation of these ideas produced tangible results which became part of the tradition: a multipurpose institution in a pluralistic society, free education if necessary, a school that was proreligion, with a wide reputation for quality and a service function to the locality.

Chapter Two

THE BRAINERD ERA

S T. Lawrence Academy needed a builder, a maker, a developer in 1828. Isolation from the stream of American life would be a matter of choice, not fact. The traditional academy had no place in the America of the future. If the school was to offer more than a retreat from reality, it was imperative to have a leader who sensed the role of education in a society that was being transformed by the dynamic forces of the frontier—industrialism and democracy. At the same time, this man must be a realist, a man who could utilize the Potsdam tradition in attaining this objective.

The Reverend Asa Brainerd, spokesman of democracy, became preceptor in 1828. Brainerd, a native of Berkshire County, Massachusetts, was in his mid-twenties. He was a graduate of the University of Vermont and had had a successful career as a preceptor of an academy.[1]

Brainerd was an ardent champion of advanced education for the common man:

The very worst curse on the subject of education for the great mass of the people and for our civil institutions, which in my estimation could possibly be pursued, would be, effectually to remove the higher means of education from the reach of the poor.

23

This would create an aristocracy in favor of wealth indeed; as it would almost of necessity secure to the sons of the rich the stations of influence, profit and honor in the several walks of life. During the twenty-five years past, I have been constantly connected with our literary institutions as scholar or teacher; and in tracing the subsequent history of my fellow-students and of my own pupils, I have been particularly struck with the fact, and have often named it to others, that almost without exception, those who are securing the highest degree of success, who have already obtained, or who bid fair to obtain, stations of high eminence and usefulness, were poor young men who were compelled to tax their powers to the utmost to sustain themselves in a course of education.

And if aristocratic tendencies are feared, it may be well to inquire what would be the result, if those mostly who have been cradled from infancy in comparative luxury, are to be educated to occupy the stations of influence, and to give tone to the measures and institutions of our country. Will they be so likely to have a fellow feeling for the great mass of the people, to sympathize with their struggles, and to endeavor to alleviate their burdens, as those who are themselves of this mass, have endured their privations, joined in their struggles, and know by experience the ills under which they labor.[2]

Brainerd was a builder who had faith in democracy and he did not intend to accept the status quo. He endowed Potsdam with a purpose, the quality preparation of teachers. This gave the institution a long-range mission in a society committed to the ideal of progress. Someone would have to help thousands of Americans in their search for personal identity. Someone would have to guide them along the road to fulfillment. Brainerd assigned this role to Potsdam graduates.

Always a realist, Brainerd planned his program around this central purpose. In the first place, curriculum revision would be necessary to meet the practical demands of the newly emerging society. Secondly, a way of learning would have to be fully developed or perhaps even discovered to enable the individual to take the fullest advantage of education. Thirdly, new facilities and staff would be required to implement the full program. And finally, more financial support would have to be found.

Brainerd had the ability to work simultaneously on a number of objectives. Nowhere was this more evident than in the promotion of his teacher education plans. Prior to 1828 teacher training at St. Lawrence Academy had been voluntary, incidental and unorganized. But the tradition had been established and Brainerd devoted his immediate attention to the preparation of teachers to promote the growth of the institution. In this effort he was initially aided by a state law of 1827. This act provided permanent funds for annual appropriations to the Common Schools, increased the literature fund, and promoted the education of teachers. The legislature increased the literature fund by $150,000, which would mean increased aid to each academy.[3] However, the law did not specify how the education of teachers was to be effected.

Brainerd eagerly seized this opportunity to show how a teacher program should be developed. His annual reports reflect his efforts to pioneer in the scientific education of teachers:

We have endeavored to devote special attention to those preparing for instruction and no pains have been spared to make them understand themselves and to prepare them to communicate to others the reasons for everything. Twenty-five of our scholars are now teaching and others left with that intention.[4]

Brainerd possessed business acumen. He felt that the 1827 law on preparation of teachers was only a beginning. Future sources of revenue for the Academy might be found in the same place. Consequently, he wanted to present the state with an accomplished fact when further aid for teacher education might be forthcoming. He ended his 1830 report with the reminder of a continuing program: "We have sent out 40 teachers." [5]

By 1831 Brainerd had introduced a course of lectures, Principles of Teaching. In the same year the Academy supplied 80 teachers to the surrounding area and "raised the character of the district schools." [6] In another report he noted that not only had the Academy sent 60 teachers to the district schools but it had been impossible to meet all the calls.[7]

This is a good example of Brainerd's hardheaded realism. The public wanted better teachers, teachers wanted higher pay and educators wanted to establish a profession. He believed that teacher preparation could become scientific. The results in the field would provide evidence that would further all objectives. Brainerd was enough of a politician to realize that legislators were not particularly interested in theories, but did pay attention to results.

The Regents started to take official notice of the pioneering work that was being carried on at Potsdam. They expressed gratification that St. Lawrence Academy had "pursued the course of giving instruction with the special view of qualifying the students to become teachers." [8]

Sensing that a ground swell was developing, Brainerd continued to emphasize his new program. In 1832 he added a series of lectures on English grammar and arithmetic. He then conducted discussions with the prospective teachers on the philosophy of each of these subjects. At the same time various textbooks in these areas were examined: [9]

Particular attention is given to the preparation of teachers qualified for the responsible task of directing the young mind in commencing its education. Courses of lectures on the principles of teaching are based on the most improved methods of teaching and the best means of governing a school. Seventy students left our school the past year and are engaged in teaching.[10]

Another innovation was introduced in this series of lectures. Brainerd conducted teaching demonstrations. The combined lecture and demonstration took one evening a week. He noted that some students at the Academy spent most of their time on this course and failed to meet other requirements at the school.[11]

Brainerd felt that textbooks could not adequately present his ideas. Students did not have a proper frame of reference; they should see ideas practiced by a master. He firmly believed that there was a body of knowledge associated with the communication of knowledge. It could be presented professionally in an intellectually honest way. He was confident that persons genuinely interested in teaching would be attracted.

Brainerd's professional sense involved him in the statewide debate over the preparation of teachers for the common schools. Two schools of thought existed: one group favored engrafting teaching departments on the academies, and another group favored the establishment of normal schools based on the Prussian model. Brainerd was a staunch supporter of the former. He felt that his pioneer work was more than a local matter. Vitally interested in improving education in New York State, he worked incessantly for the spread of his ideas.

The preparation of teachers for the common schools was a pressing problem in the 1820's and engaged the attention of the Governor, State Legislature and Board of Regents. The Governor supported the idea of separate institutions, whereas the legislature and Regents favored the academies.

The Board of Regents and the State Legislature were convinced that the academies should prepare teachers for the common schools. With this in view, state aid to the academies was consequently increased during the 1820's. The 1827 law specifically stated that increased aid should be partly expanded in educating teachers.

In 1831 Azariah C. Flagg, State Superintendent of Common Schools, pointed out that the academies had already received $169,716 and were now receiving annually $10,000 of a capital fund of $256,000. Over $400,000 was invested in real estate, buildings, libraries and philosophical apparatus in the academies:

What more ready or practicable plan can be offered than to convert these numerous academies . . . into seminaries for training of teachers? The state has done much for these schools, and something in aid of the cause of the common schools may be reasonably expected from them. And if the required information, to fit a person for teaching, can be obtained in the present institutions, sound policy and good economy are in favor of relying upon them for the training of teachers. The teachers of these academies are represented by the Regents as well qualified to discharge the duties of their stations.[13]

The Board of Regents was quick in providing the evidence to the State Legislature:

They have now the satisfaction to present a fact, which they consider of immense importance as an evidence that the views adopted by the legislature, although dissented from at that time by many intelligent individuals, were founded in wisdom. By a reference to the abstract, it will appear that St. Lawrence Academy at Potsdam, St. Lawrence County, in the fourth senatorial district, has sent out during the last year eighty teachers of common schools, and that a part of the course of study consists of lectures upon the principles of teaching. The superiority which the St. Lawrence Academy has acquired in this respect is to be ascribed altogether to the new branch of instruction introduced into it. . . . The advantages of a regular system of instruction in the principles of teaching need no illustration.

Experience is constantly suggesting improved methods for the communication of knowledge and for the discipline of youthful minds; and works have recently been published embodying the results of observation and practice. With the aid of these and with such a course of instruction as has been adopted at the St. Lawrence Academy, teachers attain, in a very short time, to qualifications which would otherwise be the products of a long and painful experience, equally embarrassing to themselves, and fatal to the progress of their pupils. The Regents are decidedly of the opinion that the academies are the proper instruments for accomplishing the great objective of supplying the common schools with teachers . . . by engrafting upon the course of studies a department of instruction in the principles of teaching, the respectability and capacities of institutions will be increased, and those who are qualifying themselves for the business of instruction may enjoy the benefit of all the other branches, which enter into the ordinary academic courses. In every point of view it is conceived that this is the most advisable method of preparing instructors.[14]

The Regents observed that if St. Lawrence Academy had been so successful with limited funds, a much improved job could be accomplished with more aid to the academies. They presented their strongest argument:

In the neighborhood of St. Lawrence Academy, the school districts are almost entirely supplied with teachers educated at that Institution; and so beneficial has been the introducing into the schools a better class of instructors, and more efficient plans of instruction, that the compensation of teachers is already, on an average, from thirty to forty dollars per annum more than it was before the Academy had established a department for training them. The influence of these measures upon the public opinion of a small section of the country furnishes the strongest ground of assurance that it is necessary only to extend them in order to produce the same results on a more extensive scale.[15]

In 1834 the State Legislature authorized the Board of Regents to establish teaching departments in eight academies, one in each senatorial district. St. Lawrence Academy was selected. The Regents appointed a committee to draw up a master plan. This plan became a milestone in teacher education.[16]

St. Lawrence Academy acted upon the plan immediately.

The 1834–1835 catalog presented local adaptation for a teacher department:

The course of studies established for this department by the Regents of the University, comprises the following: 1st. A thorough and practical knowledge of the English Language; 2d. Writing, and Drawing as practiced in mapping; 3d. Arithmetic, mental & written, & Book-Keeping; 4th. Geography and General History combined; 5th. The History of the United States; 6th. Geometry, Trigonometry, Mensuration, and Surveying; 7th. Natural Philosophy and the Elements of Astronomy; 8th. Chemistry and Mineralogy; 9th. Constitution of the United States, & that of the State of New York; 10th. Select parts of the Revised Statutes, & the duties of Public Officers; 11th. Moral and Intellectual Philosophy; 12th. The Principles of Teaching.

To complete this course of studies, requires three years; eight pledging themselves to complete this course. The Diplomas, however, will be given to those only, who shall have completed the course and passed a satisfactory examination.

To assist those preparing to engage in the business of teaching, the sum of three hundred dollars has been appropriated and mostly expended for the purchase of Text Books: so that the Institution is now able to furnish gratuitously one hundred scholars with most of the books needed to complete the course. The Tuition, in this Department, for the eight months term of study embraced in each year, is $12.00. Those who are unable to pay their Tuition, till they shall have earned it by teaching, will be particularly favored. Let no young man of talents and enterprise, who wishes to prepare himself for the business of teaching, hesitate on account of deficiency of means, to make the trial. All those who have presented themselves, have been directed in a course by which they are enabled to sustain themselves whilst prosecuting their studies.

In addition to the above Text Books, a large list of the best works on the several subjects embraced in the course of study, has been ordered and will soon be received. The scholars pursuing these several subjects, will thus be put in possession of the means of giving them a full and thorough examination.

By an appropriation from the Regents, the trustees have been enabled during the past year, to make a large addition to the Chemical, Philosophical and Astronomical Apparatus. In addition to full and thorough illustrations in connexion, as far as practicable, with the exhibition of the apparatus, in the Recitations, Public Lectures will be delivered, at least on an average of two per week.

It is believed that this, as well as several other of our older and best furnished academies, now supplies what has long been deemed a deficiency in the organization of our literary institutions. With the means now at its command; a regular course of studies established and large classes already formed to prosecute this course systematically, the Institution affords all the facilities for acquiring an English education as complete and thorough as a Collegiate course, and at the same time a more practical character, without requiring the corresponding course of classical studies. All the scholars, whether it is their design to prepare for the business of Teaching or not, are permitted to enter these classes and prosecute the whole or a part of the course.

The Female Department continues under the superintendence of Miss Rich, whose talents and experience in teaching justly entitle her to the confidence of the public. The young ladies will enjoy all the privileges of the Institution with regard to the Libraries and Lectures; and likewise the benefit of instruction in the Male Department in those studies which can be most successfully taught here.[17]

Regents relied on "the principal of each academy to make such arrangements as to convert the intellectual force under his control and direction to the best possible use in furthering the great object in view." [18] This local autonomy permitted Brainerd to formalize quickly a program that was already functioning.

The teacher department was established in Potsdam in the fall of 1834 and was completely organized during the spring term of 1835.[19]

Following the Regents' recommendation, the teacher's

course was set for three years. The school year was divided into two terms, the first ending in November, so that students could obtain employment in district schools. Such a practice was a forerunner of the current student teaching program, but there was no supervision.

Trustees of the Academy offered as many inducements as possible to encourage people to enter the teacher program. Tuition was set at $12 per year, but it was not a hard and fast rule. Tuition was reduced in some cases, in others it was credited until the students earned some money teaching. Free texts were provided, and often the trustees reported that a student should not be debarred from the program because he was unable to pay tuition.[20]

There were 66 students in the the teacher department in 1835 and 102 in 1836. Trustees reported in 1836 that "we have not made exertions to draw in students during this year, not even to advertise, because without such exertion the rooms of the Academy are crowded, and such other rooms as could be obtained for students in the village." [21]

On November 23, 1836, the first full teaching diplomas were issued to Oscar F. Shepard of Lawrence, Frederic P. Sprague of Hopkinton, and Joseph P. Gray. These young men had to take a public examination in the presence of the principal and a majority of the trustees. The examination was held in Liberty Knowles' office.[22]

In 1837 five more diplomas were issued to Rollo O. Page of Canton, Ceylon Otis of Potsdam, Hiram H. Peck of Hopkinton, William H. Carelt of Parishville and Samuel Smith of Potsdam.[23]

Each received the following diploma: [24]

The Regents of the University of the State of New York, having established in this institution a department for the education of common school teachers,

We, the President of the Board of Trustees, and the Principal of the St. Lawrence Academy, do hereby certify that . . . . . . of the town of Potsdam in the county of St. Lawrence in the State of New York has completed the course of instruction, and passed a satisfactory examination in all the subjects of study prescribed by the Regents for the department; that he has sustained, while at the institution, a good moral character, and that he is fully qualified to teach a common school of the first grade. In testimony whereof, we have hereunto affixed our signatures, together with the seal of the institution, at Potsdam in the county of St. Lawrence this _____ day of _____ 18_____.

. . . . . . *President*

. . . . . . *Principal*

The Regents had hoped that this diploma would be accepted as certification by local district boards. However, each district jealously guarded its right to conduct yearly examinations and issue new certificates. They insisted that this was necessary "to pass judgment upon the moral character as well as the ability of the individual, who may by contracting bad habits, become totally unworthy of being entrusted with the education of children." [25]

Students soon realized the folly of completing the three-year program. Some left after completing a year, others after two years. They relied on the town inspectors giving them a certificate to teach, "a calculation which they may safely make, as a single year's instruction in a course shaped with reference to prepare an individual for teaching, will, if he has previously had a good common school education, place him far above the ordinary grade of teachers." [26]

Records show that St. Lawrence Academy was the most active participant in the new plan. In 1834–1835 there were only 118 students in teacher departments in the eight designated academies. Four of them had no students; Potsdam had 66.[27] This was a tribute to Brainerd and his pioneer work in education. His teachers were always in demand in the district schools.

This increased enrollment caused a housing problem. At the time of the establishment of the teacher department, the number of scholars, especially men, was as great as the North Academy and local facilities could accommodate.[28]

As Potsdam's reputation for quality education continued to attract students, the Board of Trustees acted. Although there was no money available for expansion, they drew up plans for another building on the same lot as the North Academy.

Local residents gave their support. The town of Potsdam raised $1,000 and the village $1,605. The trustees and Brainerd contributed $1,275 of this latter sum. The estimated cost of the building was $5,200. Unable to raise sufficient funds, the trustees applied to the State Legislature for aid. On April 1, 1841, the legislature loaned the Academy $2,000 for ten years and took a mortgage on the building, which later was canceled.[29]

The South Academy was constructed in 1836 and occupied in 1837. It was a stone building four stories high. The first floor contained classrooms and the other three floors were reserved for students' rooms, with the exception of a recitation room on the third floor. This building was used primarily for the teacher department.

Brainerd's work in teacher education was inseparable from his pioneer efforts in curriculum revision. Whereas he had no opposition in the former, he faced formidable antagonists in the latter. The faculty psychology or formal discipline theory and its adherents made curriculum revision an agonizing venture.

Formal discipline had determined the aims, subject matter and methods of teaching in the first curriculum of the St. Lawrence Academy.[30] Even though some innovations had been made in the name of social usefulness, they had slowly been engulfed by the doctrine of their disciplinary value.

The formal discipline theory provided educators with a unified pattern of assumptions. The mind was viewed as a spiritual affair, having an existence independent of the body, and possessing a pattern of functioning all its own. The mind had certain powers or faculties which performed certain functions.

Perception, memory, imagination and reasoning were the powers that performed intellectual activities. Feeling and sensations performed the emotional functions and will and volition performed the physical activities permitting man to act.

These various powers were strengthened by their own activities or exercise upon the materials of the objective world. The aim of education then was a well-disciplined and balanced mind that had been exercised properly.

A basic consideration in the selection of subject matter was its potential for exercising certain faculties. The first curriculum of the St. Lawrence Academy reflected this. Mathematics, rhetoric, the classics and grammar exercised the mental powers. Moral philosophy exercised the will to act.

The formal aspect of each subject, not its content, was emphasized. This provided the exercise for the faculty. Attention was focused on formal observation and memory. It made little difference what was observed or memorized. The social utility or personal significance of a course was disregarded.

The study of languages was focused on grammar, syntax and construction. Drill and memorization provided more exercise. The development of meaning in terms of use and understanding was neglected. Students in mathematics were drilled in rules of operation rather than in problem-solving techniques. Diagraming and definitions of parts of speech dominated English grammar. Written and oral expression were neglected.

Placement of subjects in the curriculum depended on the growth and development of the mental powers. A few subjects were considered adequate. It was not necessary to introduce new subjects since the older ones met the aims of education. If new ones were introduced, they would have to be partially justified on the basis of mental discipline.

The method of teaching theoretically enabled a person to

prepare for life. The mental discipline methodology emphasized the exercise of the faculties almost exclusively. Effort became a principle of method.

Certain techniques prevailed. The textbook dominated the course because exercises were found there. Writing provided a means of drill and memorization, and homework of this nature gave the student exercise outside of school. In the absence of textbooks, lectures could provide the same function. If students could take good notes, memorize them and pass them back to the teacher, the teacher could be sure that they were practicing the proper exercises. The question method, sometimes called discussion, might distinguish a superior teacher. But here, the teacher would only ask the questions for which she had the correct answers. This was the only way to insure the proper exercises. Questions at the end of a chapter provided admirable material for this technique.

The role of the teacher in this process did not require a great deal of preparation. He would have to know only the formal aspect of the subject, which boiled down to knowing the vocabulary found in a textbook. He would have to know how to direct students in drill and conduct memory exercises. These exercises should be as strenuous as possible; the greater the exercise, the greater the growth of the faculty. He should be a stern disciplinarian. His aim should be to condition the pupil to obedience, even if it broke his will. Everyone took the same course and the same exercises so there was no concern for individual differences.

The pupil's role depended on his capacity. It was assumed that not everyone had the same degree of faculties. The upperclass groups had more ability than the other classes. Beyond this, everyone conformed and was expected to give blind obedience to external requirements. After all, the teacher knew everything and could provide the proper exercises for personal development. There was no room for self-expression, creativity or originality. Educational opportunity for many meant the privilege of doing something one could not do or was not interested in.

The formal discipline theory was especially congenial to aristocrats. They firmly believed that they had been endowed by nature with faculties that had a greater potential than those of the average man. Knowledge for the sake of knowledge, especially the classics, provided them with the requisite exercises for development. Thus equipped they could assume their natural role of leadership in society. Once a mind had been disciplined, it would not be difficult to master new knowledge and meet new problems. The aristocrat insisted that education should concentrate on the fundamentals.

Brainerd was a product of change. As a New Englander he had witnessed the impact of science and technology on town civilization. As a Jacksonian he saw that the democratic vistas were no longer a dream. They were a distinct possibility for everyone.

Census data for New England and the eastern states provide significant indicators of the change. In 1790 there were only three urban centers of over 8,000 population in this area. In 1840 there were 33. In 1810 the population was 3,487,000, in 1840 it was 6,761,000. In southern New England in all but 50 of 479 townships there was at least one manufacturing village clustering around a textile mill. The factory system developed by the Lowells spelled doom for home manufacturing. By 1860 it had virtually disappeared in the northeast.[31]

Accompanying these industrial changes was a major agricultural revolution. For several centuries agriculture had been carried on by hand labor, with a few simple tools supplemented by animal power. Now new machines and scientific agriculture heralded the age of commercial farming. Urban development depended upon the production of farm surpluses.

Agricultural change in the northeast went through two stages. The period 1810–1840 was characterized by the growth of the home market. This encouraged commercial agriculture in the northeast. From 1840–1860 western competition caused basic adjustments in eastern agriculture. Specialization in crops such as wheat was dropped and new types of specialization appeared—truck gardening, dairying, sheep, potatoes or hops, depending upon local conditions.

The connecting link between these changes was the transportation revolution. Turnpikes were improved and extended. Plank roads provided a hard surface road to local markets. The development of a canal network hastened regional specialization and commercial agriculture. The emerging railroad network would bring all of these basic changes to a rapid fruition.

When Brainerd arrived in Potsdam in 1827, he saw that the area had fully recovered from the effects of the depression. Change was the keynote in both the rural and urban sections of the town. Brainerd knew that the forces of change would produce a mature town civilization.

The average farm contained about 48 acres. The farmer produced the same crops but now had a larger surplus for trade, due mainly to increased acreage. Some manufacturing was still being carried on in the home as evidenced by such data as 8,428 yards of fulled cloth, 9,015 yards of flannel and 3,734 yards of linen, cotton and mixed cloth.[32]

There were 24 merchants in Potsdam and 14 manufacturers.[34] Business was humming.

The biggest change had occurred in the growth of the village and the hamlets. The Village of Potsdam had been incorporated in 1831. The industrial complex had reached its apogee. The development of three gristmills, eleven sawmills, two fulling mills, two carding machines, eight asheries and three tanneries indicated a saturation point within the existing framework of science and technology.[33] Further change, as in agriculture, would result from revolutions in science and technology.

An improved network of roads contributed to a more complex pattern of trade. Goods flowed into the village from the neighboring farms. All types of finished goods were imported into the village from other areas of the state and nation. The Federalist policy of land development paid dividends.

The town's social structure had changed too. A middle class had emerged, composed of businessmen and professional classes in the village and farmers in the rural areas. The family as an institution was starting to lose some of its functions—educational, religious and economic.

There were 32 district schools with 1,212 students in the town in addition to the St. Lawrence Academy. There were 391 schools with 14,054 students in St. Lawrence County.[35]

Organized religion had grown rapidly in Potsdam. The second Great Awakening reached Potsdam in 1820. Azel Lyman, devout church member and a trustee of the Academy, recalled that "the churches began to feel that their help was not in man but in God." Prayer meetings were held on Sabbath and Wednesday evenings; the number attending increased; a great solemnity prevailed, and soon the inquiry began, "What must I do to be saved?"[36] The Methodist Church was formed in 1821 as a result of this revival. There were also Episcopalian and Universalist churches. Other groups were still served by itinerant preachers. There were strong moral overtones in Potsdam which were reflected in all phases of life.

As an ordained minister Brainerd combined his faith in the evangelical spirit of American religious life with the Jacksonian faith in the perfectibility of democratic institutions. He was a confirmed optimist and had great faith in the idea of progress. Consequently he understood the necessity of removing institutional restraints that blocked the achievement of democratic vistas for all Americans.

Brainerd knew that the removal of these restraints would involve a struggle with the doctrines of formal discipline and the aristocratic assumptions underlying an earlier American society.

Change in curriculum must have direction and not everyone was capable of visualizing the future. What to introduce and what to change was of serious consequence. A school and society have traditions, faith, dynamism and direction. All of these had to be caught up in a reform and projected forward. There was an inherent danger in unguided revision. The Jacksonian ideal could be carried too far. No school could answer all the demands placed upon it; it had to see its role relative to the functioning of other institutions. A sound reformer usually keeps one foot in the present as he takes a step into the future. Brainerd stepped carefully, but fearlessly.

Brainerd's efforts at curriculum revision were facilitated by state action. The clamor against state aid to academies being based solely on the number of students pursuing the classical studies was revived in 1827.

The State Legislature passed a law requiring financial aid be distributed to the academies in proportion to the number of students enrolled in the classical or advanced English or both. This act was unique in New York State educational history. It was the only law prescribing subjects and remained in force until 1877 and 1880 when Regents examinations were established:

> Every such distribution shall be made in proportion to the number of pupils in each academy, who, for four months during the preceding year, shall have pursued therein, classical studies, or the higher branches of English education, or both. No pupil . . . shall be deemed to have pursued classical studies, unless he shall have advanced at least, so far as to have read in Latin, the first book of Aeneid, nor to have pursued the higher branches of English education, unless he shall have advanced beyond such knowledge of arithmetic, (including vulgar and decimal fractions,) and of English grammar and geography, as is usually attained in the common schools.[37]

Regents ordinances spelled out additional detail. All of these regulations left a great deal of initiative to the local academy. Only one subject was prescribed in the classical division and none in the English. However, the Regents soon supplemented this by requiring both English composition and declamation for students in both departments.[38]

The Regents advanced two reasons for their policy. It would be extremely difficult to prescribe all the courses that should be taught, but, more important, they wanted flexibility to include new subjects if the times warranted it. They were well aware that some excesses would result:

Mathematics and physical sciences enter into it in a degree disproportioned to literature and moral sciences. The fact is not disputed and it is conceived that it is to be traced to the condition of society in the United States and the nature of our occupation. Education, like everything else, when unrestrained by positive regulation, naturally takes the direction of individual interest.[39]

The explanation advanced was that the physical sciences were tied in with the development of resources, whereas literary pursuits were tied in with wealth and leisure.

The opportunity for local autonomy offered a golden opportunity to a man of courage, imagination and ability. Brainerd welcomed the challenge and added new dimensions to the aims of education, the content of the curriculum and methods of teaching.

He reported to the Regents that new subjects were selected on the basis of "their tendency to discipline the mental faculties . . . and . . . their practical utility." [40] This revealed his approach to the traditions of the school and society. He transcended them by incorporating them, and by imbuing them with a new dynamism.

As a realist Brainerd recognized the need for well-disciplined and balanced minds; this objective was not to be attained by formal exercise on the externals of subject matter, but he added two new ideas. And he insisted that this goal could be achieved by many Americans, not just a few. He visualized the Jeffersonian ideal of an aristocracy of talent to be discovered in all walks of life.

Brainerd added utility as a new dimension to the aim of educating. This was tied in with the democratic assumptions that were challenging the aristocratic assumptions. Education should promote nationalism and democracy, prepare all citizens for work in a new society, prepare them to discharge their political obligations and promote the dignity of the common man.

Brainerd also added new subject matter that was primarily useful. The first half of the nineteenth century witnessed an explosion of knowledge, and general fields of knowledge were broken down into more specialized subjects.

Before 1800 natural philosophy had included physics, chemistry, astronomy and geology. Beginning in the 1820's–1840's it was divided into two fields: natural philosophy (physical sciences) and natural history (biological sciences). It was evident that as more and more knowledge was gathered and classified in these areas, teachers would have to become more specialized in a given area.

The same transformation occurred in moral philosophy, which had been concerned with the whole range of the political, social, and economic institutions of man. Today it would be called the social sciences. In Brainerd's day moral philosophy abandoned its interest in the social sciences and subdivided into two areas: mental or intellectual philosophy (the reason) and moral philosophy (the will in moral conduct).

History and political economy then entered the curriculum. Humanities became more prominent, and modern languages, at first opposed by the classicists, soon became common in the schools.

The classical department in the Academy remained basically the same during Brainerd's tenure. Latin and Greek were the core subjects. Traditionally, they were in the patrician tradition and were good for mental discipline. Biblical antiquities in 1832 represented the only addition to the classical curriculum.[41]

. Major developments occurred in the English division. Under Brainerd's guidance the following departments emerged: mathematics and natural philosophy, modern languages and natural science, and moral, intellectual and political science.

The Department of Mathematics and Natural Philosophy was formally organized in 1835 with the establishment of the teacher department. At this time the Board of Trustees reported that "although newly established, it has been in existence a long time in this Academy and many have taught in it." [42]

Algebra, natural philosophy and mapping had been introduced before Brainerd's arrival. He added astronomy (1831), plane geometry (1838), trigonometry (1836) and mapping (1831).[43]

At the same time Brainerd hired D. S. Sheldon, A.M., as Professor of Mathematics and Natural Philosophy. He recognized that the days of the generalist were numbered, that more specialized content would require qualified teachers. A weakness of many curriculum reforms is to permit the existing staff to teach in new areas for which they are not qualified. Brainerd's views on the philosophy of subject matter would not tolerate this type of teacher. The Board of Trustees approved his decision.

In 1836 William H. Parker was hired as Professor of Languages. The appointments of Messrs. Sheldon and Parker lightened Brainerd's role so that he could concentrate on the areas he enjoyed most—principles of teaching, chemistry (natural sciences), and moral, intellectual and political science.[44]

Brainerd was vitally interested in the social sciences. This was to be expected because the controls over science and technology and their use in American society would be exercised by individuals and social institutions.

Brainerd added the following subjects to this division: logic (1828), United States history (1829), music (1831), intellectual philosophy (1832), evidences of Christianity (1833), natural theology (1835), and law, constitution and government (1836).[45]

Both in the new and old courses emphasis was placed on two things: usefulness, and content and meaning.

United States history was useful because principles could be derived from it. And if youth was familiar with them and the morals they contained, the nation's freedom would be secure. Moral and intellectual philosophy provided the opportunity to develop the moral foundation of the nation as well as that of individuals. Drawing would be useful in mapping, and arithmetic should help those who would be engaged in mechanical pursuits. Only useful experiments should be performed in chemistry.

Brainerd led the revolt against formalism, the externals of subject matter. He felt that content was important and that it should be presented in a meaningful manner. He was deeply concerned that the integrative value of some subjects would be lost. To him this was not to be something achieved; rather it was a quality of the subject itself and integration was a result of presenting it in this fashion.

His course in physical geography utilized materials and methods from many fields. This course was outstanding for its day:

With it are necessarily interwoven matters which in strictness belong to the department of astronomy. The figure and motions of the earth . . . the seasons . . . the general features of the earth's surface, embracing a knowledge of the influence of elevation above the sea upon temperature, climate . . . the atmosphere, winds and their agency in the distribution of heat and moisture . . . the theories relative to tides; a description of the most remarkable currents in the ocean; and all those natural courses, by which the conditions of the various parts of the earth are influenced, should be briefly but clearly and carefully explained.[46]

Brainerd viewed geography as something that unified these bodies of knowledge. It was this quality that produced meaning and understanding. The external form of geography might exercise a faculty like a muscle, but this would not produce understanding.

Brainerd stressed the objectives of the St. Lawrence Academy. Elementary subjects continued to be offered, including arithmetic, bookkeeping, composition, declamation, English grammar, geography, orthography, penmanship, reading and pronunciation.

Brainerd had sound views on the relationship of elementary studies to secondary. These schools (district schools) sought to be elevated much higher than they were, but he felt that they lacked the division of labor, number of teachers and the physical equipment and apparatus to do much advanced work.[47]

Brainerd also introduced a class at St. Lawrence Academy to read the freshman studies. Thus was continued the service tradition of the institution to the surrounding area. Three considerations guided him. First, adequate and qualified staff at the Academy could do this without interfering with their normal work. Second, it would be cheaper for parents in the area. Third, many students were too young and immature to go off to college. A year of instruction at the Academy "where the instructors are accustomed to exercise a close supervision over the younger class of scholars" would prepare them for college work.[48]

Once again Brainerd was unique in his time. Immaturity and inadequate preparation of high school students is a problem in college preparation today. Without subsidies and cooperating institutions, Brainerd came to grips with the problem in his own way.

His views on methods of teaching were closely tied to his views on teacher preparation. He was a firm believer in practicing what he preached. Each course should be taught the way a teacher would want a future teacher to practice.

Brainerd added significant dimensions to this area. He proposed the very advanced idea that teachers should understand themselves before they started teaching. He urged teachers to identify their own capabilities and to embark on a program of self-improvement. Teachers should recognize and accept the fact that their own education was an on-going process. They should avail themselves of all opportunities for further study. Brainerd cited the case of a graduate from St. Lawrence Academy who returned to take the course, Principles of Teaching, after teaching seven years in the district schools. The student remarked that he had become "unhitched" and returned to teaching with new enthusiasm and perception.[49]

Brainerd felt that those who taught only after an ordinary education were apt to be poor teachers because "in teaching, as in all other kinds of business, we are most inclined to do things as we have seen them done, than to be at the trouble to strike out new paths ourselves." [50]

His second major contribution was emphasis on scholarship. He knew only too well that teachers taught the facts, drilled students in correct responses and required them to pass back this information in examinations. The school master depicted by Oliver Goldsmith in *The Deserted Village* was all too common:

> And still they gazed and still the wonder grew,
> That one small head could carry all he knew.[51]

Brainerd was convinced that this factual information could pass back and forth without passing through the minds of either teacher or student.

Scholarship meant a number of things to Brainerd. It did not equate with the vocabulary in a textbook or a certain number of courses. Rather it meant an awareness of simultaneous fields of relationships, resulting from preparation in depth. As a result he insisted on this type of course content, and as much of it as possible:

As they have not a sufficiently thorough and extensive knowledge of arithmetic and geography to prepare them to teach profitably and successfully we keep them on longer. These students spend four months with us before going out to teach for the winter.[52]

Brainerd continually emphasized the philosophy of a body of knowledge. These were the general laws or principles of a field of knowledge, and provided a framework or working model that gave meaning to the data. The art of communicating lay in the ability of the teacher to direct the student in discovering this pattern.

Brainerd's two viewpoints on subject matter were very advanced, and at the same time they implemented the twofold role of education: conservation and innovation. His emphasis on content pointed up the desirability of transmitting a body of knowledge to each generation. His emphasis on the philosophy of a subject pointed to the intellectual training inherent in a course. The emphasis on the processes of intelligence would provide the individual to identify himself, create and innovate. The elevation of a person in society placed this obligation squarely on the shoulders of education.

Brainerd's emphasis on utility fostered the development of meaning and interest. If a person were to use the principles of arithmetic in his business, he would have to understand them. The fact that he was going to use them would foster interest, and an expanded curriculum would offer a student an opportunity to do the things he was interested in.

His views on methods revolutionized the role of both teachers and students. Teachers no longer dispensed knowledge for the purpose of exercising a faculty. They would have to understand themselves so that they could present the material in a meaningful and yet intellectual manner. This emphasized the philosophy of a course rather than its vocabulary. They were requested to direct students in the learning process so that they could discover meaning, using their own resources.

Students would have to play a more active role. They would become producers rather than consumers of knowledge. The emphasis in a course would be on the use of the material, not the memorization of it.

Brainerd was one of the principals called to Albany to draw up the programs of study for the teacher departments. His philosophy and work permeated the new syllabus.

The bookkeeping course taught at St. Lawrence Academy was adopted for the syllabus. "The method pursued in the St. Lawrence Academy is, perhaps, as concise and as likely to be successful as any that could be devised." The course in physical geography also was included. "In the St. Lawrence Academy the whole subject of physical geography is systematically and critically discussed, commencing with the 'history of the science and the adaptation of the objects it embraces, to awaken interest by their endless diversity,' and running through the details of the science in a complete course of seventeen lectures." [53]

But Brainerd had his greatest impact on the philosophy of subject matter, the usefulness of subject matter and the principles of teaching.

The recommended English course emphasized that the "philosophy of language should be made the subject of minute investigation." In arithmetic the "dependence of one step on another" was emphasized as the basis of understanding mathematics. "A knowledge of arithmetic . . . should be so thorough that an application of the rules of science may be made with ease and certainty. . . . The aim should be to make it an exercise of the reasoning faculty, and not, as it has usually been, a mere exertion of memory. . . . A clear and familiar knowledge of principles is indispensable." [54]

The utility of subjects was emphasized throughout the syllabus. "Drawing is only expected to be taught so far as it may be necessary for the purpose of mapping." In arithmetic exercises should be given a practical direction "by selecting as subjects for practice those familiar operations of business, with which the pupils must be conversant in after life." [55]

Many of the Potsdam educator's views on the preparation of teachers were adopted, including his theory that the examination of prospective teachers should include more than knowledge of subject matter:

The possession of knowledge does not necessarily carry with it the faculty of communicating knowledge to others. It is for this reason that the best methods of imparting instruction should be made a subject of instruction to those who are preparing themselves for the business of teaching. They should know how . . . to communicate the results of their own researches and experience in the manner best calculated to make a lasting impression on the mind, to lead their pupils into the habit of examining for themselves, instead of being directed at every step of their progress by their instructor and thus to observe, investigate and classify objects, to combine the fruits of their observation, and draw conclusions from the facts which they have obtained.[56]

Brainerd's emphasis on demonstration lessons gained a prominent spot in the report. Injudicious systems of instruction were labeled as:

fields for collecting facts and details rather than for disciplining the faculties. . . . The great instrument of reform will be to make demonstration keep pace with knowledge. Nothing should be left unexplained; nor would anything be allowed to rest on more authority. . . .[57]

The committee's advice to teachers was a clear reflection of Brainerd's philosophy that a teacher should know himself and be willing to improve himself:

Teachers should become acquainted with their own capabilities and inspired with the feeling that they may, by their own industry, raise their qualifications to any standard. The discipline of their own faculties should not terminate with the close of their course of preparation. The intervals of teaching may be filled up by studies . . . which will elevate their own character, enlarge their stock of moral and intellectual power, and render them better qualified for success in any other pursuit of life.[58]

Brainerd was very liberal in some phases of education, but he was a conservative in other areas. His dealings with students were in line with the formal discipline theory. Students were in school to be educated. The will had to be trained and the moral foundations implemented.

He looked upon student regulations as a course of study administered by an adult. The object was to condition students to adult life. Discipline was rugged, but once disciplined the transfer to self-discipline should occur. Each regulation was intended to train a faculty:

Article 5. No student except those who room in the Academy shall be absent from his boarding house after ten o'clock P.M.

Article 8. The use of intoxicating drinks, profane language, playing at cards or any game of hazard, loitering about taverns, groceries, or any place of public resort, making tumultuous noises, and all other ungentlemanly and immoral conduct are strictly prohibited.

Proper training or exercise of these two rules should insure proper health habits, and this training would be transferred to adult life, Brainerd insisted.

To instill proper training in religion and the moral life there were these regulations:

Article 6. Every member of the institution shall regularly and seasonably attend public worship on the Sabbath.

Article 7. All students shall on the evenings next preceding and succeeding to Sabbath day abstain from all such diversions as may tend to disturb those who religiously observe either of those evenings.

The virtue of hard work could be instilled by the following:

Article 1. In addition to the ordinary school hours, there shall be from two to four hours of study each day, to be regulated by the faculty.

Article 2. No student shall be absent from his room in study hours, after 10 o'clock at night without leave.

Article 4. During study hours the students shall apply themselves closely and diligently to their studies and refrain from loud talking, playing upon musical instruments, and whatever else may tend to disturb their roommates, or others in their studies.

Bad habits could be eliminated by following these dictums:

Article 3. Every student shall be accountable for damages done his own room.

Article 8. Throwing water or any other thing out of the windows is strictly prohibited.

Article 9. No student shall enter another's room without leave of the occupant.

Article 10. The rooms appropriated to the Female Department shall not be entered by the other students without leave of the Principal.

Article 13. All tumult, unnecessary noise or disturbance within the buildings or yards are strictly prohibited, as well in the recess of study as in study hours.

Article 14. No powder, fireworks or firearms of any description shall be kept, or used in the buildings.

Article 16. The stated fines or penalties are: for tearing out a leaf, one fourth the value of the volume; for a drop of ink or grease on a leaf six cents and for every leaf after the first which it penetrates three cents, for loss or destruction of a book or one volume of a set, a new set or the value in exchange for the old; for detaining a book half an hour after the time for return twelve and a half cents and for each day's detention afterwards three cents; for lending a book one fourth its value, neglect or refusal to comply with the Bye Laws, forfeiture of the rights of drawing. Penalties not specified at the discretion of the Librarian.[59]

It did not occur to Brainerd that education should foster the development of maturity. He, like many administrators, saw little or no connection between these regulations and the regular school work. Each faculty could be exercised separately and the integration of them was something to be achieved. It was some years before the whole child was considered as an entity in the educational process.

The balance sheet on Brainerd is impressive. He continued the elements of the Potsdam tradition: the spirit of innovation, quality leadership, cooperation with the community, a multipurpose institution, a school that was proreligion, and that offered a quality education free. Along with all this went the ideal of service to the community. He embraced, updated and projected them.

Asa Brainerd imbued Potsdam with the central idea of the quality preparation of teachers. He demonstrated what imaginative leadership and teaching could accomplish with this central idea. He added new dimensions at Potsdam: new aims for education, a philosophy of scholarship and a method of teaching. And finally, he established the ideal of the pioneer in education for future Potsdamites to imitate.

It is difficult to evaluate these beliefs in terms of actual practice. Regents reports only hint at such effects and the records of the Academy are too incomplete to verify them. But records show that his graduates were in demand and received higher wages. His reports, and those of the Regents, both indicate that the standards of teaching in the Potsdam area had been improved.

His great contribution was his vision of a new learning process. He was perceptive enough to realize that an individual needed a different education in a democratic society if he were to achieve life's goals. Brainerd established a cultural reserve that was absolutely necessary for educational progress. He cast a long shadow on the future of education at Potsdam.

Chapter Three

AN ERA OF TRANSITION

S T. Lawrence Academy lost its leadership in teacher education from 1846–1869. There were three basic causes: Brainerd's resignation, state policy and the normal school movement.

Brainerd had provided imaginative leadership at both the state and local levels. He had tried to renew the Academy with quality leadership and new ideas. But this turned out to be his Achilles' heel. His leadership and enthusiasm had sustained the whole program. A more massive program was needed.

Brainerd had rocked the boat and his departure gave the lid-sitters a chance to return to the doctrines of formal discipline. But there was one difference. Now you could be wrong in the right way, and those who had supported Brainerd were in disfavor.

The intellectual exhaustion of the old school was demonstrated by the determination of some groups to return to the old discipline while giving lip service to Brainerd's ideas. Old clichés were resurrected. After all, hadn't good teachers always taught this way? So a new formalism replaced the old. Professing to practice Brainerd's ideas, teachers returned to an emphasis on the externals of the teaching process.

54

Two things were probably the cause. Brainerd had not been able to communicate fully the meaning of his ideas, and teachers and administrators did not completely understand what he said. They understood him intellectually but not emotionally. They tried to interpret him through the framework of formal discipline. This could not be done. His ideas were new for the time and required a new type of teacher.

Brainerd left a lesson for future education. Successful reform might require taking apart the "establishment" and putting it back together again in a new pattern. The real enemy of conventional wisdom is not the growth of a new idea but the inexorable march of events. A crisis occurs in education when old ideas are unable to deal with new contingencies, because the ideas are obsolescent.

Vacillation in state policy made the continuance of Brainerd's work almost impossible. The Regents' plan for teacher education adopted in 1834 was continued in its unmodified form for only six years. These six years represented the height of Brainerd's work.

The debate continued between the advocates of the academies and the proponents of the normal schools. Governor William Marcy was a strong advocate of the academy program, and in a message of 1838 he stated:

The departments for educating common school teachers erected under the patronage of the state in eight of the academies have been in operation about two years and the last reports from them present favorable results. The number of students attending them is steadily increasing; they are resorted to as sources for supplying the demand for teachers, and the services of those instructed in them are on that account considered more valuable, and readily command a higher rate of compensation.[1]

In 1837 the direction and supervision of the teacher departments in the academies was shifted from the Board of Regents to the State Superintendent of Common Schools.[2] Governor vote its continued attention to the problem.

Marcy had recommended such a move to the State Legislature because he felt that the Board of Regents was not able to de-

This move was unfortunate for the academies because it placed control in the hands of a political official. Consequently, no hard and firm policy was followed. It depended upon the attitude of the particular superintendent. Superintendent Dix thought better results could be obtained by reducing the number of departments to four, Spencer wanted to increase the number to sixteen, and Young wanted to abolish the whole system because he did not think it was producing the desired results.[3]

Soon after the passage of the 1834 law, strong sentiment grew for an extension of the system. An Assembly committee in 1835 recommended that it "should at once be sufficiently extended to adapt it to the 'exigencies of the state.' " [4]

Governor Marcy urged that the number of academies involved in the program be increased if the demand for competent teachers was to be met. Superintendent Dix advocated the founding of eight more teacher departments in the academies. The added expense could be met by applying part of the United States deposit fund.[5]

In response to these demands, the legislature passed a law requiring every academy receiving $700 or more a year from the state to maintain a teacher department.[6] Potsdam did not come under the provisons of the law but continued to maintain a department.

There was a lot of dissatisfaction with the operation of this law, and it was replaced by another act in 1841. The Legislature directed $300 to be paid annually to each of sixteen designated academies to maintain a teacher department for six months of the year between May 15 and December 15.[7]

The superintendent established three requirements. Each student had to sign a pledge that he would teach at least one year after leaving the program. Age requirements were 18 for males and 16 for females. Practice teaching was required of all and it had to be done under the direction of the principal of the academy. This program was inaugurated in 1842.[8]

By this time the Trustees of St. Lawrence Academy were alarmed. They noted that in 1841 there had been an apparent decline in the number of students in teacher departments, and, as a result, some people felt the plan had failed. The trustees had faith, however, and said that at least part of the fault lay in the superintendent's requirements.

Trustees reported that in 1841 there were fifty-two students in the teacher department at Potsdam.

The number actually educated for teachers that year, was more than 100, about one half the number refused to submit to the new and singular requirements of the Superintendent, for the mere object of being counted in that department.[9]

That year, the state made no appropriation to the teacher department.

In 1842 and 1843 St. Lawrence Academy received an annual appropriation of $300 a year to conduct its teacher preparation program. In 1844 appropriations to the academies were discontinued. The 1838 regulation was still in effect but was disregarded by the superintendent. No reports from the academies concerning the education of teachers were received until the re-establishment of teacher training courses in 1849.[10]

This policy irked the Potsdam trustees and they presented a strongly worded "memorial" to the State Legislature. They reviewed the history of teacher education at the St. Lawrence Academy, and pointed with pride to the achievements of the Academy since its founding.

This Academy was chartered by the Regents of the University on the 25th day of March, 1816. The trustees have been striving ever since, at much individual expense of time, care and money, to render it useful to the surrounding country; and they have the satisfaction of believing that their efforts have been successful to a very considerable degree. They can say with confidence that this Academy has, during almost the whole time, held a prominent rank amongst the academies of the State; that it has been the means of raising by many degrees the standard of education through all the Northern part of the state; that it has furnished great numbers of well-qualified school teachers—they believe they may say thousands; that it has educated many who have become useful and prominent in all the learned professions, and in public stations and various departments of business; that a very great proportion of its scholars have been such as sustained themselves while obtaining their education, and who could not, but for this Academy, have enjoyed the benefits of education above those of the former low grade of common schools. Your memorialists believe that such advantages extended to the poorer classes of youth in the interior, and places distant from the Colleges and other means of improvements, will do more to level up the whole mass of the people, and perpetuate our free institutions, than large endowments to a few institutions in the more wealthy and more favored parts of the state.[11]

Trustees reminded the Legislature of the many favorable comments that the Regents had made on the work of the St. Lawrence Academy, "and more than once recommended it as a model for others, in the improved methods of teaching and the education of school teachers." [12]

They also referred to the letter of General Dix, Secretary of State, giving "St. Lawrence Academy the credit of having been the pioneer in the cause of educating common school teachers." [13]

They further explained that they had cheerfully accepted the state's offer to establish a teacher department in 1834. They had acted on the assumption "that the arrangement was intended to be permanent so long as they should fulfill their express agreement." [14]

The trustees explained that they had had to erect the South Academy to accommodate the increased enrollment, and, in spite of community effort, they had to borrow $2,000 from the state with interest to be paid annually or retained out of Potsdam's share of the literature fund. The trustees had paid the interest in 1842, 1843 and 1844. This had been done even though they had received only $300 in 1842 and again in 1843 and no aid in 1841 and 1844:

The teachers have discounted liberally from their salaries, to enable us to keep up the department (teacher) and the Academy thus far. Their necessities forbid a continuation of such liberality, and justice forbids that we should ask it of them.[15]

In spite of financial hardships the teacher department had been maintained. Now it was necessary to:

come to your honorable body to ask relief, and to ask it as a matter of justice. The manner and amount of relief we leave to the wisdom and enlightened liberality of your honorable body; believing that you will concur with that venerated body, the guardians of our literary institutions, the Regents of the University, in the sentiment recorded in their report of 1841.

That to withdraw from those seminaries, which have incurred expenses in the establishment of these departments, the proffered aid which was the inducement to that expense, would be as unjust as it would be injurious.[16]

The trustees pointed out that according to OUR EXPRESS AGREEMENTS, $1,000 has already been withheld and $400 will become due this month.[17]

But the tide of battle was turning. Forces advocating the normal schools won a singular battle in 1844 when the first normal school was established in Albany. However, this did not end the battle between the academies and the normal school groups.

The first normal was experimental. Until more widely adopted, the academies still had to produce teachers. The

State Legislature recognized the problem and in 1849 made provision for its solution.

An academy could receive $250 annually for 1850 and 1851 if "instructed in the science of common school teaching for at least four months during each of said years at least 20 individuals." [18] No county was to receive more than $250.

St. Lawrence Academy was one of the academies so designated, and it continued to receive such aid until its closing in 1869. Members of the first free instructed teachers class were: [19]

Silas J. Farnsworth	E. B. Clark
Carlos Colton	Charlotte Goulding
Samuel W. Smith	Alzina Eastman
Noah Perrin	William Clark
Edwin A. Merritt	Arnold Gates
Rollin Dart	Thomas M. Barriford
Robert D. Currier	James Lenney
Durany R. Orvis	Sarah White
Josiah Bliss	Nathan W. Tupper
Franklin Gibson	Fred Blodgett

Requirements for participation in this program were minimal. The curriculum was prescribed in a general way. All the elementary studies were included and as many advanced studies as could be taught. The science of teaching could be taught by lectures, observation, or by practice teaching. All students in the program, free of charge, had to sign a pledge that they intended to teach a reasonable time in the common schools. Age requirements were 16 for males and 14 for females.[20]

In 1851 the law was amended, and the selected academies received $12.50 for each student taking the teacher course. This was to be a yearly appropriation. No academy was to receive an appropriation for more than twenty pupils or a sum of $250. The age limits of the students was raised, females from 14 to 16 and males from 16 to 18.[21]

Many academies found it difficult to meet the four-month requirements of the law. In 1852 the legislature substituted one third of the academic year as the requirement.[22]

The law was modified again in 1853 when $18,000 was appropriated for teacher training in the academies. Until then only surplus funds had been appropriated. Also, no academy was to be paid for more than 25 students. With minor modifications this became the law under which Regents administered teaching classes for the next twenty years. In 1855 the number of students was reduced from 25 to 20, and in 1864 the Regents could use $3,000 of the amount appropriated for instructing teachers "to pay the expenses of maintaining in the academies, selected courses in physiology and the laws of health."[23]

A typical curriculum of the 1850's and 1860's in the teacher course at Potsdam included reading, orthography, writing, arithmetic, English grammar and geography. Students proficient in these subjects could elect one or two of the following: algebra, geometry, natural history, natural philosophy, history of the United States, science of government and physiology. All students were required to study the theory and practice of teaching and to devote most of their time to the elementary subjects.[24]

St. Lawrence Academy conducted teacher classes from 1849–1869 under these laws. These programs were a far cry from the program established by Asa Brainerd. Fearful people do not have the security to become leaders. The Potsdam tradition was at low ebb. A new school and a courageous leader with ideas once again became a necessity.

The normal school movement offered an opportunity for the Potsdam tradition to be renewed. The state's change in policy was the result of an intensive six-year campaign which culminated in the Normal School Act of 1844.

Support for normal schools had had a long history. Governor DeWitt Clinton had supported it and even Governor

Marcy had advocated county normal schools.[25] Popular support increased as the impression spread that academies were not turning out good teachers.

In 1840 Superintendent John C. Spencer, a supporter of the academy plan, appointed Dr. Alonzo Potter of Union College and the Hon. D. H. Little to visit and report on the training classes in the academies. They were not able to visit all the academies, including St. Lawrence Academy.

Dr. Potter pointed out certain defects. His major criticism was that teacher departments were secondary to the main purpose of the academies. Furthermore, mingling of students in the two divisions of an academy provided too many diversions for those in the teacher department. The three-course program was too long and there was too much emphasis on mathematics. History, political ethics and other courses in the English division should be emphasized. But Potter did admit that the departments had contributed indirectly to the improvement of the public schools. He concluded that academies probably should be continued, but felt that the establishment of normal schools would be a distinct improvement.[26]

Little admitted that he had not had the time to visit more than four academies. But he concurred with Superintendent Spencer that academies had had a salutary effect on teacher education and should be continued.[27]

Spencer, in his 1840 report, struck another blow for the academies. He asserted that normal schools were no better for the preparation of teachers than the academies and recommended that more academies be given aid to prepare teachers.[28]

When Samuel Young succeeded Spencer as superintendent he conducted an active campaign for normal schools and had the support of Governors Seward and Bouck. He made speeches throughout the state and discussed it thoroughly in his reports.[29]

Young was instrumental in having the question debated at

statewide meetings. Of special significance was the meeting of deputy superintendents in Utica in May, 1842. Horace Mann and George B. Emerson of Massachusetts and the Reverend William Gallaudet of Connecticut were invited to present their views on normal schools to the convention. A resolution favoring the establishment of one normal school was adopted at the meeting.[30]

Superintendent Young found a strong ally in the New York State Assembly, the Hon. C. T. Hulburd of St. Lawrence County, member of the education committee. He submitted a 70-page report advocating normal schools and introduced a bill advocating the establishment of a normal school at Albany. Although defeated, a substitute bill was eventually passed and signed by Governor Bouck.[31]

Regulations for this first normal set precedents for all normal schools: [32]

1. That the first term for both sexes, commencing on the 18th of December, shall continue twelve weeks, *i.e.,* to the 11th of March.

2. That during the summer term, there shall be two daily sessions, except on Saturdays, viz, from 8 A.M. to 12 o'clock and from 3 to 5 P.M. That during the winter term, there shall be but one daily session, viz, from 9 A.M. to 2 P.M.; with such *extra* sessions in the afternoon, for *general* exercises, as the principal subject to the approbation of the executive committee, shall judge necessary.

3. That since the branches required by law to be taught in all the common schools, viz, reading, orthography, writing, arithmetic, geography and English grammar—are of primary importance, they shall receive in all cases primary attention in the normal school; nor shall the pupils be allowed to pass to the higher branches, till in the judgment of the teachers they are thoroughly prepared to do so. The instruction in these branches as far as the nature of the subjects will admit, shall for the present be given by topics, allowing to the pupils the use of any textbooks to which they have been accustomed or may have access.

4. That exercises in drawing, vocal music and English composition shall be attended to by all the pupils throughout the whole course of study.

5. Among the branches to be pursued, in addition to the above, are physiology, history of United States, natural philosophy, algebra, geometry, surveying, application of science to the arts, use of globes, intellectual and moral philosophy, with such other branches as the executive committee may from time to time direct.

6. That the state pupils shall be admitted at the commencement of any term, on presenting a certificate of their having been selected to attend the school, by the proper authorities of their respective counties. That all volunteer pupils shall, before they can be admitted, present satisfactory testimonials of their moral character from a county or town superintendent, and be able to sustain to the satisfaction of the principal, an examination in reading, spelling, writing, arithmetic, geography and English grammar.

7. That the pupil's title to a recommendation or certificate as a well-qualified teacher on leaving the school, shall depend on his moral character and literary attainments, and not on the length of time spent in the school; though the pupil shall be entitled to such recommendation or certificate who shall not remain in the school one entire term, and no certificate except one of full qualifications shall be given.

8. That the internal regulations of the school shall be left to take their form and character from the circumstances as they arise; and that such regulations as the teachers may hereafter suggest for the government of the school, shall be submitted to the executive committee for their approval, before they shall go into effect.

F. Dwight, Secretary

Albany Normal was established as an experiment but was soon converted into a permanent institution. Its graduates quickly proved the value of this type of training and soon sentiment grew to establish other normal schools in the state.

The State Legislature accordingly authorized four additional normal schools in May, 1866.[33] The Governor, Lieutenant Governor, Secretary of State, State Treasurer, Attorney General and State Superintendent of Instruction constituted a commission to determine locations and to receive and accept proposals.

Certain guarantees had to be made by a community applying for a normal school. It had to guarantee site, buildings, furniture and certain items of equipment free to the state.[34]

The march of events exposed the obsolescence of the "establishment." There was no Brainerd to step into the breach and lead the fight for the renewal of the Potsdam tradition. But the community again provided the leadership and support as it had done in the days of Benjamin Raymond.

General Edwin Adkins Merritt led the fight. General Merritt was Quartermaster General on Governor Fenton's staff and a very close friend and supporter of the governor. The general had taken an active part along with Victor M. Rice, Superintendent of Instruction, and Malcolm MacVicar of Brockport, in obtaining passage of the bill authorizing four more normals.

General Merritt suggested the Board of Trustees of St. Lawrence Academy act immediately and on December 26, 1866, the board authorized General Merritt to present an application to the State Commission on Location. The local board promised to convey to the state the property of the St. Lawrence Academy and the Presbyterian Church property. Fulfillment of the proposition was guaranteed by Potsdam village authorities.[35]

Other communities also wanted a normal school but General Merritt left no stone unturned. He invited Governor Fenton, the Chairman of the Committee on Location, to visit Potsdam, and the Board of Trustees of the Academy was given adequate time to present a detailed history of Potsdam's role in teacher education.

General Merritt suggested that the governor address the

student body. The convocation was held in the chapel. At the close of the address Principal Sweet presented the governor with a bouquet of flowers, the gift of the student body. Each student was personally introduced to the governor, and when he departed the faculty and student body escorted him to the train.

The General then inaugurated a campaign to raise additional money necessary for the location of the school, and received an appropriation of $10,000 from the County Board of Supervisors. Returning to Albany he presented a resolution to the Committee on Location, but many other localities in the state were aware of the advantages of having a normal school and it became evident that a larger sum of money must be raised by St. Lawrence County. At the annual meeting of the Board of Supervisors, in company with A. X. Parker and Dr. Fisher, General Merritt asked for an appropriation of $40,000 and a resolution was passed appropriating $25,000, if a school was located in St. Lawrence County.[36]

At the next meeting in Albany of the Committee on Location, all the communities that had filed applications were represented. Large offers of money were made by the cities. Undaunted by these tactics, General Merritt pointed out that it was the purpose of the law to accommodate, as far as practical, all parts of the state, and that location rather than money should be the determining factor in the selection of site. If a community was deemed desirable by these criteria, it should be given a reasonable time to supplement the amount of money originally offered. The committee decided to locate a school at Potsdam, if assured the locality would provide $22,000 in addition to the academy buildings. The town and village of Potsdam contributed the necessary funds.[37]

Construction work was started early in the spring of 1868. The Academy buildings were torn down and the Presbyterian Church was incorporated into the normal building as a chapel. The Normal was erected in front of the church, making a three-story building 227 by 113 feet. Impressive corner-stone ceremonies were held on June 24, 1868.[28]

After the Academy buildings were demolished to make room for the Normal buildings, the Board of Trustees had to find temporary quarters for the Academy. They arranged temporary quarters in the Firemen's Hall, formerly the Methodist Episcopal Church. The required alterations were made in the spring of 1868 and the Academy was quickly reopened under the principalship of George H. Sweet.[39]

A great deal of interest was manifested in the construction of new buildings. According to a local news item:

> Workmen are rapidly completing the Normal Building, and it is expected to be ready for use by the 1st prox. The seats and desks were all made here and do credit to the workmanship of our mechanics. The seats are made of cherry, with iron castings, and are very comfortable. All who have seen them pronounce them to be the best they ever saw in a school building. The rooms and galleries are all finished with ash, the walls are stained a delicate pink color, and the ceiling a sky blue. The rooms are high, well lighted, and, when finished and furnished, will be beautiful and convenient. The building is a magnificent one, and when the grounds are properly graded and fenced and the rubbish cleared away, the whole will present a very attractive appearance.[40]

Classes were formally opened in the unfinished buildings on April 27, 1869, for a ten-week term with the following faculty: Malcolm MacVicar, Principal; George H. Sweet, Vice Principal; Henry L. Harter; M. Annie Allen; E. Darwin Blakeslee; Ellen J. Merritt; Eleanor E. Jones; Lucy A. Leonard; and Emma L. Qua.[41]

The first Local Board was named by Superintendent Victor M. Rice, August 10, 1867, as follows: Henry Watkins, Charles O. Tappan, Noble S. Elderkin, Aaron N. Deming, Jesse Reynolds, Eben Fisher, Roswell G. Pettibone, John I. Gilbert,

George Ormiston, Mr. Ormiston declined to accept the appointment, and Abraham X. Parker was appointed in his place.[42]

December 3, 1867, the board organized as follows: Henry Watkins, President; Charles O. Tappan, Secretary; Jesse Reynolds, Treasurer.

The residents of Potsdam had another item in their cultural knapsacks that eventually made a major contribution to the college's history. This was their musical heritage.[43] Unfortunately this has escaped the attention of most historians, especially educational historians.

Forerunner of all public school music and choral work in the North Country and New England was the old-fashioned singing school. Singing masters covered regular circuits and met in churches, schoolhouses and private homes, working with all age groups. Singing schools were known of as early as the 1840's and were popular organizations for years.

One famous singing school master was Jack Chandler, who also was a fine violinist. Probably the most famous singing master of the North Country was Mylon Lewis, who brought Nick Goodall, the eccentric but startling violinist, to the section. In a training similar to that given Beethoven by his father, Goodall's father forced him to practice twelve to fifteen hours a day and to this tyrannical pressure was attributed his mental derangement. Goodall's father was director of the orchestra in Ford Theatre, Washington, at the time of Lincoln's assassination.

Charles Dove of Potsdam, a nephew of Mylon Lewis, said that Goodall followed Lewis back from the central part of the state in the late 1870's and refused to return to his home in Boston. Goodall was described as an outstanding violinst and an excellent pianist. When he had the impulse to play the piano, he would stop wherever he happened to be, inquire about a piano and play for hours. There seemed to be nothing written for violin or piano too difficult for him to perform. He was ever perverse—not performing when expected to, and playing on and on without stopping, often the wrong kind of music.

At various times Goodall lived in Malone, Potsdam, Gouverneur and Canton. He spent his last days in Watertown, where he was finally consigned to the Almshouse and died in 1881 in his thirties. He has been described by Irving Bacheller in his novel *Eben Holden.*

Pioneers in the early nineteenth century had little music. They had stern duties to perform and their Puritan ideas interfered with musical development. Much of the early music of this section came from Vermont. The early instruments were drum, trumpet and jew's-harp. Later the violin grew in favor, but for a long time it was frowned upon because of its connection with the dance. Soon the flute and cello came into more frequent use. The cello was allowed in the church, but for years the violin was not tolerated. A story is told of the attempt of a Sunday school superintendent to use a visiting cornet-playing friend to help with the hymns. When one of the Scottish Presbyterian elders saw the instrument, he rose to his feet and said, "There'll be no horn in the kirk in the morning."

About 1845 the lap melodeon, held on the lap and worked with the elbow, made its appearance. These early instruments were manufactured in Concord, New Hampshire. This was followed by the melodeon, which was a lap accordion on legs. Throughout Jefferson County, especially, piano dealers allowed credit for the melodeon on a trade-in toward the purchase of a piano.

After the big day of the melodeon, the reed organ was developed and became very popular in the 1850's. Reed organs were very common and were a tremendous factor in creating and developing musical interest. At this time there were very few pianos and many young musical enthusiasts walked miles for an opportunity of playing on a piano.

Throughout this period bands and fife and drum corps were popular throughout the North Country. It is said that as early as the 1820's Watertown had a brass band. It always performed at one of the most exciting events of the time—public hangings. The composition played for such occasions, oddly enough, was Schubert's "Rose Tree."

One of the most important contributing factors of Northern New York's musical heritage was the Northern New York Musical Association, begun in 1861. In January of that year a meeting was held in Ogdensburg to form a musical association for Northern New York. The constitution and nominating committee consisted of nine men from different towns.

The Northern New York Musical Association's objective was the elevation of musical taste and the promotion of a more general cultivation of musical skill, especially in vocal music. Any person could become a member of the association by signing the constitution and bylaws. The first president was the Reverend H. C. Riggs of Potsdam. The working committee had the responsibility to get a good attendance at each convention of the association and report to the chairman the probable number who might attend from their locality.

The first annual gathering of the association was held in Potsdam from January 21–25, 1862. An amendment to the constitution at this time stated: "Anyone may become a member of this association by the annual payment of a membership fee of $1 for gentlemen and 50 cents for ladies." Throughout the four days of the convention, business meetings, typical singing schools and rehearsals under Professor Baker of Boston were held mornings and afternoons in preparation for two evening concerts. It is significant to note that 44 towns then had working committee members, compared to 27 the first year. The objective of the association was restated: "The advancement of music as a science and an art within the field of its influence." The first concert of the association was described as brilliant, and at an early meeting on the following morning the members present voted a purse of $25 for Professor Baker, listened to some sweet songs by Mrs. Little of Boston, and then indulged in hearty handshakes and goodbyes until the following year. Members recorded in the secretary's book indicate there were 261 present from 49 towns—43 in New York, two in Canada, three in Vermont, and one (Boston) in Massachusetts.

A total of twenty-five conventions of this association were held from 1862 to 1891. Fifteen were held in Potsdam, six in Malone, two in Ogdensburg, and two in Canton. Records indicate that the festival of 1878 cost $2,259.48.

An early constitutional revision stated that deficits were to be made up by members of the association and anyone neglecting to pay his dues for two successive years had to forfeit membership. Some residents of Potsdam have said that eight or ten wealthy men would make up the inevitable deficit during each of the last several years of the festivals. This explains the fact that such ambitious programs could be undertaken and that so many famous visiting musicians could be brought in. The secretary in 1874 recorded the following expenses: L. O. Emerson, director, was paid $100 and expenses for the week's work; Mrs. Carter, soprano soloist from Boston, received $75; Mrs. Spring, contralto, $50; J. P. Cobb, baritone, $100; the Beethoven Quintet Club of Boston, which furnished accompaniment, was given $350 and expenses. Season tickets were $2 for men and $1 for ladies.

Prominent directors of this musical union were G. F. Baker of Boston, L. O. Emerson of Boston, George F. Root of Chicago, J. H. Mony of Concord, John P. Morgan of New York, H. G. Blaisdell of Concord, and Carl Zerrahn of Berlin and Boston, the most famous director and for many years director of Boston's Handel and Haydn Society.

As many as five hundred persons congregated annually for the meetings and spent a week in one of the area towns. It is certain that the musical heritage was enriched more than the first members of the Association anticipated when they set the advancement of music as a science and an art as their objective.

The year 1878 ushered in what might be termed the golden

era of performance for northern New York. A period of eight or nine years, from 1878 to 1887, saw Potsdam attract world-famous artists such as Annie Louise Carey, contralto; Emma Thursby, soprano; Adelaide Phillips, soprano; Ida Hubbell, contralto; and Signor Brignoli, the Caruso of his day. In 1877 the Roze-Mapleson Company, managed by Henry Mapleson of London, and featuring Mlle. Marie Roze and Signor Brignoli, presented opera at the Potsdam Opera House. Clara Louise Kellogg, one of the country's great singers, brought her own company to the Potsdam Opera House for a series of performances. It is said that Ole Bull, Norwegian violin virtuoso, appeared in Gouverneur during this era.

A member of the Association, Daniel Donahue, recalled a vivid picture of the splendor of the festivals:

Now that I look back nearly 65 years I marvel at the courage and enterprise of a really small group of music lovers to put on a week's music festival in midwinter with the R.W. & O.R.R. as the only means of transportation, snow drifts 15 feet high and temperatures as low as 40 below zero. It was truly wonderful to assume such a tremendous financial responsibility to bring artists with national and international reputations and orchestras like Bernard Listamin's of Boston and Blaisdell's orchestra of Concord, N.H., with their 50 or 60 musicians. I can see in my mind's eye Prof. Carl Zerrahn, the Director, escorting Miss Kellogg, Miss Carey, Miss Thursby, Miss Wyant and the others to the footlights in that grand Chesterfield way that he knew so well. Miss Thursby at that time was soloist at St. Thomas' Church, New York, at $10,000 yearly, the Vanderbilt Church. There was another opera Bouffe artist, Mr. Cobb, who was very popular, and of course Martha Dana Sheppard the really great pianist and accompanist. It was even more remarkable when they did Gilbert & Sullivan's light operas with entirely local talent. We also had concerts from world artists like Theodore Thomas and his 60-piece orchestra with soloists, Gilmore's Band, Ole Bull, Camilla Urso, Remenyi and scores of others. No other town in the country could match this.[44]

Such a festival must have been an inspiration to those who attended. In one week one could hear recitals and concerts performed with eminent conductors, and attend performances of such a choral masterpiece as *The Messiah* or *Elijah* with symphony orchestra and soloists imported from distant cities.

In time the financial burdens of the festivals became too great for a few to carry. The pressures of commercialization and enterprising managers added to the yearly deficit. This, together with more advanced and better means of transportation that permitted persons to travel to large cities, spelled the end of the Association. The musical activities, concerts and recitals at the Crane Institute of Music, then part of the Normal School, provided an outlet for music lovers in Potsdam. The Association planted seeds for future festivals before terminating activity. The Spring Festival of the Arts, an extremely important part of the current curriculum and activities of the Crane Department of Music of the State University College at Potsdam, owes its origin and tradition to the festivals of the Northern New York Music Association.

This musical heritage was responsible for the introduction of music into the curriculum of the St. Lawrence Academy as early as 1831. Miss Catherine McIntyre of Canada was the first music teacher.[45]

In 1840 Samuel Partridge was engaged as a teacher of both vocal and instrumental music. For three years he had been a member of a teaching class in the Boston Academy of Music and also had several years of teaching experience.[46]

Music was important to the people in Potsdam and figured strongly in educational thought. As another phase of the Jacksonian dynamism, it was inevitable that music would find its place in the curriculum. The significance of these courses became evident when music was included in the curriculum by public authority.

Chapter Four

THE MacVICAR ERA

IN 1869 Potsdam Normal needed a builder and a developer for the second time in its history. Again Potsdam was at an educational crossroad. A leader who could sum up the Potsdam tradition and project it forward was necessary if the Normal School was to play a positive role in a new period of transition. The Normal School opened on the threshold of the emergence of modern America. The threefold dynamism unleashed in Jacksonian America and accelerated by the Civil War propelled America toward an urban-industrial society. Potsdam and northern New York moved into another period of history under the impact of these forces, and education was faced with new challenges.

The continuing industrial, agricultural and transportation revolution caused basic changes in the institutional structure of the area. The mature town civilization of Brainerd's day was a thing of the past. Outwardly Potsdam looked about the same, a village surrounded by a rural hinterland. But a man with a sense of history could see the inexorable force of change.

Census data revealed the change in the industrial foundations of the Potsdam area. The movement of industry out of the home was virtually completed by 1870. The supplementary industries in the urban nuclei started to decline and eventually disappeared. The fulling mills, carding machines, distilleries, gristmills and tanneries also disappeared—their future value was mainly a source for historical markers or nostalgic poetry or folklore.[1]

This phenomenon was part of the centralization of industry in America. Under the impact of science and technology the factory system spelled the doom for small local industries and dislocated local economies.

The foundations of the area's agriculture changed under the impact. The day of the self-sufficient farmer producing a small surplus of grain and other products and trading and bartering in the villages declined. Potsdam was part of the national economy. The New York Central and Rutland railroads exposed area farmers to far-flung competition. Survival lay in commercial agriculture. The process of adaptation to this competition was arduous and many turned to the production of butter and cheese, potatoes, and livestock. Change from a relatively simple rural existence to an urban-industrial economy was swift.[2]

During Brainerd's day farmers put most of their cleared acres in crops. Two changes occurred by the 1870's. Individual farmers stopped clearing additional acres and thereby closed an era in American farming. By the mid 1870's a total of 41,672 of 47,965 acres in the town of Potsdam were devoted to pasture or meadow. The number of livestock increased and the pounds of butter and cheese were increased dramatically.[3] This heralded the North Country's initial adaptation to the national agricultural pattern.

The changing agricultural pattern had repercussions in the industrial picture of the countryside. Butter and cheese factories dotted the area. Soon there would be complaints from the farmers about high freight rates on the Rutland and New York Central. The vagaries of the national market caused new headaches. Since horses were used extensively on the farms, harness shops and blacksmith shops became very common. Small agricultural implement industries appeared, such as hoe and rake shops. Villages had to adapt to change or perish. Factories producing sashes and blinds, coaches and wagons, and chairs took up the slack in some areas. Feed stores became prominent in the village.[4]

Village life became more significant as it played a vital role in the distribution pattern in the new economy. The middle class became more numerous, stronger and more vocal. Merchants and local lawyers, bankers, newspapermen, and other members of the professional class dominated the rural scene. Farmers had to deal with these various groups and in many cases were dominated by them. These urban groups were wedded to the business philosophy. This had important repercussions in the political, economic and social institutions of the area.

Social institutions in Potsdam felt the force of these changes. The use of horse power and machines displaced a certain amount of human labor. For the first time some of the young people in the area left the old homestead to carve out new careers. The rate of population growth leveled off and remained basically the same until the middle of the twentieth century. Older people, remaining behind, tended to dominate life in the rural areas and in the hamlets and villages.

The old-time family unit lost more of its functions and influence. The morals, values, attitudes and behavior patterns of the people were molded less and less by the family. The rural churches felt the same forces and saw their force on people lessened. The sociological foundations of life for the younger generation were much different from those of their parents. As a result education faced many new challenges.

Some rural areas of the state and nation were unable to adapt to these changes and slow stagnation set in, accompanied by human erosion. Continued growth depended upon human resources. The character of the people of

Potsdam was revealed by their vigor in adapting to change. Continued adaptation to change would depend upon flexible people. Thus education faced a major challenge to prepare this type of person to live in a new urban-industrial complex.

The Potsdam tradition in education had been molded primarily by Brainerd in a town civilization pattern. Its main ingredients were the quality preparation of teachers emphasizing scholarship and the art and science of teaching, new content and methodology, and emphasis on moral foundations, a spirit of innovation, strong leadership, a multipurpose approach to education and close cooperation of people in the town.

Could this tradition face the new challenge of a society in transition? Was a Normal School the solution to the transformation of the school? This question was on everyone's mind and especially on the minds of about thirty students gathered in the corridors of the New Normal Building.

"What was a Normal School anyway? Our ideas were vague about it. The most we really knew was that tuition and textbooks were free and that wonderful teachers from far away were coming to turn us into teachers." [5]

Entering the Normal was a sobering experience for many students. "Most of us were somewhat scared by the dignity of the Normal and academic teachers, by the size of the chapel, and by the tremendous responsibilities which we soon found resting on our shoulders." [6]

The big question on everyone's mind was the entrance examination. Miss Julia Ettie Crane, one of the group, recalled that the first day at the Normal was a day of examinations, "an experience new to us all. We had heard of examinations in the old academy, but we had never taken any." [7]

The students were instructed to assemble in the academic girls' room. In a few minutes Dr. Malcolm MacVicar, the new principal, entered. From the moment he walked in, students sensed that here was a strong man who intended to run the school in his own way. At the same time he was warmhearted and patient, and as one student said, "He tried to make us understand what we were there for and gave us some ideas about examinations." [8]

The examinations reflected MacVicar's contention that scholarship was a vital part of teacher preparation. He knew that many students leaving the common schools were inadequately prepared. They were immature and lacked the discipline for advanced work. He used the examinations for two purposes: admission and placement. He realized that students had some fear of this new "device" and he spent much time explaining them.

One student recalled that she and her friend were thunderstruck when they were actually given instructions for taking the examination:

We had never heard before that helping one another in such a time of need was cheating. We honestly thought it was obeying the Bible injunction to do to others as we would have them do to us. My "trusty crony" and I, who together had safely weathered all the inquisitorial storms of district school and Academy, had divided up our subjects, she giving particular attention to one half, I to the other, thus feeling reasonably sure what one did not know, the other would. Imagine our consternation then at being told that the slightest communication would be considered a criminal offense and our despair when we found we would not even have a chance to be criminals, for we were seated a long distance apart and watched every minute. We had only "wireless" communication and that must have helped us through for we were both put into the advanced class.[9]

In retrospect these examinations appear archaic but in a sense they created the same terror that Regents and entrance examinations do today. A typical examination covered the following material:

NEW YORK STATE NORMAL SCHOOLS.
Entrance Examination, February, 1893
First Paper.

QUESTIONS

Prepared by a Committee of Normal Principals, and published by the State Department of Public Instruction.

Write the subject of the examination, your name, and the date at the head of your papers.

The work should be written out in full in the answers.

Correct answers will receive 10 credits each, and a proportionately less number will be allowed as the answer approximates correctness or shows knowledge of principles.

In order to secure admission, candidates must gain an average of 70 credits in the three branches and not fall below 60 credits in any one of them.

Use care in spelling, writing, and general neatness of appearance.

ARITHMETIC

1. Define (a) prime number, (b) factor, (c) fraction, (d) percent, (e) proportion.
2. Find the G. C. D. and the L. C. M. of 12, 18, 27, 28, and 63.
3. Five times $\frac{2}{11}$ of 77 is $\frac{14}{15}$ of how many times 25?

GEOGRAPHY

1. Define river basin, isthmus, continent, gulf, geyser.
2. Name the zones and give the width of each in degrees.
3. Bound New York State and locate five important cities in it.

GRAMMAR

"When the natives of the island beheld the ships hovering on their coast, they supposed them monsters which had issued from the deep during the night. They crowded to the beach and watched their movements with awful anxiety. Their veering about, apparently without effort, and the shifting and furling of their sails, resembling huge wings, filled them with astonishment."— Washington Irving.

1. Write the unmodified subject and predicate of each proposition (or clause) in the above sentence.

2. Define a verb and make a list of the intransitive verbs in the selection.
3. (a) Change all transitive verbs to the passive voice.
   (b) Give the principal parts of all the intransitive verbs.[10]

If students wondered what a normal school was, they soon received a clear picture, for MacVicar had been active in teacher training in New York State for many years. As a teacher and principal at Brockport Collegiate Institute from 1859–1867 he had played a prominent role in the teacher training class. But he became convinced that this method was inadequate, so he acted. Along with Victor M. Rice, State Superintendent, he proposed to the State Legislature in 1865–1866 a bill for the establishment of a normal school at Brockport. The bill was subsequently modified to provide for four schools instead of one and a committee on location was named to decide where the schools should be located.

Brockport was selected as one of the sites for a normal school. The Superintendent of Instruction named MacVicar to reorganize the Collegiate Institute into a normal school. With few modifications this plan became the basis for the four new normal schools.

The normal school movement had not as yet won complete public support. There was still a strong body of sentiment supporting the academies. At this time there were only two normal schools in the state—Albany (1844) and Oswego (1866).

Albany had been established as a five-year experiment. It soon proved its value and became a permanent institution. Even then it had its critics. Many educators were critical of its curriculum and felt that it was too short.

Oswego had a widespread reputation due to Edward Austin Sheldon's work on object teaching. Sheldon had been city superintendent of schools in Oswego since 1854. After five years he became dissatisfied with the teaching-learning process in the city schools.

Visiting the National Museum in Toronto, Sheldon saw a display of teaching materials used in the Home and Colonial School in London. This was a training school for teachers and represented an adaptation of Pestalozzi's objective teaching. Sheldon purchased the whole display.[11]

He immediately started an in-service program in Oswego based on his own version of "object teaching." Every Saturday morning for three hours all teachers were required to study the new method and plan the next week's work.

In 1861 the Oswego Primary Teachers Training School was opened. Miss Margaret E. M. Jones of the London School was in charge and when she returned to London, Sheldon assumed personal control.[12] In 1863 the State Legislature voted an annual grant of $3,000 and in 1865 the state assumed control of the school and converted it into a normal school.[13]

Oswego became the mecca for object teaching. Criticism soon developed about its heavy emphasis on pedagogical training and many educators complained that Oswego graduates lacked scholarship.

The long debate over teacher preparation was reaching its climax in New York State. Both academies and normal schools had been given the opportunity to prove their claims. The period of discussion was over and all interested parties were interested in positive evidence.

It was a time for leadership by men who had the courage of their convictions and who could implement their ideals. The State of New York found such a man in Malcolm MacVicar.

Like Brainerd, MacVicar was vitally interested in devising new and better means of education. He worked tirelessly locally and also worked for statewide reform. In August, 1865, by appointment, he read a paper before the annual convocation of the Regents. This paper on the "Internal Organization of Academies" was the first step toward the establishment of regents examinations.[14]

The chancellor of the University of the State of New York appointed him chairman of a Committee of Principals of

Academies to examine and report on the results of the newly established regents examinations.

The Board of Regents recognized MacVicar's outstanding ability by awarding him the degree of doctor of philosophy the following year at their convocation. In the summer of 1869 his alma mater, the University of Rochester, added the degree of doctor of laws.

MacVicar became principal of the new Brockport Normal School. He established a curriculum and supervised the erection of new buildings, but his health suffered under the pressure. He wanted to resign at the end of the school year 1867–1868 but the state superintendent persuaded him to take a year's leave of absence. While vacationing in Leavenworth, Kansas, in 1868–1869 he became superintendent of schools and completely reorganized that city's school system.

When he returned to New York he was appointed principal of the new Potsdam Normal School.[17] Fortunately the building program was almost completed and his main job in Potsdam was to establish the curriculum and the practice school.

MacVicar's plan for the Normal curriculum was described in a "Circular of the State Normal and Training School at Potsdam, New York." [18] Abram B. Weaver, superintendent of public instruction, sent it to school commissioners and city superintendents of schools throughout the state. According to law each county was entitled to twice as many students in each normal school as it had representatives in the State Assembly.

COURSES OF INSTRUCTION
ELEMENTARY ENGLISH COURSE.
First Year

FIRST TERM:
  Arithmetic,
  Grammar,
  Geography,
  Reading, (last half,)

Spelling and Impromptu Composition
Linear Drawing, daily,
Penmanship, (last half,)
Vocal Music, (first half,)
 Light Gymnastics, daily,
SECOND TERM:
 Arithmetic,
 Grammar and Analysis, (first half,)
 Botany, (second half,)
 Rhetoric, (first half,)
 Reading, (second half,)
 Physiology and Zoology, (first half,)
 United States History, (second half,)
 Object and Perspective Drawing,
 Composition, semi-weekly,
 Penmanship, (1st half,) Vocal Music, (2d half,)
 Light Gymnastics, daily,

Second Year

FIRST TERM:
 Philosophy and History of Education,
 School Economy, Civil Government and School Law,
 Methods of giving Object Lessons, and of teaching the subjects
 of the Elementary Course,
 Declamations, Essays, and Select Readings,
 The Object Lessons include Lessons on Objects, Form, Size,
Color, Place, Weight, Sounds, Animals, Plants, Human Body, and
Moral Instruction.
SECOND TERM:
 Practice in Training School, Essays, Select Readings or
 Declamations.

ADVANCED ENGLISH COURSE.
First Year

FIRST TERM:
 Algebra,
 Natural Philosophy,
 General History,

Light Gymnastics,
Geometry,
Compositions,
Declamations,
Botany, (half term,)
Select Readings.
    Rhetoric and English Literature, (half term,)
SECOND TERM:
Algebra,
Book-keeping,
Physical Geography,
Chemistry,
Geometry and Trigonometry,
Light Gymnastics,
    Compositions, Declamations, Select Readings.

Second Year

FIRST TERM:
Same as the First Term of the Second Year of the Elementary English Course.
SECOND TERM:
Moral Philosophy,
Compositions,
Mineralogy and Geology,
Practice in Training School,
Methods in higher studies,
Light Gymnastics,

CLASSICAL COURSE

Students, to be admitted to this Course, must pass a satisfactory examination in all the studies of the First Year in the Elementary English Course.

First Year

FIRST TERM:
Algebra,
Geometry,
General History,
Light Gymnastics,

Botany, (half term,)
Latin,
Compositions, Declamations, Select Readings,
SECOND TERM:
Algebra,
Light Gymnastics,
Book-keeping,
Latin,
Physical Geography, and Astronomy,
Geometry and Trigonometry,
Compositions, Declamations, Select Readings,

Second Year

FIRST TERM:
Latin,
Light Gymnastics,
Natural Philosophy,
Greek or Modern Languages,
Compositions, Declamations, Select Readings,
SECOND TERM:
Latin,
Moral Philosophy,
Chemistry,
Light Gymnastics,
Greek or Modern Languages,
Compositions, Declamations, Select Readings,

Third Year

FIRST TERM:
Latin,
Philosophy of Education,
Greek or Modern Languages,
Light Gymnastics, Methods of giving Object Lessons, and of
teaching the subjects of the Elementary English Course,
Compositions, Declamations, Select Readings,
SECOND TERM:
Latin,
Composition,
Greek or Modern Languages,

Methods in higher studies,
Mineralogy and Geology,
Practice in training school.

MacVicar viewed the primary purpose of the normal school as quality preparation of teachers. As a result of his experience he felt that certain qualities identified such a teacher and he had a definite program to achieve this objective.

Teachers should possess the following characteristics:

They should possess a reliable, transparent and unimpeachable character, and a strong personality, marked by tact and common sense.

They should possess a commanding presence, accompanied by a sympathetic nature guided by a sensitive conscience, and a firm and controlling will.

They should be true to every duty and personal conviction, yet generous and fair in their treatment of the conviction of others, recognizing in the fullest sense the principle of "soul liberty," and maintaining in acts, as well as in words, the Golden Rule as the true standard of life's conduct.

They should be sympathetic to their pupils, giving to them their confidence, and rendering them effective help whenever necessary.

They should be entirely impartial in their dealings with their pupils. Their course in this respect should be so transparent that no student can fail to recognize the just and unbiased character of their actions.

They should be models to their pupils in all things that pertain to personal conduct, or that pertain to any line of school work in which pupils are engaged. They should never fail to sustain by their own acts, every requirement they make of their pupils.[19]

No one would disagree with these qualities but MacVicar went far beyond such a general list. He believed that scholarship was a prime requisite for sound teaching, that teachers should possess an "exhaustive knowledge of the subjects on which they give instruction, and also of subjects on which these are dependent." [20] He also believed that continuity and articulation of subject matter provided key guides to the successful development of content.

On the surface this did not appear to be much of a departure from the formalism of the formal-discipline theory, which attempted to arrange subjects according to the emergence and development of the various faculties. Perception, memory, imagination and reason emerged in that order and subjects that exercised them should be planned in that sequence.

MacVicar believed that continuity and articulation were a logical outgrowth of the systematic organization of each body of knowledge. A teacher who possessed an "exhaustive knowledge" of a subject would organize a course around the basic principles of a subject, the key idea in Brainerd's philosophy.

But MacVicar realized that the fatal weakness of any methodology or theory was its potential for shallowness. He did not want teachers to feel that a method could do the work for them. He wanted teachers to be intellectually honest and thus insisted on sound scholarship. A methodology may protect students against poor teaching, but does not insure good teaching.

Like Brainerd, MacVicar placed heavy emphasis on teachers knowing themselves. He felt that teachers should be required in every course of study "to analyze and trace with great care and accuracy their own mental processes in reaching results." [21] This was MacVicar's point of departure for further advances.

Brainerd had pioneered in the nature of organized bodies of knowledge and made this the basis for scholarship in the preparation of teachers. MacVicar now added two more dimensions: nature of the growing child and nature of society.

He believed that true success in teaching depended on the teacher's "ability to put himself in a real sense in the pupil's place and to look at every difficulty and every line of work from the pupil's standpoint." [22]

The teacher should "study the actual infant, child, youth

and man under normal conditions and amid the various changes through which each passes in the process of development."[23]

This knowledge of the child and thorough training in content should be supplemented by an understanding of sociological forces.

Teachers should "possess the power of forming, intuitively, a reliable estimate of the real character of their pupils, and of the forces by which their conduct is directed and controlled."

MacVicar was one of the first American educators to sense the impact of sociological forces on the child and the learning process. He felt that this was especially significant in the 1870's because of the impact of change on American institutions. Knowledge of these forces and their effects contributed to empathy and the effectiveness of the teaching process.

MacVicar's advanced views in this area represented a frontal assault on the old school. If one were just to "educate" the students, the hard approach was necessary. The new teacher, who considered the student and other forces in the educative process, was often accused of being soft and easy.

MacVicar sensed this and emphasized a complete approach which brought the past and present into a new synthesis.

Teachers "should possess a correct knowledge of the present attainments of their pupils, their present and past environment, and of the connection which the subjects under consideration sustain to the knowledge previously acquired."[26]

MacVicar combined his ideas of child development with continuity and articulation of subject matter. If a teacher had worked out the patterns of relationships in a field of knowledge, he became part of that knowledge. By placing himself in the student's place, and being aware of the sociological forces, he should be able to put the student into the subject matter. This reversed the traditional process of placing the subject matter into the student.

Dr. MacVicar's views on the qualifications of teachers set a high standard for the profession, and were well in advance of the times. Even though he realized that these would rarely be combined in one person, he insisted that they were the ideal for every prospective student.

MacVicar believed that true teaching power is largely a natural gift. But he was thoroughly convinced that this power could be made more effective under the guidance of experienced instructors. This job should be entrusted to normal schools with an experienced staff. He felt that the work in the academies had been inadequate. At the same time, he was not happy with the training plan at either Albany or Oswego. MacVicar required a different type of school to prepare his teachers.

In renewing Potsdam's tradition of quality preparation of teachers, MacVicar had the advantage of starting with a new institution. He also was able to employ a staff that could advance his ideas, and he expected them to set the tone of the school. He created the atmosphere for them to work in.

His program rested on three things: the nature of an organized body of knowledge, nature of the child and nature of society. He asserted that all subjects in a normal school should be presented in a way that would exemplify these principles. However, he relied on method courses and the practice school for actual training of prospective teachers.

MacVicar believed in method courses with one major qualification. A method could not do the work for the teacher, but there was a science of teaching and there were techniques. But this was only part of the story. Effective use of a method rested on sound knowledge and an understanding of the child and society.

MacVicar sensed that object teaching was an advance over the old telling and exercising method. But in the hands of ignorant people it could be reduced to an empty formalism. He wanted people with depth to offer his method courses.

This was the Brainerd tradition and was essential and still is to quality preparation.

MacVicar hired three teachers from Oswego to introduce object teaching at Potsdam: Miss Amelia Morey, Principal of the Intermediate Department; Miss Ellen Merritt, Teacher of Methods; and Miss Eleanor Jones, Principal of the Primary Department.[27]

He was a firm believer in having qualified people training teachers. He tried to avoid Brainerd's mistake. Some teachers could understand object teaching intellectually but not emotionally. Without emotional involvement MacVicar was convinced that any method would be ineffective. Reinforcing his views on scholarship, MacVicar set a high standard for those involved in method courses.

He was convinced that too much emphasis could be placed on the science of teaching:

He held in a very real sense that the study of man is man, and hence that however valuable the study of books on psychology and the science and art of teaching, such study cannot take the place in the training of teachers of the careful and exhaustive study of the living specimens. The teacher, he maintained, can be properly trained only when required, under the guidance of experienced leaders, to study the actual infant, child, youth and man under normal conditions, and amid the various changes through which each passes in the process of development.[28]

MacVicar made the practice school the heart of his program. Like Brainerd, who pioneered with his demonstration lessons, he felt that observation of the art of teaching and then practicing it was the only way to train a teacher. MacVicar was willing to decrease the amount of time given to method courses and devote it to the practice school.

The art of teaching could only be acquired by "persistent practice under favorable conditions." He believed that "it is the act of doing under experienced guidance that the clearest and most valuable scientific knowledge upon any subject is acquired." [29]

MacVicar's criteria for experience were high. They were a combination of scholarship, science and art, and he felt that the number of years teaching did not necessarily prepare a teacher for this type of work.

There was a strong strain of Puritanism in MacVicar, which throws some light on a paradox of his administration. He was a traditionalist in believing that character development was a major objective of education. He regarded it as a course of study and placed it under the heading of scholarship. Even though MacVicar held advanced views on the nature of the child, empathy and sociological foundations, he still felt that he had to educate students in the moral foundations of society.

He made his position very clear by stating his philosophy on student regulations in the school catalog:

Mental discipline alone is not the measure of success in practical life, nor is it the measure of the highest form of manhood or womanhood. The power acquired through the study of various subjects under the guidance of teachers, will be effective in after life, just to the extent to which strength of character and the power of self-control have been developed. In view of these facts, character and proper deportment are regarded as the crowning excellence of true scholarship, and receive the first attention of the teachers. The various regulations of the school are not arbitrary rules, intended simply to secure order that the teachers may perform their work successfully, but they are a course of study and instruction, designed to cultivate correct views of the relations of the governing to the governed, correct habits, and the power of self-government.[30]

Rules were stringent under MacVicar and they were rigorously enforced. Students came away with vivid memories:

During our study hours, we were obliged to keep to our room and were not even to communicate with each other. We usually got on very well. At other times it was a hard matter to keep still. Sometimes we heard footsteps in the hall. Heavier footsteps than were accustomed to pass through there. Then a tap at the door of an adjoining room, occupied by teachers. Then frequently would be beautiful sounds floating to our ears, and accompaniments on the violin. Somehow or other these unusual occurrences had a very disquieting effect on us. They always seemed to inspire my roommate to say a great many funny things to the stove.

I think I should have been happier if I had always remembered that we could not go down town in the evenings without permission, unless on Thursday night. One night in front of the Albion House I met the preceptress. Perhaps some of the rest of you have done the same thing, and you may know just how small I felt. One of our chapel experiences stands out very clearly in my mind, when our good Dr. MacVicar used to stand up in all the majesty of his righteousness. Then woe to the student who had a conscience. How we used to tremble in our places when the command came. "All who have not kept study hours stand." Well, I always stood. The memory of those strains of music and conversations with the stove always brought me to my feet.

I don't remember of ever appearing to advantage on the occasions but once. The subject of discussion was, why we were there, the motive that brought us there, etc. Several were called and their answers were unsatisfactory. Finally I raised my hand and was given the floor. I arose and said, "we are here to be educated." Well, the faculty nodded approval and I sat in triumph. I did not think it necessary to tell them that a short time before I had attended a teachers institute and there gained my information.[81]

Student life during the MacVicar regime was restricted. Social life was held to a minimum and students were under military discipline. During school hours students were not permitted to communicate in any way. They marched from class to class in straight lines and strict study hours were imposed. Students could not make or receive calls. Visits to the village were strictly regulated. Mail was brought to the school and distributed at morning exercises, so there was no excuse for going near the post office. About once a month each student had to confess his or her sins at morning chapel service and woe to those with a conscience.

There was no dancing during the MacVicar regime. There was no such thing as an undergraduate reception. Now and then there was a "sociable." The reception room, office and library were thrown together for a parlor and the hall and chapel served for promenading. Highlight of the sociable for a girl was to be invited by a boy to "walk" up and down the aisle of the chapel. At times partners were exchanged. "In this exciting though innocent way we spent two hours and reached home in time to go to bed by half-past nine." [32] There were no games, dancing or refreshments. "The flapper and necker were unknown as such and clothes were worn to adorn and not to reveal the human form." [33]

Charlie Hotchkiss was the school clown. While MacVicar conducted chapel exercises Charlie entertained students by starting from his seat in back of the old Normal Hall and going under the seats to the front of the hall. Suddenly he would appear seated in the front row, composed and dignified.[34]

But students were students and there were highlights. There was a traditional day off every October and students rushed off in two directions: either up the river or to Allens Falls in Parishville. The "Falls" have been silent witness to much of the unwritten history of Potsdam.

Any type of exercise could easily be converted into a casual social. Gymnastic exercises were popular in the late 1860's and 1870's. Many visitors came to watch the simple performances with rings, dumbbells and wands in a room on the third floor of the Normal.

The girls thought a great deal of their precious gymnastics.

"We had no suits, but dresses, something like a comfortably short and loose shirtwaist suit. These first ones were made of black alpaca and elaborately trimmed with bright plaid; red plaid for the dark haired, blue plaid for the light haired and green plaid for the red haired. Just as they were all finished a sociable was announced for our class. We thought those dresses beautiful and we decided to all wear them to the sociable and to the sociable we went in our gymnastic dresses. One aristocratic lady was overheard saying 'did not the poor things know any better?' But we did not care for that because the boys asked us to 'walk' with them more that night than they ever had before, showing that they were as barbaric as we were, and that they appreciated our brilliant reds, blues and greens against the black background." [35] College boys have not changed.

Student organizations emerged in the 1870's with the formation of three literary societies. Francis Baconian and Roger Baconian were founded by the boys and Alpha by the girls. They were a far cry from modern fraternities and sororities. During MacVicar's tenure they were primarily intellectual societies conducting debates and similar exercises.

MacVicar's disciplinary methods were criticized and there was a lot of grumbling among students. But the testimony of these students in later life bears witness to the results:

Few teachers labor as earnestly to develop character in their students as Dr. MacVicar. In his effort to turn the steps of his students into paths of righteousness he counted no toil or sacrifice too great. His methods of discipline were often criticized but he fearlessly used the methods he believed to be the best for the accomplishment of his noble purpose, viz: the development of true manhood and womanhood in his students.[36]

When students received severe rebuke in the presence of the entire school, when examination papers were forfeited because a watch had been held up to communicate to a friend the time of day, when whispering was a sin, and lending a lead pencil a misdemeanor, sensitive souls lived in a kind of terror. . . . But when the lines were drawn so sharply, clear views of right and wrong were gained, and many who received the training live to thank Dr. MacVicar for definiteness of purpose, clearness of perception and a loyalty to right which his upright character nurtured in their minds.[37]

He was gifted with vigorous original thought and a vivid expression of it. He was a humble and sincere follower of the Great Teacher and stamped his personality upon his students in an unusual way. He catered to no narrow views in educational processes but declared that the work of teachers has to do with modeling every phase of the nature of the pupils, including the physical, intellectual, moral and spiritual. And the training imparted to teachers must include this fourfold work.[38]

At the most critical time in youth I fell under the sway of his commanding personality, and shall never cease to be grateful for this. When I walked up the steps into the Old Normal, a funloving, careless lad, I could not appreciate the Teacher who there waited to probe into our inmost hearts, and to proceed to his one task—the creation of character. He knew us better than we knew ourselves. I do not regret that he laid a strong hand on us. It needed to be. He would bring us to choose the right, to substitute personal honor for obedience to the letter of the law. No easy task. I well remember how he inspired us with hatred of all cheating and dishonesty. We did break some rules, but we did not lie. His rugged strength fascinated, while at times it alarmed us. But all of the time we were coming up to higher levels, and he knew it. He was thoroughly and intensely Christian and appealed to the highest motives. Often did he converse personally with me on the question of my personal example and influence, and show me what I ought to be.[39]

He used to say with his unique accent: "Am I understood?" We thought we understood him, but we did not. In these distant days, after toil and struggle, after victory and defeat, we begin to dimly comprehend what the teacher was trying to do for us. He would equip us for life. How few such teachers! Here and there a Mac-Vicar but multitudes who make knowledge the end of all education. I confess I used to shrink a little, when his flashing eye rested on me, and when the probe was thrust in, but now I am profoundly grateful.[40]

He won by his kindness, integrity and scholarly mind the loyal and enthusiastic support of all his teachers. No one ever questioned his sincerity and rarely his judgment. His greatness of heart and nobleness of character usually went a long way in winning for him any cause in which he was engaged. The discipline of the school was comparatively easy, for each student found his own moral perceptions keener and his moral judgments clearer by means of the emanations from Dr. MacVicar's moral character. Concerning the right or wrong of any contemplated action, to raise the question, "What would Dr. MacVicar think of it?" was usually sufficient to dispel any haze with which sophistry might have surrounded it.[41]

If I were to contribute one token to his character as a teacher it would be this: He always endeavored to impress upon us the necessity of studying and acquiring a store of knowledge, the use of which in after years would make life interesting. What higher tribute could one offer? Possibly that with it all, and more important than acquirements that would make this life interesting, he taught to build up a character that one could take into the spiritual life and beyond this world; which would even adorn that infinitely more interesting life yet to come. And so he always taught that there should be no time wasted, every act and every movement should have in view usefulness.[42]

In addition to preparing teachers MacVicar had to establish an academic department in the Normal School. When the people of Potsdam and St. Lawrence County gave financial support to the Normal, they acted with the understanding that an academic department would be established.

The 1870 circular from the state superintendent's office contained the following information about the academic department: [43]

Applications for admission should be made either in person or by letter to the Principal of the School and should be accompanied by a careful statement of the character, habits and present attainments of candidates. No idle, insubordinate or dissipated pupil will be tolerated.

Students will be received at any time, but in no case for less than a quarter except by special arrangement; and no deduction in price of tuition will be made for those who enter within the two, or leave within the last three, weeks of the term, nor for absence during the term except for sickness.

Classes out of the regular course cannot be organized for the accommodation of students entering this department.

The courses of study are:

First—The Advanced English Course. Second—The Classical Course. These are identical with the same course in the Normal Department, except that they embrace no professional training.

Cost of Tuition:

Pupils will be charged the following rates of tuition per quarter: English course, $6.00; Classical $7.00; Diploma and Graduation Fee (extra) $5.00.

The debate over the merits of normal schools in preparing teachers reached its climax in the mid 1870's. The State Assembly appointed a committee to make an exhaustive examination of all the normal schools. Their report of 1879 represented a victory for MacVicar's views.

The committee members visited each normal school and then submitted a 70-page report to the legislature.

They identified four specific objects for the normal schools: [44]

1. Culture of pupils—physical, intellectual, moral.
2. Knowledge of subjects.
3. Instruction in methods of teaching.
4. Actual practice in methods taught.

The committee was in fundamental agreement with Mac-Vicar's student personnel policies. Members were impressed with the excellent demeanor of the pupils. They felt that learning to govern oneself was a prerequisite for good teaching. The fact that students could sit in chapel unattended impressed them.

MacVicar's emphasis on scholarship, methods of teaching and practice school received hearty endorsement. The Normal Department provided background in content and in theories of teaching. But it was in the practice school that the theories were put into use.

The classes in the normal schools were under "experienced" teachers. But the actual teaching was being carried on by normal students under the supervision of these "experienced" teachers:

Sometimes other normal pupils observe the teaching as done by one of their own number, and in this way we found recitations going on at the same time in different rooms in reading, spelling, arithmetic, grammar and geography, some of the normal scholars having charge for the time being of each class. After that, and usually near the close of the day, these pupils who have been acting as teachers, as well as those who have been "observing," meet, and one of the normal critics who has been watching their work, reviews it, pointing out and explaining not only the errors, but the excellencies observed. In addition, the pupil-teachers question and are questioned as to what is well or ill done, and suggestions are made by way of improvement.[45]

The investigating committee felt that the practice school, the heart of MacVicar's program, gave reality to teacher preparation:

Without it the abstract instruction elsewhere given in the science of education and the art of teaching would necessarily lose much of its value. No one would think of learning any other art without trying to practice it, and that, too, with one who had already learned it.[46]

In addition to being impressed with the efforts of normal departments and practice schools, the committee put its finger on that great intangible—the art of teaching. MacVicar had fought long and hard for this important fact. Solid scholarship—yes, methods—yes, but in the last analysis teaching "is one human spirit working upon other human spirits, awakening and directing thought, evolving power, forming habits, shaping character, and helping to determine the motive and the result of all subsequent life." [47] Thus, the state returned to the central idea of the Potsdam tradition, quality preparation of teachers.

The committee's report indicated the confidence the state had placed in MacVicar. It also indicated clearly that the state would in the future rely upon the normal schools for its teachers. This was a significant victory. Education for all, sponsored by the state, required adequately prepared teachers in increasing numbers. Quality of education equated precisely with the programs in the normal schools.

MacVicar and men like him had won a singular victory, but it really was only a beginning. Soon someone would have to lead these institutions into the twentieth century.

The balance sheet on Malcolm MacVicar is impressive. He did an outstanding job in summing up the Potsdam tradition and applying it to the normal school. Brainerd's central purpose of the quality preparation of teachers was firmly re-established. The school's multipurpose and service functions were continued with the academic department. MacVicar placed great emphasis on moral education.

The spirit of innovation found unique expression in Mac-Vicar as he added new dimensions to teacher education. He added knowledge of child development, empathy and the impact of social forces on the educative process. He imported new teachers to update the Potsdam curriculum. Unknowingly he sowed the seeds for new dimensions in student relationships.

MacVicar walked in Brainerd's shadow and between them they pioneered the three basics in the modern curriculum: knowledge of the child, knowledge of society and knowledge of organized bodies of learning. The way was firmly prepared for modern administrators and imaginative teachers.

Chapter Five

THE STOWELL ERA

A new type of leader was needed at Potsdam Normal as the twentieth century approached. One man could no longer dominate as Brainerd and MacVicar had in the past. A leader was required who could view everything as part of the educative process. Faculty and students would have to be more actively involved in the processes of the school. The Potsdam tradition would have to be expanded if it was to have a meaningful impact on education. The danger of a post-Brainerd period could not be repeated. Modern and enlightened leadership was needed.

Dr. Thomas B. Stowell was Potsdam's first modern-type administrator. He had an encompassing view of the Normal as an institution that had evolved around a central idea. He was aware that schools do "not spring up spontaneously, they do not come with a mushroom growth in a night, they are rather the unfolding or evolution of something which has gone before. The existence of institutions depends upon previous or still earlier institutions." He pointed out the spirit and initiative of the early settlers under the inspired leadership of Benjamin Raymond in establishing the St. Lawrence Academy. Stowell acknowledged the contribution of quality leadership in the development of Potsdam, especially that of Asa Brainerd, "a man noted for intellectual greatness." Teachers prepared by these leaders had always been in demand and "often times, at higher salaries than those of other schools." [1]

Stowell identified the quality preparation of teachers as the central idea of Potsdam, the idea that gave it permanence. He believed "that institutions survive long after those who founded them and promoted their interests are forgotten. Institutions are permanent because of their spirituality—they are not material and their immortality rests in the fact of their spirituality. . . . All institutions develop around some central thought or idea; particularly is this true of the development of educational ideas, and it has been emphatically true of this (Potsdam) Normal School." [2]

Stowell had a sense of this tradition and felt that he was part of it. He had worked and lived with MacVicar in Kansas before he moved to Cortland Normal. When MacVicar came to Potsdam he tried to lure Stowell away from Cortland, but Stowell said he had made a commitment and couldn't break it. But he did recommend the hiring of Professor Blakeslee, his son-in-law. As Stowell remarked: "And so I have had from the earliest work of the school a peculiar relation to it, and while I have been here but twenty years, I have really been here the whole forty years of its history. That is why I came intimately in contact with those of you whose memories relate to this early date." [3] Stowell also said:

> But while an institution is founded upon a central idea, it is necessary to have some physical expression of that idea to give it permanency and efficiency. Individuals are necessary. . . . What has saved the State Normal School at Potsdam and brought it to the front is not the central idea of the institution alone. It is because of the personalities of the men and women who have gathered around this center and have added their personalities—removing the weaknesses and adding strength to the efficiency of the school.[4]

The breadth of Dr. Stowell's vision was illustrated by his concept that Potsdam alumni could continue to play this role. An alumni association had been organized on January 28, 1873, with Miss Amelia McFadden as first president.[5] The association held periodic meetings, usually at commencement time. For the most part it was fraternal in its functioning. Stowell wanted to invigorate it.

In an address to the association he realistically pointed out that it was alumni, not faculty or students, who gave Potsdam its reputation. "Your lives are what the world outside sees and meets. They know us not." [6]

While acknowledging the past glories of Potsdam, Stowell did not intend to apply the backward look to the Normal School. It was no time to rest on the laurels of Brainerd and MacVicar. Stowell believed that education should reflect society, and therefore it would have to be altered by the forces that were shaping that society.

Stowell knew that the program and function of the public schools would have to change to meet the demands of the new urban-industrial complex. Like MacVicar, he sensed the impact of sociological forces on the educational process. Schools would have to be concerned with such things as physical education and vocational training. New programs in the sciences and social sciences would have to be included if education was going to help all Americans share in the promise of American life.

But more than this, Stowell believed that the masses should share in an enriched cultural life. Even though a scientist, he felt that music and art programs should be included in public school curriculum. Someone would have to train teachers for this new work. Proper instruction was necessary lest democratic tastes should become vulgarized.

In making these adjustments Stowell realized that much of the Potsdam tradition should be continued. Brainerd's ideas on systems of knowledge, and MacVicar's theories on the nature of the child and society could contribute significantly to change. But they would have to be combined with new intellectual currents. The result should be an approach that would remove the institutional restraints that hindered individual discovery and fulfillment.

Stowell visualized his role as providing a climate that would favor innovation. In some areas he personally set the pace. But to some extent he hoped that this climate would encourage teachers to do what they should be doing, self-improvement. Theirs would be the main responsibility to update all phases of the curriculum.

He also was determined to change student policy. School life should provide opportunities for students to develop into mature people. The proper application of new pedagogic principles made this a necessity. Future teachers should be living examples of the new ideas so they could inspire their students.

Potsdam became an exciting place in the early 1890's and 1900's. Experimentation and active research became standard policy. Faculty and students worked enthusiastically under his direction. Potsdam graduates were more in demand than ever before.

Stowell saw himself as a catalyst of change. In some areas of the curriculum he personally provided the leadership. This was especially true in his efforts to update Potsdam in the field of science.

Dr. Stowell was a recognized scientist. He had studied under the famous Agassiz. He spent his summer vacations in the Anatomical Laboratory of Cornell University under Dr. Burt G. Wilder or in the field collecting material for research. "To his familiarity with nature and love of her ways must be added his strength as a teacher of the natural sciences." [7]

Stowell was well versed in new scientific information. He conducted many investigations in the field of histology (vegetal and animal), and comparative neurology. He presented papers before learned societies, using original drawings descriptive of the cranial and spinal nerves of the domestic cat as a basis for neurological study. Stowell published an outline course in anatomy and physiology, a special book on the effects of narcotics and other works.

Stowell regarded science as a mine of ideas for utilization. He was vitally interested in the scientific method as a bridge between scientific ideas and the ultimate product. He emphasized method as a disciplined attack upon problems. "The enthusiasm with which his students pursued their laboratory investigations, was born of contact with a soul, which was in close communication with the heart of nature and to whom she gladly disclosed her secrets." [8]

The curriculum felt the impact of Stowell. In the English Course, botany, zoology, physiology, mineralogy, geology, physics and chemistry were offered. General science methods, including lessons on plants, animals, the human body, physics, etc., were offered in the third year. A new course, the Scientific Course, was offered. This was the same as the English Course with the addition of two years study of any two languages—Latin, Greek, French or German. Some science appeared in the Classical Course—mineralogy, geology, chemistry and science methods. [9]

The movement for manual training was gaining momentum throughout the country, but Potsdam had neither the facilities nor staff to prepare teachers for this work. So Dr. Stowell made arrangements with the Thomas S. Clarkson Memorial School of Technology for selected Normal students to take work in sewing, cooking, forging, whittling and joinery. [10]

This was a good example of Stowell's concept of action research. He saw the need for such courses and developed a program. To understand the work fully, he himself enrolled in the whittling course and became quite adept at it. "Dr. Stowell and Professor Graves are members of this class and both show marked evidence of becoming good whittlers, though it is necessary to keep them in the front seats." [11]

The manual training was in two parts.[10] During the first part of the period the students made a projection drawing with simple instruments of the model to be cut. A reproduction of the drawing was made on thin wood "and then the real fun with the jack-knife begins, and we think we can see possibilities with the simplest of cutting tools, which we had not realized." [12]

By 1901 the course in manual training was an integral part of the Normal program. It was designed to prepare teachers to handle classes in manual training in the public schools. There were two courses: elementary cutting and knife work leading to wood-carving for the boys and a sewing course for the girls.

In the practice school manual training began in the fifth year of the primary department. The classes were taught by the practice teachers under supervision of the critics. In the lower grades the work was the same for the boys and girls; in the higher grades the boys did bench work and the girls sewing.

Stowell was very realistic as to what one man could accomplish. "If there were in an institution but a single man, a single thought, the institution would soon get into grooves or ruts, and would become visionary and impractical." [13]

Stowell's faculty policy stimulated imaginative teachers to make some of the basic adaptations that were necessary. Miss Julia Crane, the famous music pioneer, described the policy in these words:

In his relations with his faculty he has shown an absolute confidence in their ability to carry on the work of the department to which each belonged that has given an individuality and strength to the school which is seldom surpassed. While willing to advise and ever ready to help he has given each member of his faculty absolute sovereignty in his own domain.[14]

Stowell looked for certain things in his teachers: scholarship and depth, imagination, excitement, flexibility, inspiration, knowledge of self, of students and of society and a dedicated professional sense. He recognized that the great danger of intellectuality was its stockade potential. One may retire here secure in his own righteousness.

Stowell believed that teaching in Potsdam was a special type of privilege with extraordinary responsibilities. The privilege was at least twofold: to convey one's enthusiasm and understanding as well as knowledge to the future generation, and also to improve one's profession by experimentation and by working in the field. Classroom performance was only a part of one's obligations. Stowell himself was a living example of this type of faculty member.

Stowell set the pace with his experimentation and action research. Imaginative faculty members followed his example. Julia Crane in music, Professor Flagg in history and literature, Alice Bristol in the kindergarten, and Professor Morse in art set the pace. Their spirit and leadership were contagious. Many students caught the spirit. Potsdam Normal became a stimulating place. The result—Potsdam moved rapidly to adapt itself to the ideas of Herbart and Froebel and the other intellectual currents sweeping America. As Stowell had remarked: the permanence of Potsdam's central idea was that individuals added their personalities to the central idea—"removing the weaknesses and adding strength to the efficiency of the school." [15]

MacVicar had insured the introduction of the ideas of Pestalozzi by importing teachers from Oswego to incorporate object teaching in the curriculum. Professor Edward W. Flagg, especially, made sure that the ideas of Johann Friedrich Herbart were included in both content and method courses at Potsdam.

Herbart had placed a great emphasis on moral education and had advocated the use of literature to lift student morals. Disciples of this school believed than a person's social responsibilities depended upon the society he lived in. One's past relations with people, and experience with things, determined people's interests and activities. A creative study of history and literature would illuminate these principles, but it would take a creative teacher to stimulate thoughts other than those on the printed page before him.

Flagg's work in literature and history illustrates the application of Herbartian ideas. Flagg believed that a student reading history or literature should show as much individuality as the writer. To do otherwise would make him a slave to the writer's views and would make reading an end in itself. Reading should be more than mere exercise. Memory work was not real learning.

Flagg pointed out that "unless the reader's individuality rises dominant over the writer's thoughts there will be no essential and permanent growth. It is what we put between the lines—the associated thoughts, the experiences of our lives which are made more impressive in these new lights, and the fresh experiences of other lives—which constitutes the value of right reading." [16]

His lesson plan on the character of Elizabeth, from Green's *History of England* was a particular example of his technique:

The wilfulness of Henry VIII, the triviality of Anne Boleyn played over the surface of a nature hard as steel, a temper purely intellectual, the very type of reason untouched by imagination or passion. . . . Elizabeth seldom saw her course at a glance, but she played with a hundred courses, fitfully and discursively, as a musician runs his fingers over the keyboard, till she hit suddenly upon the right one.[17]

Flagg showed how a mere reading of this passage according to old formal discipline theory was meaningless. Creative reading of the passage required a great deal more. The reader should become acquainted with Henry VIII and Anne Boleyn, historically and individually. The metaphors and their application would have to be understood. Students would have to make a thorough study of Elizabeth and the period she lived in. Flagg also insisted that the full meaning of the passage could only be found and interpreted by knowing what happened before and after this particular period. It was clear that Flagg was familiar with the culture-epoch theory formulated by Tuiskon, Ziller and others.

Flagg insisted that reading the great writers was valuable because they, "besides adding to our knowledge of life, throw new light upon what we have already seen; and with the greatest writers every reading brings its new realizations." [18]

Flagg also introduced Herbart's educational psychology into his method course. Employing Herbart's doctrine of interest, he taught teachers in the five steps of preparation, presentation, association, generalization and application. Fortunately for Potsdam the method course was taught by a man imbued with scholarship.

Herbart's five steps soon degenerated into an empty formalism in the hands of people schooled in the doctrines of formal discipline. But Flagg involved his students emotionally and they realized the true value of a methodology. With this type of training students knew that Herbart's five steps could not do the teaching for them. There was still an art to teaching and they had the privilege of sitting at the feet of a teacher who practiced and exemplified this art.

Stowell imported Miss Alice A. Bristol to incorporate a kindergarten program. She was a graduate of Teachers College, New York City, and had been teaching in the Model School of the School of Pedagogy, Buffalo, New York. She had also observed kindergartens on the continent and was noted for using the most advanced methods.[19]

Alice Bristol was convinced that Froebel's ideas would revolutionize education from the kindergarten to the university. But this could only be achieved when everyone would work for "the same end and that end something larger, higher, nobler than the ability to do puzzles in arithmetic and later in the higher mathematics, to give dates and name battles, to classify and learn scientific names, etc. . . ." [20]

Her kindergarten work placed a great deal of emphasis on activity, self-development and the socializing force of group dynamics. She felt that the activity should spring from the child's own interests, to form a spontaneous world of fantasy, play, clay and paste. The activities should also strengthen the natural creativity of the child.

Her program in the kindergarten provided opportunities for the harmonious development of the child as he engaged in all of these activities. Harmonious development depended on the threefold development of spiritual, mental and physical natures.

Miss Bristol believed that the kindergarten represented the life of the world in miniature, "with the social idea the great idea—a means to a great end." Children were "taught not only to respect the rights of others, but to be generously kind and helpful to each other. They are treated justly themselves and so learn to recognize and practice justice toward others. In their play they imitate the industries and activities of life and are led to sympathize with labor, to see its dignity and beauty, and our dependence upon each other. They are taught personal responsibility, self-control, conservatism and concentrating energy." [21]

Bristol, like all Froebelians, made the story the center of all activities. The story needed to be well chosen and well prepared, and much depended on the art of telling it. [22]

Miss Bristol believed that the work in the kindergarten contributed to overall educational development. Outcome of the work should be the formation of tendencies and habits that provided the foundation for future education.

She asserted that the kindergarten provided training in readiness for reading and language. She also emphasized creative interpretation:

The child is told a story, within his experience of course, and sent to the board to illustrate or he is taken to the door and has his attention called to the action of the wind, the fluttering leaves, flying birds, etc., and asked to tell the story with chalk. He is gaining and giving expression to ideas with nearly every mark he makes. Not your ideas but his own. It is a natural and most helpful introduction to reading and language.[23]

Hattie Leete Clapp, one of Miss Bristol's disciples, perceptively noted the major obstacle to the spread of these ideas —lack of preparation by teachers and lack of appreciation by school boards. Furthermore, no one could run a kindergarten without thorough preparation:

This cannot be accomplished by textbooks. One must see the actual working kindergarten, in master hands, and hear the scheme unfolded by one who knows it from A to Z and watch the development of the child life and manipulate the various materials under skilled direction. Many think they can do work by reading a guide or copying patterns.[24]

Stowell had sensed this and did not run the risk of having a new program based on a new philosophy perverted by a textbook approach. He realized that the knowledge and the art went far beyond a methods text.

He "unhitched" Miss Bristol and she boldly led Potsdam into the twentieth century. Perceptual psychology, the training of the whole child, respect for all life, and Dewey's idea that life in a school is really life in miniature are recognizable in the work of this creative teacher.

Professor Stansbury Norse was another teacher who flourished under Stowell. Believing that the masses should have access to art, Stowell encouraged Norse to found a school of design in 1895.[25] Once again Stowell demonstrated his conviction that just not anyone could teach a subject, and, furthermore, he wanted children protected against this type of teaching.

Soon Norse's course in Principles of Drawing became very popular, attracting thirty to forty students each term. Norse gave a special Drawing Teachers course that would qualify people to teach drawing. This course included "special instruction in design, color, perspective, charcoal and crayon drawing, observation and teaching in the training school and the study of the history of art and psychology." [26]

This department attracted students and teachers from wide areas of the state and beyond. In 1897 two teachers from Bridgeport, Connecticut, enrolled. At the same time it was noted that Miss Rena Wright of New Rochelle was making great progress in her work, which "shows a peculiarly delicate and delightful handling." [27]

In 1897 Professor Norse published *How To Learn Drawing*, a manual for art students. The first section of the book contained his philosophy of art education. He believed that certain principles should govern all art teaching and he discussed fully the mental activities brought into play and how they should be developed. "Perception, resumption, conception, apperception, and judgment are defined, and the training of the mind by the proper methods." [28]

Physical culture programs drew more and more attention from 1860 on. The Civil War had partially punctured the myth of the health and vitality of American youth, especially in the North. Inventories of belongings of youth going into the Union forces revealed a pill for every ache and pain. American schools were more and more expected to provide some type of program.

Once again Stowell fostered the development of a program that would prepare future teachers to fulfill their obligation to American youth. He recognized that few graduates would be teaching in a school with a gymnasium so the course of instruction emphasized "free exercises." No effort was made to produce athletes but the main effort was to develop the body. "To this end exercises are taken to give symmetry of form, grace of movement, and as much strength to every part of the body, as is demanded by student and teacher life." [29]

Originally the elocution teacher handled physical culture but in time concentrated on voice culture and physical expression.

Adequate facilities hampered the development of a physical culture program. The local community once again showed its loyalty to the school. In 1896 a gymnasium was opened in the Ives block for use by the Young Men's Guild of Trinity Church. Many of the Normal boys were invited to join.[30]

In May 1892, Mary Lord Bacon opened a women's gymnasium which used the Ling-Posse (Swedish) system of physical culture. In 1895 Mrs. E. A. Everett permitted the large ballroom on the third floor of her home on Elm Street to be outfitted as a women's gymnasium and Baron Posse of Boston sent Miss Ada Membury to direct classes.[31]

The objective of this program reflected the concern of the school with the development of the whole child:

The aim of the work has been to cultivate the equal development of the leading muscular qualities of the body as a whole, to improve the organism in its functional activity. No attempt is made to cultivate the knotty or excessive contractility of the muscle of the athlete, or the loose-jointed extensibility of the circus performer, but a harmonious combination of the three with the result of a well controlled, co-ordinated force; a progression of work proportioned to each individual of the class, everything in its proper relation according to the laws of physics, physiology and psychology with a result of present exhilaration and health for all time.[32]

In 1888 and 1889 the Stowell Annex, a three-story building on Main Street, was erected. This was connected to the main Normal building by a corridor. It also contained a new gymnasium, 83 feet by 50 feet, provided with running track, apparatus, lockers and showers.[33]

Organized athletics made their appearance during Stowell's tenure. The school fielded teams in football, basketball,

baseball and track. The Normal used the local fairgrounds
for their football games. The following item discussed a game
in October, 1907:

The first football game of the season in the school was played
on the fair grounds October 2, between the Clarkson Freshmen
and the Normals and the score at the close of the last half stood
0 to 0. The weather could not have been better and the gate
receipts were good. The Freshmen tried the new forward pass
several times, but showed lack of practice and lost the ball re-
peatedly. The Normals did not try forward passing as they seemed
to realize they were not ready for it, that is, had not had enough
practice. Neither side made more than 20 yards at any one time by
scrimmage. There was a great deal of punting done.[34]

In 1900 the Normal School, Clarkson Tech and St. Lawrence University began a series of triangular track meets. But
disputes over eligibility and the conduct of the meets soon
brought an end to the meet.[35]

Basketball became very popular at the Normal and the team
compiled enviable records. In November, 1907, they defeated
Ogdensburg Free Academy by a score of 82–4,[36] heralding the
day of the tight defensive play of the Potsdam Bears in the 1960's.

The Normal took great pride in upsetting the better-known
schools:

On the evening of January 2, the "Little Normal Five" met and
defeated Hamilton College at Clinton by a score of 33 to 21. . . .
The players are to be congratulated upon their good work as the
opponents greatly surpassed our fellows in strength and height.[37]

Potsdamites were enthusiastic spectators. In 1903 a Canton
resident observing their presence at a basketball game in Canton between St. Lawrence and University of Pennsylvania said
that they created "too much excitement." [38]

An early harbinger of the later enthusiasm over hockey games
is contained in the following:

The management is always willing to welcome Potsdam crowds, but their presence does not add materially to the scientific playing of basketball.[39]

In addition to recognizing the force of a teacher's personality on the life and ambition of students, Stowell placed great faith on "the reflection of the undergraduate student upon the teacher. . . . So the reflections of the spirits of the young men and young women who have come from this northern land upon us who have been the teaching force have given to us the greatness of the school. And so the character of the undergraduate body is what has made the school." [40]

Stowell developed two policies to try to improve the caliber of the students entering Potsdam: advanced placement and a recommended course of reading for entering students.

The college catalog contained the following description of the placement program:

After admission to the school, either upon one of the prescribed evidences of proficiency or upon examination at the school, students will be given such advanced standing as, in the judgment of the principal, their qualifications warrant. The principal will give such value to the diplomas of other institutions of collegiate or academic grade, and to state certificates issued by the Superintendent of Public Instruction, as he thinks proper in determining whether the student shall be advanced in standing.

In all science subjects nothing but laboratory work will be accepted. In mathematical subjects the reason for every step must be understood. Mere ability to work examples is not sufficient. In Grammar and Rhetoric mere rules and definitions will not suffice. Ability to analyze thought and to write correctly are indispensable.

Pupils who are so advanced without examination will, if on trial found deficient, be required to take up the branches in the school. Thorough, careful preparation in the various branches is indispensable, in order to take up the discussion of methods successfully, and it is always unfortunate for any one to be passed who has not such preparation. Pupils who contemplate being advanced in this way should bring certificates from their teachers, stating definitely the character and the extent of the knowledge gained.[41]

As Stowell continued to raise the standards of the school, he realized that many students lacked adequate preparation in some fields. So he recommended a reading list for prospective students which would help them in the literature and rhetoric courses required at the college:

I. Dickens' *History of England;* Abbott's *Elizabeth, Richard III, William the Conqueror;* Shakespeare's *King John;* Scott's *Kenilworth, Ivanhoe;* Thackeray's *Four Georges, Henry Esmond.*

II. Higginson's *U.S. History;* Kingsley's *Westward Ho!;* Stowe's *Uncle Tom's Cabin;* Cooper's *Last of the Mohicans;* Longfellow's *Miles Standish;* Irving's *Knickerbocker.*

III. Hawthorne's *Tanglewood Tales,* and *Wonder Book; Stories from Iliad and Odyssey; Stories from the Grecian Dramatists;* Merivale's *History of Rome;* Cox's *History of Greece;* Plutarch's *Lives;* Froude's *Caesar;* Trollope's *Cicero;* Bulwer's *Last Days of Pompeii;* Eber's *Uarda;* Macaulay's *Lays of Ancient Rome.*

IV. Hugo's *Les Miserables;* Taylor's *Faust;* George Eliot's *Romola;* Goldsmith's *Vicar of Wakefield;* Dickens' *Tale of Two Cities;* Warner's *Back Log Studies;* Holmes' *Autocrat of the Breakfast Table;* Longfellow's *Evangeline;* Alford's *Queen's English;* Moon's *Dean's English;* Miller's *My Schools and Schoolmasters;* Milton's *Paradise Lost;* Emerson's *Representative Men;* Lamb's *Tales from Shakespeare;* Hawthorne's *House of Seven Gables;* Yonge's *History of France;* Yonge's *History of Germany.*[42]

Stowell viewed student life as an integral part of the educative process. Like MacVicar, he believed fundamentally in character development but achieved it in a different way. People remembered MacVicar pointing his long finger di-

*Edwin A. Merritt, leader in community efforts to establish Potsdam
Normal School*

Dr. Malcolm MacVicar, first president of Potsdam Normal School

Dr. Thomas B. Stowell, president of Potsdam Normal School, eminent scientist and progressive administrator

First Potsdam Normal School building, 1868–1919

Professor Edward W. Flagg with his Yale University classmate, former President William Howard Taft, at Potsdam Normal School, October 21, 1915

rectly at everyone and saying, "Be good men and women." He had rigid discipline and firmly believed in its efficacy.

But Stowell recognized that the forces altering American society and American education called for a change in policy. Students had to be treated in a more mature manner if they were going to be successful teachers. Stowell's official statement on student discipline included:

The discipline of the school is based upon the largest liberty but not license. Pupils who do not wish to do good and faithful work are not desired. This institution is dedicated to study, and to professional training. We believe that where little is required from pupils much should be expected. Personal discipline is placed among the most important accomplishments of a Normal student.[43]

Faculty members noticed immediately that to achieve this end Stowell used different means from those used by traditionalists like MacVicar. Miss Crane said that Stowell believed that students were best led by positive, not negative teaching. So he showed them the desirability of the right course of action instead of the wrong:

Then came the rather revolutionary idea that matters of discipline were not public property even for the faculty; and we discovered that underneath what seemed an arbitrary ruling, was the principle that prejudice is often engendered in one teacher by the opinions of another. . . .[44]

Miss Crane was impressed by Stowell's quiet, confident, unassuming manner in dealing with students. She noted that he worked "quietly and with a determination to find the best in each one, and nourish that best to its highest possibilities." [45]

Students reacted positively to his approach. Many students were lifted out of discouragement and acquired higher ideals. "Some who have started on the downward road have been made to see the light which brightened for them the ascending path. . . . " [46]

Some people called Stowell's discipline lax, but "those who have seen more clearly have realized that the hearty cooperation of students and teachers, the entire absence of viciousness, the cheerful obedience and loyalty of the students which are marked characteristics of the school are the direct result of his ideals of discipline." [47]

Stowell encouraged faculty participation in this new approach. Miss Bristol was one who played a conspicuous role in this development. She insisted that the social life of the school should be as important as any other feature. This would develop a closer feeling between the faculty and students. Informality was the keynote of her social gatherings in the kindergarten room.

For the first time in Potsdam's history, student life became a prominent feature of school life. Stowell had won his point. A student could be human and enjoy life without destroying his character.

The literary societies continued their discussions and debate. Now, however, there were union or joint meetings of male and female organizations. Debates were prominent at these meetings but they became more and more social in the new atmosphere. "The Alphas and Delphics spent a very enjoyable evening recently in dancing at the Normal Gym" became common.[48] "The annual ball of the Delphic Fraternity occurred December seventh, 1908, was a grand success, it being the finest social event that has occurred for sometime. Eighty couples who enjoyed themselves greatly were in attendance." [49] "The annual banquet of the Francis Baconian and Calliopean societies occurs Friday evening, January 15th, in the gymnasium. A delightful time is anticipated." [50]

The strains of an inspiring two-step drifted from the gymnasium. "Soon the floor was filled with merry dancers, and from that time until 10:30, the hour set for parting, waltzes and two-steps succeeded each other rapidly." [51]

In February, 1908, the ladies of the faculty gave a reception for the basketball team.[52] A Calliopean wrote: "Our worthy friend of the Delphic . . . seems surprised to learn that the Calliopean society entertains a friendly feeling for the fraternity. Is it strange and unlooked for. . . . " [53]

Allens Falls by then had competition. "Potsdam now has its steamboat ramble among the islands. Hiram H. Swift has placed upon the river a launch so that one can have a three mile excursion among the Thousand Islands of Potsdam and all for 25 cents." "Straw rides seem to be the order of the day." [54]

Dr. Stowell rose to make an announcement. "Now the ice is very good for skating [on the Racquette River]. I thought perhaps you were not aware of the fact. I hope you will avail yourselves of every opportunity to go skating. Never mind classes or lessons—just skate, and skate, and skate, but don't turn into a skate." A student recalled that "most of us took this announcement literally and perhaps we would have turned into skates (skating out of Normal for good) if Dame Nature had not intervened and sent a regular northern New York blizzard to prevent such a catastrophe." [55]

Symbolic of the new faculty-student feeling was the annual Halloween party in the Normal gym which was decorated to "represent everything that was weird and uncanny." Professor Flagg was the perennial master of ceremonies. "Ancient games, contests and 'stunts' of all kinds were cheerfully entered into by all." The stunts usually were full of puns at various members of the faculty and student body.[56]

Stowell's faculty and student policies created an unmistakable spirit which visitors were quick to notice. Dr. Sheldon of Oswego was overwhelmed by it. After visiting the Normal for two or three days and mingling freely with faculty and students, he said to Dr. Stowell:

My dear boy, you have got here the greatest school I have ever witnessed in my life. Are you aware of the spirit of this school? There is nothing like it to be found in the country. I would give anything if I only had the spirit of this school in my school. We haven't anything like it, and I don't think it can be duplicated anywhere else.[57]

Stowell was well aware of this spirit. He had deliberately fostered it, feeling that it would impart a new dynamism to Potsdam's ideal of quality preparation of teachers. Like his predecessors Stowell based his program of teacher education on scholarship, the science of teaching and the art of teaching.

Like Brainerd and MacVicar he placed great emphasis on the practice school. The key to the successful operation of this school depended upon the experienced teachers in charge. By 1900 a real problem had emerged in Potsdam as elsewhere— a demand for teachers specially trained to teach methodology, to give criticism and to supervise training classes.

Recognizing the need Stowell established a graduate course for the special training of method teachers and critics. From the outset the course received favorable comments because of the needs it met:

To learn how to adjust mind to subject matter is quite distinct from learning how to instruct others how to make such adjust-ment. It may be safely affirmed that few persons have the qualifi-cations inherent or acquired, which fit them for teachers of methods, and fewer still make effective critics and supervisors. . . . Criticism is both science and art; it requires active sympathy, keen appreciation of the needs of pupils, ability to totalize self, quick command of resources, fertility of expedients, and especially a desire to be helpful united with positive experiental knowledge of success in helping others. These special qualifications pre-suppose the general, such as manliness, high conceptions of the possibilities of human nature, experience with children and ap-perceptive knowledge of mind, the interdependence of mind activities, the characters referrable to heredity and to environment, vivid imagination and power of visualization.

Methodology is not a series of model lessons, or an elaboration of speculative pedagogics. The question should be asked of every teacher of methods, "have you personally tested your theories; are you ready to summon a class before your teachers-in-training and vindicate your claims?" Methodology presupposes clear and comprehensive knowledge of pedagogical psychology, and ability to present work which will be intelligible, inspiring and helpful. . . .[58]

Stowell was hopeful that this type of teacher would help develop a teacher as much in demand as in the days of Asa Brainerd.

Potsdam graduates made their mark in two distinct areas: advanced work in other colleges and in the teaching profession. A president of a college confided to Stowell that "Potsdam was the only Normal School in the State that sent them qualified students."

A school man in New York City confessed that he obtained more superior women from "the Potsdam Normal School than from all other sources combined, and the marvel to me has been how it was possible, and I have come up here to see, and I find the secret. . . ." [60]

Testimonials of this nature attest to the success of Stowell's administration. Brainerd's shadow still cast its spell on Potsdam but crucial days lay ahead in the twentieth century. Stowell brought Potsdam Normal to the threshold of modern times. Would there be new people who could add their personalities to the Potsdam tradition, removing weaknesses and adding strength to the efficiency of the school?

The balance sheet on Dr. Stowell was impressive. He retained the best of the Potsdam tradition, updated it and made it more functional. He demonstrated how a school could maintain its leadership by adapting to change. He raised the warning signs for those who would stand still.

Stowell's great contribution was the development of the Potsdam "spirit." This was a direct result of his faculty and student policies. His encompassing view of the total educational process infused the Potsdam tradition with a new richness. Any future could hold promise with a Dr. Thomas Stowell directing the school.

Chapter Six

JULIA E. CRANE

JULIA E. Crane represented the flowering of the Potsdam tradition. The basic ideas of teacher education that had been developed since the days of Asa Brainerd found full expression in her pioneer work in music education. She was a brilliant example of what an imaginative teacher can do under the leadership of a stimulating administrator.

Julia Crane was a Potsdam native. She attended Potsdam district schools and was one of the first students to attend the Normal School, graduating in 1874.

Her musical talent was evident at an early age. She began studying the piano at 11, and by 14 had a reputation of possessing a "resonant, pure voice and an inborn feeling for effective interpretation." She soon became an outstanding vocalist and performed in school, church choirs, singing schools and in local music festivals.

After graduating from the Normal she taught in the Potsdam public schools and at the Shippensburg, Pennsylvania, Normal School. In 1881, General and Mrs. Merritt invited her to be their guest during General Merritt's tour of duty as Consul General in London. She accepted, and used the opportunity to study voice under Manuel Garcia, celebrated teacher of Jenny Lind.

Returning to Potsdam, she opened a private voice studio for two years and at the same time continued her active participation in North Country musical activities.

In the spring of 1884 the music teacher at the Normal School resigned. The music teacher at this time led hymns at chapel, prepared music for public exercises and devoted much time to private lessons. Students desiring voice or instrumental lessons took them on a private basis.

The board offered Miss Crane the position. At first she was reluctant to accept it because her voice studio was prospering and she wanted to continue her concert work.

Mr. Watkins, president of the board, pleaded, "the Normal School position requires only one period of class teaching per day, conducting the singing in chapel and preparing music for commencement and other school exhibitions. You may have all the rest of the time to continue your voice work. We will furnish your studio and pianos for your own use and for the practice of your pupils." [1]

Miss Crane's major objection to the offer was her conviction that one class period per day was not sufficient time in which to do the work in music that ought to be done in a Normal School. She said that she would take the job under one condition:

The only thing that would tempt me to take the position would be the privilege of working out a plan which had been in my mind from the time I completed my Normal course. My Normal School instructors had made me very enthusiastic over Methods of Teaching, and I had realized that it ought to be thought possible to give similar instruction in Normal music classes. The thought had often been in my mind that with proper training, Normal graduates might be as well fitted to teach the music of the grades as they were to teach reading or history. [2]

Mr. Watkins seized this opening. "Miss Crane, if you will take this position, I promise you that I will do everything in

my power to make it possible for you to work out your ideals." [3]
She accepted the offer at a salary of $300 per year effective
September, 1884.

Miss Crane was a pioneer and innovator in the image of
Asa Brainerd. She had a plan to implement, backed by zest
and courage.

She studied the music course in the Normal School, then
wrote a letter to the State Superintendent, stating that
neither time nor funds were adequate to train people to
teach music.

Miss Crane then presented a plan for training teachers of
music and sought permission to try it. "The permission
came and I started a piece of work the results of which . . .
I did not foresee, even in my dreams," [4] she wrote.

When Dr. Cook, Principal of the Normal School, met
Miss Crane he asked how she expected to prepare music
teachers in one period of instruction per day for twenty
weeks. She agreed that it was impossible.

Dr. Cook was so intent upon making Miss Crane's program
a success that he adjusted the schedule to permit a daily
singing period, as well as a short period for teaching music
reading, in the primary and intermediate departments. This
second period was so arranged that Normal students were
freed from all class responsibilities in order that they might
observe and teach music at that time. It was also possible
for a "Normalite" to study music throughout an entire course.

Miss Crane's efforts were successful in both her Normal
School course and in her private studio. Soon the increased
demand for music instruction resulted in the creation of the
Normal Conservatory. The Conservatory, later called the
Crane Normal Institute of Music, was a private school that
supplemented the music program in the Normal School. It
had a faculty of three: Miss Crane, teacher of voice, methods
and survey; F. E. Hathorne, teacher of piano, organ and
harmony; Mr. Watkins, son of the president of the board, in

charge of orchestra. Miss Crane taught theory and methods in the Normal and voice in the Conservatory. It was her personality that made the programs mutually supporting.

During the first two years some of Miss Crane's private voice pupils enrolled in her Normal School course so that they could teach music in the public schools. This was the beginning of the music supervisor's program. From this program, inaugurated in 1886, were graduated seven candidates in 1888, the first special music teachers graduated from any Normal School in the United States. Like Brainerd's graduates, Miss Crane's students were soon in demand, for they raised the standards of music teaching.

The basic curriculum of this pioneer course was simple concentration on musical studies, professional courses for understanding children, public school orientation and methodology, and practical application of the whole program. The course required two years. The main items were:

Twenty weeks of notation and terminology.
Forty weeks of music history.
Forty weeks of musical form.
Eighty weeks of ear training.
Eighty weeks of sight singing.
One hundred weeks study of part songs by standard and classic composers, in chorus class and Phoenix Club.
Forty weeks of harmony.
Ten weeks of acoustics.
Forty weeks of methods of teaching.
Twenty weeks of psychology.
Ten weeks of history of education.
Forty weeks of observation.
Teaching in the practice school.
Teaching in the graded schools of the town.
Supervision of other teachers.
Conducting of choruses.
Teaching extra classes in ear training, voice training, theory, etc.
Private lessons in voice culture.

All music classes had two recitations per week, Psychology five, and History of Education five.[5]

Miss Crane constantly devoted more of her time after 1888 to training music specialists. A realist, she sensed that the impact of her ideas would have to become known through these persons. She also realized that the time had come for the massive execution of her ideas. In her own way, she was avoiding Brainerd's mistake of not being emotionally understood.

Although she was convinced of the soundness of her views and her program, she wanted to study the methods of other music institutions and other school systems. In 1891 she took a one year leave of absence and traveled extensively throughout the United States, studying music education programs.

She studied schools in Denver, Colorado, and then moved on to California. She presented papers, gave talks and sang at teacher meetings in Pasadena, San Diego and Riverside:

She was invited to talk to the teachers at Riverside. Afterward Superintendent Keys wrote to Superintendent Monroe of Pasadena: "You must ask Miss Crane to talk to your teachers. My experience has been that among 1,000 music teachers about 800 know music, but nothing of schools, 150 know music and have had some successful experience in schoolwork, 40 have added to these qualities the ability to sing or play, 9 are fine performers, good teachers and understand fairly the pedagogy of their work, and one is a beautiful singer, plays the piano, understands music, is a born teacher, and so clear in her knowledge of the pedagogy of her work that she can impart her knowledge of the art of teaching to others. This one is Miss Crane.[6]

Miss Crane continued her trip through the Midwest, winning the plaudits of educators in Minnesota and Wisconsin. The records of the Crane Normal Institute showing graduates from these areas bore testimony to her influence.

Miss Crane returned to Potsdam with new ideas that added

new dimensions to her program. Soon the continued popularity and expansion of the music program created a space problem. Miss Crane purchased a house next to the Normal School on Main Street, which served as her residence and a home for the Institute. The vocal studies, practice room and business office were located here. Classwork was still conducted in the Normal building. But by 1910 more space was required. Her request came at the same time as an offer was made to move her Institute to Syracuse:

The classes in music history, harmony, sight singing, etc. were still conducted in the Normal Building, but in cramped and inconvenient rooms, until the year after Dr. Thompson came to the school as Principal. Dr. Street had invited me to move the Music School to Syracuse and had offered us the title "Crane Normal Institute of Music in Connection with Syracuse University." At this time, the local board of the Normal School agreed to provide better quarters if we would remain in Potsdam. It was then that the large chemical laboratory of the second floor of the Science Building was cut into four rooms, and the school found itself provided with three class rooms, a library and study room, a cloak room and an office, all convenient of access to Science Hall in which chorus and orchestra work could be done.[7]

Concomitant with the expansion of her program and the increased demand for Crane graduates was the problem of staff:

As the demand for teachers grew, it became evident that there was need of a broader training, and that one teacher could not teach all the music of the Normal School, and at the same time, give the special students more attention. The Local Board of the Normal School first engaged someone to help me by looking over papers and doing other clerical duties, but finally increased my salary and asked me to engage such help as I thought suitable. My first assistant taught music history and helped with the voice pupils; later Miss Austin and Mrs. Bryant were engaged, Miss

Austin teaching some Normal Classes—Music History and Harmony to the special pupils—and Mrs. Bryant taking the voice pupils for whom I no longer had sufficient time.[8]

The Crane Institute continued the Potsdam tradition of service to the community. Recitals, concerts and other musical programs became important cultural events in the school and community, and local residents were particularly interested in lesson demonstrations at commencement. These were commonplace between 1888 and 1916. Children from the primary and intermediate departments formed a class and Crane graduates directed them in sight singing, rote singing and other musical activities.

Recital programs in the 1890's were confined to the piano students of Miss Crane and Mr. Hathorne. Greater variety was added in the early 1900's: instrumental and vocal recitals, "class" and "all-school" recitals, faculty recitals and others of special interest.

The annual concert was presented each spring as a culminating activity, with music students, Normal students, faculty and professional guests participating. Later the high school chorus and orchestra were added. Miss Crane conducted these concerts for more than twenty-five years.

The founding, early growth and success of the Crane Institute were due primarily to Miss Crane's personality, philosophy and recognized abilities. The active encouragement and support of the local Normal Board and the State Education Department were strong contributing factors. The quality of Crane graduates, and their success in teaching, widely advertised the work of the Institute. Miss Crane observed:

The success of our graduates must be accounted for by the thorough and practical quality of the work done in the school. It had been the policy of the school to allow each teacher to specialize in the line of work for which his talents and training best fitted him, and once in his right place, to allow him absolute freedom to work out his highest ideals. While this has required a larger faculty than is usually found in a small school, it has proven the wise course, as each teacher has been enthusiastic and happy in his work, as well as constantly growing in breadth of culture and skill.[9]

Finally, there was the *Music Teacher's Manual.* Soon after founding the school, Miss Crane fulfilled a definite need by publishing a simple "Outline of Work" used by students of the early classes. In time the "outline" was revised and enlarged to contain a complete discussion of all work done in the regular normal classes, including subject matter for classes in theory, an outline of the preparatory work in teaching. The entire work for methods, a complete course of study for the primary and intermediate departments, lists of music and music reading systems, and philosophical and psychological principles at the foundation of music teaching were included. The first edition was available in 1887 and the last edition, the eighth, was published in 1923. The *Manual* was widely distributed and used as a text in several music teacher institutions across the United States.

Miss Crane brought together the strands of the Potsdam tradition and she inspired many students. The welfare of the student was the base of her philosophy, placing heavy responsibility on the teacher to provide the proper setting for self-realization. She believed that the teaching of music required deep understanding of music and values:

It is not necessary that I prove my ability as a music supervisor through the performance of operettas and dramatic entertainments, which involve endless labor and practice and add little to the child's musical equipment. But if I would prove the value of music in the schools, I must lay the same foundation for future work that is required of the teacher of reading and arithmetic.

What would be thought of a teacher of reading who found it necessary to parade the children of her grade in poems and dramatic prose learned by rote, and yet failed to prepare them for the intelligent reading necessary for the study of literature and history? How absurd would be the attitude of a teacher who trained her pupils in showy tricks with figures, sending them on to the teachers of advanced arithmetic, algebra and geometry unable to add, subtract, and multiply. And yet is this any more unwise than the use of the school music period for the repetition of ditties unworthy of the name of music, whose sole end is a school entertainment?[10]

Miss Crane insisted on presenting music in an intellectually honest way. Any other attempt would defeat her purposes, She developed a curriculum and a method to accomplish this purpose.

She was also deeply concerned with the problem of balance. "Until music supervisors realize that their work is an integral part of a great whole and that it has not served its purpose until it acts in harmony with the other parts of that whole, it is certain that music will never take its rightful place in the scheme of education." [11]

Her emphasis on scholarship did not blind her to the dangers of intellectuality. If music were to contribute to the increasing power, abilities and tastes of an individual, its use would have to be intelligently planned:

These ideals and this power are not gained merely through acquiring a knowledge of the three R's; neither are they obtained through the addition of art and music to the courses of study. In other words, the course of study through which one passes is not the sole agent that determines his ideals, neither does it give a man the power to live up to those ideals. But a wisely planned course of study, plus honest and intelligent effect in mastering it, do wield a mighty influence over character.

For this reason the answer to the question "what are the best means for accomplishing the ultimate ends of school music?" seems even more important than a definition of the ends themselves.[12]

Miss Crane felt that music had unique qualities for the development of the emotional aspect of a child's potential but that desired results depended on the quality of teaching:

We use music in our school not only for the musical ability which pupils acquire through its study, but for the development of character toward which we think all education should aim. We believe that music has a power to reach the emotions which other branches of study do not possess, and that it is therefore not only a desirable factor in education, but an absolutely necessary element for fully rounded development. While I thoroughly believe that music has this power, I also feel that it must be properly presented to the pupil in order to reach the highest results. So while I long to see the day when every child shall be brought under its benign influence, I do not advocate compulsory music; in other words, I believe that the teachers must be prepared for the work before they are required by law to teach music.[13]

She recognized that the aesthetic values of music complicated the problem of teaching. In the hands of charlatans the masses could be kept in ignorance of the true values of music:

Superintendents, supervisors, and teachers should be convinced that schools build for the future, and that music is only part of the curriculum. The element which music contributes to education is an aesthetic element, and because of this, dishonesty of practice gives it an influence antagonistic to the beneficent influence it should exert. Better no music, than music taught by dishonest methods.[14]

Miss Crane felt strongly that music and education should try to develop refinement, taste and the intellect. Properly taught music contributed to the cultivation of the senses, of the ear and the eye and awakened a sense of the beautiful. At the same time music contributed to mental discipline.

But fortunately she was aware that the ideas of Rousseau, Pestalozzi, Herbart, Spencer and Froebel had widened the horizons for educating the whole person.

She believed also in a therapeutic value of music. "An element which lifts the thoughts above evil things, which makes obedience a pleasure and creates a love for the good, the true, and the beautiful, assists in the moral training of the young. That music does this, none deny. Good music arouses a spirit of good will, creates a harmonious atmosphere, and where harmony and good will prevail, the disobedient, unruly spirit finds no resting place." [15]

Miss Crane believed that joy in learning was the result of successful achievement on the part of the student:

> If a child takes pleasure in the work he is doing (and he will if the work is adapted to his stage of development) then we may decide that the plan of teaching is a good one. But if his pleasure arises from the glamour cast over the work by ingenious devices of the teacher, what will be his condition when he is brought face to face with work, stripped of all its garnishings.
>
> It is a false hypothesis upon which to base a plan for teaching, that children enjoy play better than work. Work properly adapted to the capacity and development of the child may bring him the highest pleasure; and the earlier in life he learns these pleasures, the better for him.[16]

The best results could be achieved by applying one of Brainerd's principles. Music should be presented in a manner permitting self-discovery, which in turn would lead to self-realization:

> No subject taught in the public schools is more capable of giving to the child real, active, independent work than music rightly taught. In its study he may see himself day by day acquiring power—the power to do today what he could not do yesterday. He may find himself skillful where once he was awkward, quick

where once he was slow. It is easy to do the work for the children, to make the pretty toy and present it complete, in the form of a beautiful song. But it takes skill, tact, real teaching ability, to make the child an independent worker in the field of music. . . . Beware of any method of teaching which has as its basis an effort to amuse. Our race must be educated to sturdy effort, and whether we teach music or the carpenter's trade, our success is in proportion to the desire for independent effort which we awaken in our pupils.[17]

The method of presentation was the key to whether a student would be led to self-discovery and on to fulfillment:

The fact that truth is beautiful and attractive in itself, does not, however, do away with the fact that the manner of presenting the truth is of highest importance. All honor then is due those earnest and enthusiastic teachers who discover or invent new and beautiful modes of presentation, or who search out relations that give new life to old ideas.

When the work of the day, or perhaps it is better to say the work of the whole course of study is so arranged, and so intelligently presented that the facts of history become an inspiration for a higher and purer living; when nature study brings pupils closer to the vital principles of life; when reading and music become a means for learning the thoughts and emotions of the great masters of poetry and art, and later, a beautiful expression of one's own best thoughts and feelings; then may we say truly that there are teachers who have solved not only the problem of correlation, but the problem of education.[18]

Miss Crane prescribed no fixed set of rules to attain these ideals, but recognized that the basic criterion of any procedure was its ability to awaken latent ideas and talents:

I do not know the best methods; but I have meant to say that in all education there seems to be a tendency to an enervating sensuous habit of work, which is as destructive to good results in teaching as the life which leads to it is to the progress of the race. In all our search for right methods we need to remember that showy structures are not always based upon stable foundations, and that, while time and storms may wear off the gilding and chip off florid ornamentation, the house that is built upon the rock will stand. And it seems to me not an indefinite or vague standard that I am setting up, for in simple language it reads: Keep your eyes open for the light; work with sincerity of purpose; have no fear when your pet theories are demolished; for nothing that is right can be destroyed, and the destruction of the false makes way for the true.[19]

Perhaps Helen Hosmer has best expressed Miss Crane's basic approach: thorough preparation to introduce and explain the subject matter, in the sense of unlocking a door to a room, into which the students entered to find answers for themselves. This was followed by a guiding and drawing process to clarify, deepen and enrich student experience, along tried and proven educational principles.[20]

Miss Crane believed that methods rested on the child's taste, his various states of mind and the development of his body. The growth processes of the child provided insight necessary for the application of fundamental principles. She decided sense training and technical facility should be correlated with the growth of the child. In the first grade music should be presented to the child almost exclusively through the ear, insuring a foundation for interest, taste and appreciation.

Formal and technical training should be presented at the time that the child acquired techniques in his other courses. Music reading, notation and ear training were essential for future discovery:

To fail to give a child the power to read music in the years when he is gaining the technique of all his other studies, puts him in an embarrassing position as a high school student, and later in college, creating a feeling regarding music, which makes the development of appreciation next to impossible.[21]

Miss Crane sensibly realized that there was no one type of lesson for all teaching situations. So a prospective teacher should have experience in all types. Her *Manual* provided material on eight different types of lessons. Students learned descriptions, illustrations and simple lessons for each type, then applied them in actual teaching.

The lesson in appreciation was the last type presented. Although appreciation of the art of music represented the culmination of the study of music for Miss Crane, she considered every lesson as a preparation for future awakening within the child a love for beauty in music. The preparation of the lesson was geared to give the child a feeling of personal association with the composer and his music. Correlation played a large part in providing a sense of affiliation. Therefore, reading, art, history and geography were useful in contributing to the lesson. Music selected for listening purposes was to be of highest quality both as to musical integrity and artistic excellence. The overall effect of the experience was determined through questioning on the part of the teacher to ascertain the interest and understanding of the children.

Another portion of the *Manual* was devoted to specific problems in teaching music along with suggested techniques for solution.

The problem of music reading was approached as a matter of pitch and rhythm discrimination and the plan for the study was in three phases: imitative, recognition and representation. Any new learning was to be presented by getting the child to repeat back what he had heard. Recognition of the material was followed by the student actually notating the music. Basic to the study of pitch was familiarity and facility with the scale. The use of syllables was advocated as a primary means to establish relationships of pitches within a tonality. In a statement dated 1896, Miss Crane said:

The problem of the public school teacher is to give to pupils who have never played an instrument, a unit of measurement, a means by which, when they are in doubt, they may measure the scale relations with accuracy. . . . Twelve years ago, I too feared the results of syllables. I was converted from my doubts by actual experience in the public schools, and for the last 8 to 10 years, have used syllables exclusively for elementary work. . . . as I test pupils who have come up under this treatment, I find that the syllable singing has been disregarded like the burr from the ripened nut, its purpose served, its day of usefulness over. Until this stage is reached, I should as readily try to teach children to measure cloth by the eye without the use of a yardstick as the scale without definite names to sing.[22]

Sample outlines or lesson plans were included in the *Manual*. These plans were never intended to structure a class. Her philosophy could be followed by any enthusiast as a lesson plan:

Any plan which can be made before teaching the class is necessarily inadequate. Each day's work should be planned from the needs of the individuals in the class with the purpose to be accomplished clearly in mind, and with the aim of making the lesson a helpful link between the work already done, and that which is to be done in the future.

The teacher should aim to give the child a clear idea of the end toward which they are working, arousing a desire in each pupil's mind, to accomplish the tasks set before him. In all drill work, state the purpose, and call attention to the gain made through this drill. Teach nothing that cannot be used in future lessons.[23]

Miss Crane's deep concern for the individual was revealed in her treatment of boys' changing voices:

Formerly it was the custom to have the boys cease singing entirely during the period, with the result that the boys lost all interest in music and that after their voices were settled they would not sing, and furthermore boys who possessed fine alto or soprano voices had poor voices after the change. She formed the boys into separate classes and kept them singing, choosing music especially adapted and within the compass, with the result that the boys took increased interest in their music. Many of the boys became leaders after the period of mutation. The best child voices became the best men voices. There was no roughness and no break and the period of mutation passed almost imperceptibly. Many boys failed to know when the change came. She said that it is evident that to keep boys singing during the mutation period helps the voice, lessens the length of the period and avoids roughness in the voice afterward.[24]

Miss Crane believed that voice training was primarily a matter of emotions and that singing was the whole being, working in harmony with the music. The condition of the mind and the consequent expression of the body produced a characteristic tone. A happy, free, buoyant tone was the quality desired. She felt that this could be attained by adhering to the following guidelines: children cannot be scolded into singing; a happy quality of tone can come only from a happy heart; a change of facial expression will change the quality of tone; if children sing badly, make them happy and they will sing better; before beginning a song, see that the children are comfortable and in a happy frame of mind; a pleasant smile from the teacher, a cheery word, or a well-chosen story, may all be time saved in the end, as the results cannot be right if the spirits are dull; choose songs of a bright and lively character, varying with lullabies, or other quiet songs, but never using somber, sad songs with young children . . . ; choose songs of high pitch rather than low pitch . . . ; naturally children sing sweetly, and need only to be kept singing naturally to sing well . . . ; require correct pronunciation, clear vowels, and short, distinct consonants, with no running of one letter into another, but at the same time, no jerking of sounds.[25]

Miss Crane placed a great deal of faith in music as a science but also emphasized that it was an art. "Music is an art, but this art may be shorn of all its power by a lack of proper attention to the science upon which it is based. Our problem then seems to be to steer wisely between the Scylla of imitative work requiring no initiative on the part of the pupil, and the Charybdis of intellectual drudgery over facts that never function in the life of the masses, into that joyous haven where mastery of self and of necessary technical difficulties has developed the power to stand by the lofty ideals to which the artistic appreciation of music may uplift." [26]

The role of the teacher was paramount in attaining this ideal. At no time should a teacher place her aspirations before those of the student. Successful accomplishment was the key to results. The student should recognize for himself that pleasure came from self-achievement, for the duty of the teacher was to put the positive before the student by leading him into the best possible learning situation and then drawing from him the understanding of basic truths.[27]

Julia Crane was Brainerd's democratic disciple. Believing as she did in the contributory role of music toward the development of the full potential of an individual, she insisted on music for all the students. To her this was a logical fulfillment of equality.

Like Brainerd, she felt that democracy depended upon access to this equality. She pointed out on more than one occasion that music did not belong solely to the aristocracy. Music had become mixed up with the schools; and once in the school, it belonged to the masses.

Miss Crane realized that music was part of the North Country heritage—it had been part of its people. It was this universal appeal that helped music win a place in the schools.

Her innovation was that music could be studied by the masses and be beneficial to them:

What place has music in the life of people? It is recognized as a harmonizing influence in the home; our churches demand it as a vital part of the service; we ask for it to enliven our pleasures and to assuage our griefs, and in these latter days the hospitals are employing it as a therapeutic agent. Is there any one thing more universally demanded by mankind than music?

On the other hand, is there any field in which the charlatan thrives with more security from detection? Is there any field in which the best that art can furnish is less appreciated? Is there any field in which a stone can be palmed off for bread with greater ease? Why is this true? Because of the ignorance of the masses. Is it necessary that the masses remain ignorant? Is the musician's art complex and beyond the appreciation of the public? I think no one who has seen its effects will disagree with me in the statement that nothing ever introduced into the public schools is so simple, so easily comprehended, nothing brings greater return in real understanding and development, for the time spent, than music.[28]

Julia Crane felt that certain qualities would enhance a teacher's success in performing this role. Humility was high on her list of qualifications:

Would there be any doubt of the dignity of the profession if all teachers were animated by the same spirit that gave Arnold of Rugby his world-wide fame? And what is this spirit but the spirit of humility, the "love that seeketh not her own"? Surely this spirit, understood and demonstrated, would long ago have given school teachers not only rank but power, a power born of the "love that never faileth."

But what, say you, has all this to do with the insignificant problems of the music teacher? I have stated this fundamental principle upon which all true teaching rests, because I am convinced that it is only by its application to our problems that even the minutest of them is correctly solved, and only as these are correctly solved so we merit the rank of "God-ordained Priests for teaching."

It is often noted that the "newly rich" show the most arrogant pride in wealth; the college freshman is only exceeded in pride of learning by the first year high-school lad; and we as school music teachers, the newest accessions to the teaching force, are the surest of our methods, the most arrogant of our learning. The teachers of the three R's have seen too many changes in the methods of teaching to feel that the last word has been spoken for them, and with their humility comes the possibility of still greater progress. As we examine the various stages of development from the old alphabet method of teaching reading, through the phonic, word, and sentence methods, down to the methods of the present day, we realize that it has been the teachers of sufficient humility and love to catch the mental processes of the child at his work, who have brought about these improvements.[29]

A successful teacher had definite obligations and responsibilities:

The teacher or supervisor of school music must today be a musician of no mean attainments; he must sing well, understand the care of the voice, play the piano, and understand the orchestral instruments sufficiently to be able to conduct a high school orchestra. He must understand the history and theory of music, for many high schools are offering elective courses in these subjects. . . . He must be well versed in the pedagogical literature of the day and must know the most approved methods of teaching, not to be able to teach other subjects, but because the grade teachers far better use his plans and instructions if he can illustrate the methods of teaching with which they are familiar. . . . He must be the most successful disciplinarian in the school.[30]

She was well aware that a music teacher was a functional member of a faculty and a community:

The supervisor of music must then know the needs of the community, must know the relation of the school to the community, must see the trend of modern education and realize his own relation to the work which the schools must do in order to reach their goal.

Then the problems of the high school should be shared with the pupil teachers. No one should enter the field as a supervisor who has not seen the high school from the teacher's standpoint. And it is not the music in the high school that requires exclusive attention, but the relation of the music to the rest of the schedule, the reaction of the music upon the life of the school, both scholastic and social.

Until music supervisors realize that their work is an integral part of a great whole and that it has not served its purpose until it acts in harmony with the other parts of that whole, it is certain that music will never take its rightful place in the scheme of education.[31]

Like Brainerd, she emphasized growth in the profession. This depended upon the teacher's own initiative:

The place in which one does his teaching does not decide his success, nor his reputation. Who is it that has said something to the effect that though your place be in the wilderness the world will wear a path to your door if you have something to give that the world wants. I hear so many reports from teachers who find their positions "undesirable, narrow, no opportunity for growth," that I wonder if it ever occurs to them that we really grow from the inside out, not from the outside in.[32]

A teacher should broaden her experience, be aware of the need for self-improvement and be willing to accept and try the new:

One of the most interesting as well as one of the most helpful things a teacher can do is to visit schools. Find out where there are teachers at work who are getting results, then go to see how they accomplish those results. Don't look for perfection, and don't stop to find fault with the things you can do better yourself. These are not the profitable things for you, but pay your most earnest attention to the lines of work which are better than your own.[33]

She left a warning for all those who prefer to retire behind their intellectual stockades:

Some fine day you will wake up to the sad consciousness that the world has moved on and left you in the rear. Then it will be a much more difficult matter to begin your education anew, and you will wish you had never stopped growing. You will discover that the money you saved by staying at home is like that which of old was "hidden in the earth" when it should have been "put to the exchangers." The interest received on the investment made by teachers in attending conventions and conferences, visiting schools and keeping in touch with new movements in education would be difficult to reckon in *per cent,* but is certainly greater than the returns from any other investment a teacher can make.[34]

Miss Crane was a firm believer in the Brainerd-MacVicar tradition of scholarship. She devised and evolved a curriculum which she felt met this test. With this as a background, the science and art of music teaching could be practiced.

The heart of her curriculum was a balanced program of music studies and practical application in teaching. Weighted course work in theory provided the basic language and material of music before one could practice the art of teaching.

Knowledge of subject matter was matched with professional courses and observation and teaching that provided the experience necessary to formulate a personal method, founded on sound educational principles.

Miss Crane stressed music reading, ear training and theory as the fundamentals of music. Basic principles of teaching were applied to this foundation. The course was systematic and progressive.

The curriculum at all times remained flexible in two respects: first, as conditions in the music field changed, the curriculum could adapt very readily to it; and second, there was opportunity for depth studies for those students who had the necessary talents and skills.

By 1900 the basic outline of the course of study in music for Normal students had been fixed and remained essentially the same through the next quarter century. The first three terms were required content with elective subjects available for selection thereafter. A prominent feature of the training, although not listed as a course in music but included as one aspect of the Normal department, was observation and practice teaching. This part of the curriculum was somewhat flexible, allowing for individual differences and wishes of the students.

As curricular patterns in the Normal changed to meet the demands of public education, Miss Crane kept pace. After the adoption of a primary and kindergarten course, she designed a course in music to meet their specific needs. This remained basically the same until 1925.

In 1912 a course was devised in the Normal that combined classroom teaching with music. The curriculum outlined a course providing for two-thirds study in elementary courses and one-third in special music training. The music part of the program included: Music Methods; Study of Children's Songs; Notation; Melody Writing and Musical History; Sight Singing and Ear Training; and Voice Culture.[35]

In adapting the Crane curriculum to meet the needs of training teachers, she used the following guide:

Some new work has been added to the course every year, and each addition has been the result of a real demand for more practical and more extended training, suggested by a careful study of the needs of the public schools. While the theoretical course is not so extended as that given by some of the best music schools, it is thorough and broad, and intended to lay a foundation for future study, and at the same time is fully adequate to the needs of the public school music teacher.[36]

The 1911 curriculum showed specialized studies in melody reading, children's songs, accompanying, oratorio and a thesis. Emphasis remained on ear training and sight singing.[37]

In 1913 a course was introduced to prepare teachers in high school music as well as for higher education. This course contained greater depth and required three years for completion.

This course was discontinued in 1916 after only two students had been graduated. The program was too advanced for the times and better facilities were necessary, especially for programs in instrumental music. From 1916–1924 the subjects of the third year were offered as electives, thus permitting more work in depth.

After 1922 only two courses were offered at the Normal School: elementary teachers course and the special music course.

Students were permitted some leeway in these programs so that they could grow in their own way and to the extent they chose. They were first given an overview of the whole program and were then permitted to concentrate on certain grade levels.

The Institute, not a part of the Normal, provided opportunities for the development of skills in vocal and instrumental music. This unique feature of the total Potsdam program contributed to the quality of all graduates.

Until 1916, courses in general education were omitted from the Crane curriculum on the assumption that the background of the students was sufficient. In 1916 a course in general history appeared, but only as a background for music history. "Neither the biography of the great masters nor the history of the development of the science and art of music can mean much without some knowledge of the age in which these masters lived. . . ."[38] This was the beginning of the remedy of a fundamental defect in the music curriculum, a process continued until this day.

Professional studies occupied a reasonable portion of the student's time and provided both general and specialized subject matter. Courses such as history of education, principles of education and psychology were taught by Normal School faculty, aimed at giving the music students a general understanding of the background, principles and organization of the educational system. Special courses in methodology, conducting, materials and the like were presented by the Institute staff as studies in the special work of teaching music. Both the general and specific were made meaningful by a thorough experience in observing and practice teaching in the classroom. No other aspect of the course of study was allotted more time than this phase of the work, and clearly revealed a philosophy of "learning by doing."

Methods classes and practice teaching were closely knit. During the first year an overview of the elementary music program was made, lessons of various types were illustrated and peculiar problems were analyzed. The following year the plans and methods of procedure were tested in actual teaching in the grades. Students examined materials and studied latest methods. Later, the same procedure was followed in the high school music program.

The purpose of method was to present an inclusive and encompassing course rather than a restrictive or imposed method. The following statement from the circular of 1916 emphasized this point:

 While the method class presents general educational principles, applying them to the teaching of music, definite plans or work are outlined, subject matter systematized and methods of procedure suggested, students are clearly shown that no method works itself. Behind methods and systems and plans there must always be a teacher who thinks, one who studies the conditions of the community, the demands of the school, the needs of the individual pupil; there must be a teacher who knows music and who is always alert to discover the best material that is available for school use. . . . The method class should certainly teach definite plans of work, but never the idea that the final dictum has been discovered. It must, instead, seek to make each teacher an investigator and discover for himself.[39]

The course work was dominated by studies in music theory. Ear training and sight-singing were emphasized, along with analysis, harmony and form. The underlying purpose was the fundamental belief that the work of a teacher of music, regardless of the level, required that he be able to use musical notation as accurately and as skillfully as a teacher of mathematics used numbers, or a teacher of English used grammar. Similarly, the work of a music teacher required the same facility in reading music and understanding the musical score as a teacher of English needed to read and understand a poem or novel. The circular of 1916 stated that the aim was not:

to train composers, but rather to give each pupil a practical working of fundamental harmonic usages, and to make these not merely exercises . . . but real tone combinations; in other words, to teach him to hear with the eye.[40]

A review of course outlines and lesson plans showed that, although depth in study was reached, the type of work was limited to a theory based upon a nineteenth century style of composition. Neither the complexities of modern harmony, counterpoint or form, nor the study of contrapuntal techniques and the harmonic structures of the music of the seventeenth and early eighteenth centuries was included. At the end of the second year, inversion of triads and seventh chords, dominant sevenths, enharmonic tones, modulation, figured bass, diminished chords, suspensions, had been investigated and studied thoroughly. By comparison, the course was more thorough but less encompassing than those offered in the Crane department at the time of this writing.[41]

Skill in performance, by private study or participation, was always a requirement. Flexibility in scheduling permitted this.

Each teacher was the judge as to whether a student's progress was satisfactory. There does not seem to have been a set standard.

Ensemble participation was a prominent feature of the curriculum. Choral and instrumental groups from the Normal were augmented in the early days by the addition of local and high school musicians.

Various school groups presented concerts, the choral club and the orchestra being the first to do so. In 1890 a chorus of 15 singers and an orchestra of 12 performed. By 1901 the chorus had increased to 78. An orchestra of 14 provided the accompaniment for Mendelssohn's *Hymn of Praise*. In 1905 *The Creation* and *The Messiah* were performed.

The Phoenix Club, a women's vocal ensemble, was formed during these years. A little later a men's group was formed. Its members were high school boys and townsmen.

Students at the Institute were expected to attend concerts, recitals and lectures. School circulars announced the policy. "Pupils must come to the school planning to attend every lecture and concert given, that no opportunity for culture may be lost."

Entrance requirements remained substantially the same from 1886–1926:

No one is fitted to teach in the public schools of today without at least the preparation furnished by the course of study in a good high school. The fact that one is to be a special teacher of music in no way relieves him of this necessity. Students who wish to take the Special Music Teacher's Course in this school, must have the equivalent of a good high school education as a foundation for this work. If it is not convenient to complete such a course before coming to Potsdam, students may enter the high school here, and complete the course while carrying on the work in music.[42]

Examinations were given in sight-singing and theory to determine placement and schedule of work.

Julia E. Crane

Miss Crane pioneered establishing the first training school for music teachers in the United States. The reputation and influence of the Crane Normal Institute spread rapidly, and the school received widespread publicity throughout the country. Crane graduates were one of the school's biggest assets:

Over 250 have been graduated from the school. Of these over 80 per cent have taught in the public schools. Nineteen different normal schools have chosen their teachers here, and in some of them as many as four different teachers from this school have followed each other. These normal schools are situated in 10 different states. In addition to the normal schools which have been furnished with teachers from this school, its graduates have taught in the schools in nearly 100 different towns in 21 states of the Union.

The success of the work in the various parts of the Union is manifested in the students who come from these places to prepare for teaching music. At the present time the school has pupils from New York, New Jersey, Massachusetts, Pennsylvania, Minnesota, Wisconsin and Ohio.[43]

The school developed an enviable national recognition. Not only did it send teachers throughout the United States, but it drew students from widespread areas.

Facilities limited student enrollment to 65 and an average of 17 were graduated each year. The faculty was expanded slowly; it numbered 10 at the time of Miss Crane's death in 1923.

Miss Crane was very active in state and national professional organizations. She served on numerous committees, presented papers and led discussions, and in 1920 was elected first vice president of the Music Supervisors National Conference.

Her services were in constant demand. In 1916 she was on the summer faculty at the University of Wisconsin, and in 1918 at the University of Southern California, where Dr. Stowell was head of the Education department.

Like MacVicar, Miss Crane rendered valuable service to

the state. Probably her most outstanding contribution was the work she performed on the Music Council of the State Education Department. High school graduation requirements in music for admission to state normal schools and writing the state high school syllabus for music were two outstanding contributions of this council. Miss Crane played a leading role in each and also served on the State Examinations Board from 1909–1912.

Miss Crane renewed the Potsdam spirit in education. Its central idea of quality preparation found a fitting exponent in this imaginative, dynamic woman. Her work was soundly based on the pioneer work of Asa Brainerd and Malcolm MacVicar. She worked closely with Dr. Stowell and together they set a pattern for another great team that was to follow.

Chapter Seven

THE INTERREGNUM

Dʀ. Thomas Stowell and Miss Julia Crane applied the Potsdam tradition to the twentieth century. Imaginative leadership again was demanded as "the ninteenth century bowed out around 1920." [1] The need for strong leadership again was evident during the Potsdam interregnum, a quarter century of transition.

Like all institutions, Potsdam faced the problem of renewal, especially during transitional periods. Potsdam's interregnum fell into two phases. During the first phase the old guard, apostles of the backward look, struggled to stay in power. In their hands promising new innovations and experiments became a dull orthodoxy. Their pedagogism shielded Potsdam from change and the dull routine of running a school became identified with progress.

But at every turn, persons with new ideas fought what they termed shallowness and unrealism. Admittedly, they were not crystal clear in their prognosis of change, but they did sense the absolute necessity of restoring the cutting edge of innovation. By 1930 this group was able to start renewing the Potsdam tradition and injecting an air of excitement into an atmosphere not yet identified by many educational leaders.

Regardless of the leadership an interregnum always presents

needs. Potsdam needed to meet these challenges as it had in the past when Brainerd and MacVicar had been sensitive to change and had provided dynamic leadership. Stowell and Crane had made sure that earlier programs were only steps out of which other new changes flowed. Both had developed imaginative programs.

In the past, when educational leadership at the school defaulted, strength in the community furnished a vital impetus.

Certain basic needs demanded attention during this period: the continuance of the Crane Normal Institute of Music after Miss Crane's death, a building program, experimentation and innovation in curriculum based on the tripod of the Potsdam experience and a renewal of the spirit during the Stowell regime.

The first crisis came in 1923 with the death of Miss Crane. During the last years of her life she had inaugurated a movement to incorporate her institute as a department in the Normal School. Such a proposal had been adapted by the local board of the Normal School and a resolution had been presented to the State Legislature.

The resolution proposed that the state purchase the Crane Institute for $20,000 and incorporate it as part of the Normal School. It also requested an annual appropriation of $17,500 to carry on the work of the new department.[2] A bill was introduced in the State Legislature during the spring of 1923, but was defeated.

Miss Crane's will created a problem. It stipulated that the Crane Institute be offered first to the State of New York and then to any private purchaser who might wish to carry on the work as a private school. The will further stated that the money paid for the plant and equipment would go into a trust fund for her sisters. After their deaths the residue was to be used to establish scholarships for students in the school.

Executrix of the will was empowered to continue the

Crane Institute for two years, pending negotiations, in order to give all music students opportunity to complete the course.

In spite of a well-organized campaign, the bill for purchase was again defeated in the Legislature in 1924. This time conflict over the purchase price, faculty and office personnel hindered passage.

Again a group of local residents stepped in to keep the Crane Institute in Potsdam. Attorney Frank L. Cubley, a Normal alumnus, presented the following request to Frank Graves, Commissioner of Education:

As you are probably aware, efforts were made to have the legislature appropriate sufficient funds to purchase and operate the Crane Normal Institute in connection with the Potsdam State Normal School. These efforts were unsuccessful during the Legislatures of 1923 and 1924.

In order to save the closing of the institution and preserve in its present condition until the legislature may see fit to make the necessary appropriation, a company of business men of Potsdam are ready to subscribe the necessary amount to form a corporation and maintain the school. To that end I am herewith enclosing a proposed certificate of incorporation upon which I would like to have your approval, pursuant to Section 6 of the Stock Corporation Law, which requires the approval of the Commissioner. Upon the last sheet of the certificate, I have drawn a proposed approval. If there are any further details you want regarding this matter, I would be very glad to furnish them to you.[3]

The proposed certificate was returned to Mr. Cubley on July 3, 1924, for filing with the Secretary of State. The local corporation was organized with the following officers:

> Charles H. Sisson, president.
> Ruth Scott Frelick, vice president.
> Lewis D. Dewey, secretary and treasurer.
> Horace N. Clark, director.
> Frank L. Cubley, director.[4]

Mr. Sisson signed the contract to purchase the property and equipment of the Crane Institute on August 1, 1924. This insured the continuation of the school for the ensuing year. The deed and bill of sale were presented to the corporation's officers on January 1, 1925, and exactly one year later the mortgage was paid in full. Eleven thousand dollars was paid for the real property, $4,000 for the furnishings, supplies and equipment in the Crane Institute.[5]

The corporation continued the struggle for state purchase of the institute, but disagreement in Potsdam delayed introduction of the bill. Dr. Congdon wanted certain details, such as clerical personnel, cleared up first. The corporation wanted to sell first and then work out such details.

Exasperated with Dr. Congdon's dilatory tactics, Mr. Cubley wrote the following letter to Harry Ingram, chairman of the St. Lawrence County Republican Committee and executive officer of the Public Service Commission, and also the corporation's liaison man in Albany:

Regarding the Crane Bill, I have had two or three conferences with Mr. Sisson and he had one with Dr. Congdon. . . . Mr. Sisson and I have decided that the thing for you to do is to introduce the bill as it stands. . . . This is a matter which the Crane Corporation desires to handle without interference from anyone and the thing for us to do is to go ahead as you think best and handle it purely as a business proposition for the corporation. We cannot afford to let any of these side issues affect the sale. . . . You therefore have authority from Mr. Sisson and myself representing the Crane Corporation to bang ahead.[6]

But all efforts failed again. The Legislature still refused to pass the bill, so during the next year the campaign was intensified. In April, 1925, Mr. Cubley met with Commissioner Graves and the Board of Regents. They reached agreements on all issues. The Crane Alumni Association staged an active letter writing campaign to members of the Legislature, urging passage. The bill finally was passed and signed by the Governor on May 13, 1926.[7]

Joint action by the State Department of Education, the Institute Corporation and the Normal School Board was necessary to carry out the terms of the act. Such action was taken on July 26, 1926, and the Crane Normal Institute became the Crane department of music of the Potsdam Normal School.

Space was at a premium earlier in the 1900's. First attempt for a new building came in 1906 during Dr. Stowell's tenure. In that year, Assemblyman E. A. Merritt, Jr., introduced a bill to appropriate $125,000 for a building. Governor Higgins vetoed it. A similar bill was introduced each succeeding year until 1915, when an appropriation bill of $300,000, introduced by Assemblyman E. A. Everett, was signed by Governor Whitman. This sum was for the main building and an additional $75,000 was voted in 1917.

Additional allocations were voted between 1918–1920 for improvements and additions to the physical plant. The final appropriation of $100,000 to complete the main building was signed into law by Governor Smith in 1920.[8]

The old Normal buildings were demolished and classes were held in the Stowell and Cook annexes while the new building was under construction. Extra rooms were created by erecting numerous partitions; but even so, double sessions were necessary. The high school and grade school convened in the morning and the Normal students in the afternoon. A high school student described conditions this way:

Being of a very generous nature, the High School deprived itself of the pleasure of school in the afternoon and loaned the building to the Normals during that time. Even afternoon study hall was not allowed to some of its oldest patrons in the High School. Some of the Normals considered themselves ill treated because they were obliged to stay until 5:15 but we, of the High School, feel assured that if they had to get up, get ready for school, eat as much breakfast as their limited time would allow, be at school at 8 and have to wait until 12:20 before they could finish their breakfast, that they would consider our tale of woe the longer and worse to hear.[9]

A nostalgic note of construction of the new building:

In constructing the walls of the new Normal the stone material of the old Normal was all used in the inner lining; and as the old Normal had in a similar way utilized the stone of the Academy building, we have now in our latest building both the Academy and the old Normal ever presesent in body even as the spirit of education that flourished in them pervades the school of today.[10]

The cornerstone was laid in the summer of 1917. Although the building was not entirely completed, the 1919 commencement exercises were held in the new auditorium. The fiftieth anniversary banquet of the Normal School in 1919 was also held there.

Classes opened in the new building in September, 1919, but there was no heat, and when a cold wave came classes were changed back to double sessions. School No. 8 was used for training classes and the "dried out" portions of the old Normal were used for the high school and Normal until the new boiler house was completed.[11]

The north end of the new building housed the practice school and primary department on the first floor, intermediate department on the second floor and junior high school on the third floor. The south end was used by the Normal for offices and special classrooms. The senior high school was in Cook Annex and part of Stowell Annex. The gymnasium was maintained in Stowell Annex and was used by all departments.[12]

By 1927 crowded conditions caused new problems. There were approximately 500 students in the practice school and enrollment in the Normal was up to 728. The State Education Department requested a new practice school and the State Legislature appropriated about $254,000 for the new building, which was dedicated in 1931 to Randolph Congdon, principal of the Normal.[13]

In 1934 Cook Annex was rebuilt for use by the music department. A private residence and lot adjoining the Normal campus also were purchased as practice rooms for voice and piano. In 1936 the state purchased a ten-acre tract of land, Congdon Field, on Pierrepont Avenue for use as a sports field. In 1944 options were taken on an additional twenty-five acres adjacent to the sports field as a site for a proposed new college, the present State University College at Potsdam.[14]

Curriculum change and adjustment provided the major problem of the interregnum. This problem was met only superficially in the Normal department, but the Crane department, under the imaginative leadership of Helen M. Hosmer, made a full-scale renewal of the Potsdam tradition.

Miss Crane's work had created an irresistible movement in music. It moved everything before it. Both the state and the Crane Institute, later the Crane department, were heavily influenced by her philosophy.

The first phase of the interregnum was devoted largely to filling out existing programs. The Elementary Teachers Course remained basically the same during the period 1923–1930. Work was focused on materials and methods of teaching, music reading, notation and terminology.

Entrance requirements for this course were upgraded during this period. The original requirements included:

All students are examined upon entrance, and such as are unable to sing familiar songs, or imitate songs sung to them, as well as those unable to read the simplest melodies, are assigned to a special class for intensive instruction. A daily period of such instruction is given for a term of 20 weeks. The work of this class consists of ear and voice training, song singing and the fundamentals of music reading.[15]

As music became more widely used in the public school curriculum, a need arose for more specially trained personnel in the upper grades, and under Marie Schuette's guidance, entrance requirements for the Elementary Teachers Course were upgraded:

As explained elsewhere, the first year of the course is alike for all students. During this year, a decision is reached regarding the grades (kindergarten-primary, intermediate, or junior high school) for which special preparation will be made during the second and third years. Final admission to the kindergarten course will be in part dependent upon the possession of an acceptable singing voice.[16]

The Special Music Course, designed for dual preparation in classroom and music teaching, underwent little change during this period.

The Crane Music Supervisors Course was changed in 1926 when the Board of Regents decided to extend the length of course preparation in special fields to three years. The courses offered in the extended program reflected those planned by Miss Crane in 1913.

Participants had to meet a dual set of requirements, for the Normal School and for the Crane department:

Applicants for admission to the Crane Music Supervisors Course must have natural music ability. They must be able to play the piano sufficiently well to accompany at sight a song of moderate difficulty. Although no previous training in voice or upon an orchestral instrument is required for entrance a test is given each applicant to determine the degree of proficiency along both of these lines. *A personal interview during the spring or summer before the proposed time for entrance is urged since only in this way can the degree of native musical ability be ascertained.*[17]

Emphasis remained on music theory and ear training, observation and practice teaching, performance ability and ensemble participation. The added year gave needed time for more depth (a Potsdam tradition) and for instrumental studies, a reflection of the growing interest in music in public schools.

In 1926–1927, a system of practice teaching was established. Music students had charge of the music instruction in a considerable number of area schools and in all local schools.

Miss Crane's belief that music should be instilled in the lives of the students was continued in two ways: student attendance was required at concert and recital appearances given by noted artists and ensembles and by individual performance and participation in Crane musical organizations.

Performances by the Russian Symphonic Choir and the violinist Jacobbinoff were some of the outstanding events. The number of Crane organizations was expanded to include the Normal Orchestra, Crane Orchestra, Chapel Orchestra, Junior Orchestra and a Normal Band. Existing organizations like the Phoenix Club increased in membership.

To be sure, there was duplication of performers, especially in the instrumental groups, but the important thing was that everyone was engaged in producing music. Furthermore, it was expected that group participation would not be limited to one area but that students would participate in both a vocal and an instrumental group when possible. From this grew a unifying spirit of performance excellence which welded the students and faculty together through a realization of the full sweep and impact of music upon their lives. The tradition continued while the degree of enrichment grew through greater awareness of the means of musical production. The voice and the instrument, the chorus, the orchestra and the band, the piano and the organ became means to the same end. The Crane department of music was unified by an expanding curriculum because of the fundamental belief that music as a part of one's life could find expression in a variety of ways.

The tradition of service to the area was continued by the Crane Institute during the interregnum.

Maude DeGan Groff, a music missionary associated with

the education foundation of the Lake Placid Club, Lake Placid, New York, visited Miss Schuette in 1925–1926. She had two projects in mind: improvement of choirs in the Adirondack region by an annual choir festival, and the improvement of teaching music in area public schools by means of student teachers. Implementation of both programs depended upon the cooperation of Crane. Miss Schuette gave it.[18]

Both programs were inaugurated under the auspices of the education foundation at Lake Placid, and the teaching program met with an enthusiastic response.

A report on the program gave the details: "No town has failed to take a music teacher when one has been offered and none have given up their music, many raising the salaries of the teachers for the second year." [19]

This program pointed up the value of the music supervisor's course at Potsdam:

This campaign also opens up a new outlet for music teachers. For it requires initiative, as well as knowledge, executive ability and spirit, because the "missioner" will have to help the rural people. As most of the towns have no choirs, choruses, or other form of music teachers must be able to sing for demonstration and solo work, play the piano well, and one orchestral instrument. They must also have a working knowledge of all of the instruments in the orchestra, and be able to lead a chorus and put on an operetta.[20]

The promotion of music festivals, the other facet of Mrs. Graff's original proposition, met with instantaneous success. The first such festival was held in the fall of 1925, featuring area talent in a short series of recitals and lectures.

The Crane Institute played a leading role in these festivals from the beginning:

The Phoenix Club of Crane Institute, together with Mrs. Ellen Snyder Morgan, Misses Schuette, Hosmer, Beaudry, Hewitt; Messrs.

Bishop, Doubleday, Maxcy, Stevenson and C. Premo, motored to Lake Placid Tuesday afternoon, October 6, to give a twilight recital at the Agora, Lake Placid Club. . . . An excellent program, under the direction of Miss Helen Hosmer, choral director of the Crane School, was presented, impressing the audience with the ideals of the Crane School.[21]

The Adirondack Music Festival gradually expanded its activities and objectives. As much as a week's time was devoted to concerts, lectures, instruction and competitions. The directors hoped to elevate musical standards and to generally improve singing and playing, especially in church music. They also included a children's day, hoping to stimulate school music.

The increased activities soon led to two annual festivals— a fall festival stressing music for worship, and a spring festival directed toward improving school music. Reaction to the spring festival indicated a great potential for future growth:

No musical event in Adirondack history is known to have made as deep an impression on auditors and participants as the school festival held on June 4. Over 800 from nearly 30 schools took part. The competition was most spirited in each of the three classes. Both choruses and orchestras won high praise from music leaders for apparent long and thorough training and high quality of rendition. . . . Many school superintendents, district superintendents and other high educational officials were present. The Phoenix Club of Crane Institute, now the Crane music department of Potsdam Normal School, attended in body as festival guests and rendered several highly appreciated programs. An important conference of music leaders with the festival committee, was held after the day's program to discuss future school festival policies. A number of the festival patrons were present and by their counsel did much to guarantee the success of the competition.[22]

The participation of public schools in the program soon necessitated another sponsoring group. It was only logical to move the school festival to Potsdam under the sponsorship of the Crane department of music.

Miss Crane's policies were solidified in the 1920's. She had met the initial needs for qualified music instruction in the school. Consequently the Elementary Teachers Course and the Special Music Course were strengthened. But the promise of Julia Crane demanded more than this. Her work had to be updated and projected into the future. The Crane department was at a crossroad. Bold, new, imaginative leadership was needed.

Dr. Helen M. Hosmer provided this leadership. To know Miss Hosmer is to understand the Potsdam tradition. Handicapped by the times and the leadership of the times, she infected the Crane department with dynamism. She, personally, was the bridge between that tradition and its ultimate application to modern education in Potsdam. Her greatest work came under the presidency of Dr. Frederick W. Crumb, but her initial work in the 1930's and 1940's should have provided an impetus for The State University College at Potsdam.

Helen Hosmer moved to Potsdam when she was eight years old. John Hosmer, her father, a long-time resident of Potsdam, held a position in Albany with the New York State Department of Agriculture and the Treasury Department.

Her outstanding musical talent was recognized in the fourth grade in School No. 8 when she was singled out as having a rare and unique talent as an accompanist. Soon she became a central figure in the musical functions of the school and the community. It was good for Miss Hosmer to grow up in Potsdam and the North Country. Her natural talents, absolute pitch and an incredible ability to play the piano flowered in a community with a rich musical heritage.

She was graduated from the Normal School and the Crane Institute in 1918, completing both courses in three years. Voice was her principal area of study. Miss Crane's traditions, hopes and aspirations for music were passed on to her.

Miss Hosmer spent four years in Winsted, Connecticut, as city supervisor of music. She resigned in 1922 and returned to Potsdam. Two years earlier Miss Crane had offered her a position on the Crane faculty, but she had declined, feeling that she had not had enough experience.

The situation had changed. Her mother was ill, and this time she accepted a teaching offer from Miss Crane. A telephone call insured the eventual continuity of the Potsdam tradition.

After her mother's death in 1924, Miss Hosmer spent the summer in France studying voice at the American Conservatory at Fontainebleau. It was the beginning of a long friendship and association with Mademoiselle Nadia Boulanger.[23] It was a deep friendship, based on mutual respect and admiration.

In 1926–1927 Miss Hosmer took a leave of absence from Potsdam and received a bachelor of science degree at Columbia University. During the summers 1928 and 1931 she taught and pursued a graduate program at Columbia. She received a master's degree and also organized the music department of New College at Columbia.

The experience at Columbia was another turning point in her career. Alice Bivins, a former teacher at Crane, was Peter Dykema's assistant at Columbia and was in charge of a summer experimental school for children in performing arts. Miss Bivins hired Miss Hosmer to teach intermediate children. When Miss Bivins died two years later, Miss Hosmer was placed in charge of the project designed to integrate the arts. More than anything else, it stimulated Miss Hosmer's interest in such an approach. The seeds of future Potsdam programs were sown then.[24]

Her work at New College was stimulating; it was an experimental college based on the theories of Dr. Thomas Alexander. The curriculum was very flexible and the methods were creative and progressive.

The 1920's had been a period of growth for Miss Hosmer.

No one was a better example of Asa Brainerd's advice to teachers to grow professionally. She got her chance to demonstrate her rare gifts in Potsdam when she became acting director of the Crane department in 1929, while Miss Schuette was on a leave of absence. The following year she became director.

Miss Hosmer thrived on innovation, and the fine cutting edge of change was restored to the Potsdam tradition. Like the giants before her, she came to the task with specific, long-range objectives in mind.

First she sought good publicity to acquaint more people with the quality of work in the Crane department (as had Asa Brainerd). Her broad experience had convinced her of the unique opportunities at Potsdam. She felt the right kind of publicity also would attract a fine faculty and better students.

Also, Miss Hosmer saw the need for a broader, more modern, curriculum. More complete acquaintance with the varieties of musical expression should be ensured by a full complement of bands, orchestras and choirs. More men students and more instrumentalists were needed.

She represented an opportunity for the musical tradition of the North Country to be revitalized through the Crane department. She was the living embodiment of the role of music in human life and was dedicated to furthering these cultural activities. Dr. Stowell's dream was on the verge of reality through quality achievement.

Finally, her dedication to scholarship led to her determination to improve academic standards so that Crane could become a degree-granting department of the Normal School. The turning point had arrived. Almost alone, this unusual woman inaugurated programs that were in the best of the Potsdam tradition.

In brief, her accomplishments in curriculum were "a gradual tightening of the curriculum to produce a specialist teacher. The Elementary Teachers Course, which allowed for only six required hours in 1930, specified only four credits in 1946. The Special Music Course, designed for dual preparation in classroom and music teaching and a long-standing feature of the course offerings at Potsdam, was eliminated by 1946. The length and depth of the Music Supervisors Course was expanded over these same years gaining early recognition and status as a specialized course of study."

The full function of Miss Hosmer's heritage, education and experience, found its first, and possibly richest expression, in the experimental group and European study trip. Impatient, she set out to demonstrate that a richer education could be obtained outside the existing ground rules. Her dynamism and enthusiasm were irresistible and Dr. Congdon and the Board of Regents gave their consent. She lost no time.

In September, 1933, at a meeting of the Crane freshmen, she asked for volunteers to enter an experimental program. Only sixteen volunteered. Today she would be overwhelmed by volunteers. Ten were eventually selected on the basis of their backgrounds and as being representative of a cross section of their class.

She held the first meeting at her home on Hamilton Street, Potsdam, on October 24, 1933. The following goals were identified through group discussion.[25] Students

1. Should be skilled in one line, but should have vision and be broadminded.
2. Should have real musicianship.
3. Should have both specialization and general knowledge.
4. Must have ability to put the subject across.
5. Must have authority and also personality to balance it.
6. Through a study of psychology and people, should learn to deal with others.

Asa Brainerd, Malcolm MacVicar, Thomas Stowell and Julia Crane might have smiled down on this meeting.

At first, the ten students did not create an unusual stir. Their weekly seminar meeting, however, was working like a yeast. Soon they began to question standard procedures on campus and began discussing alternatives in their evening meetings. Soon a new plan emerged, a curriculum, a method and a procedure. By the end of the first semester, February, 1934, the plan was submitted to Dr. Hermann Cooper, assistant commissioner of education, and it was approved.

There were imaginative innovations in this experiment.[26] Subjects were studied in blocks of time instead of following the regular schedule. This permitted more concentration and study in depth. The course was divided into five lines of pursuit, involving professional aspects of the major field, music background, general cultural background, education and music skills. Except for skills which were continuous, one week was devoted to each group in rotation, so that at the end of the semester three weeks would have been spent on each group. This provided sixty hours for each subject, instead of the minimum, thirty-six, previously required.

The following was a plan for a semester's work:

February 26–March 2	School Music Teaching I (3 projects)
March 5–March 9	Harmony
March 12–March 16	English
	Health Ed. ⎫ Reports
	Physical Ed. ⎭
March 19–March 23	Psychology
April 9–April 13	School Music Teaching I (Observation—Participation)
April 16–April 20	Harmony
April 23–April 27	English
April 30–May 4	Psychology
May 7–May 10	School Music Teaching I (Observation—Participation)
May 14–May 18	Harmony
May 21–May 25	English
May 30–June 4	Psychology
June 4–June 8	Review

Personality and character development were stressed and an interesting form of therapy, "truth meetings," was devised to bolster individual weaknesses and to erase arrogance. They were in marked contrast to MacVicar's moral sermons in morning chapel.

Dr. Stowell must have smiled again.

Inevitably the program focused on music as a special field. But it was an encompassing view as attempts were made to integrate it with other disciplines.

The traditional marking system was abolished and a system was adopted, based on subject matter, attitude, personality, cultural status and musicality. The registrar recorded no grades but simply gave credit for the courses.

Another innovation was that of utilizing the faculty on an individual conference basis and studying subjects in blocks of time for depth. Subjects such a psychology, history, literature, music history and science were studied over a period of one to ten weeks of concentrated effort. Although classroom attendance was not required, it was the student's personal responsibility to meet privately with the instructor concerned, receive outlines and assignments and submit reports and papers. Each student's findings and research were shared with others.

Seminar sessions were made more stimulating by having the instructors share in the discussions of their topics or subjects and so as to provide clarification, depth and perspective. At examination time tests were taken along with the regular students, and evidence of results generally indicated a more superior knowledge and understanding of the material by those in the experimental group.

This block system could not be employed for every subject. Skill subjects were covered in regular class work, while specific problems relative to them were covered in seminar. Members of the regular Crane faculty were involved in the experiment. Miss Hosmer typically assumed the heaviest teaching responsibilities. Guest faculty, visiting educators, musicians and outstanding personalities were utilized, wherever possible, to enrich the experiment.

The curriculum, determined by the students, differed only slightly from the required one. Some courses were combined, some expanded, but none eliminated. Goals established under the guidance of a master teacher ensured a sound program.

Motivation for learning was competence motivation. It was an individual's own responsibility to meet the established standards, but the generative quality of the program produced an intellectual curiosity that guaranteed results.

The highlight of the experiment was one semester of study in Europe. Eighteen students made the trip. Three members of the experimental group could not go, so other members of the Crane department were permitted to go.

The faculty for the trip was superb. Miss Hosmer, Miss Mildred Lewis of Kentucky and Dr. Vincent Jones of Temple University joined the American complement. Nadia Boulanger of Paris, Charles Kennedy Scott of London and Dr. Georg Kartzke of Berlin formed the European counterpart.

The New York Times printed the following article on the departure of the group for Europe:

A noteworthy step in the training of music teachers is being taken in the Crane Department of Music at the State Normal School at Potsdam, N. Y. For the first time in the history of teacher training in the United States, a normal school is offering a semester's work in the various centers of Europe. . . .

Eighteen students are now visiting Germany, France and the British Isles on the first study tour in charge of Miss Helen M. Hosmer.

French, German, history of art, history of music, music literature, harmony, conducting, European history and comparative education make up the curriculum. . . .[27]

The itinerary included festivals at Bayreuth and Salzburg. At Bayreuth, students attended performances of the *Ring of the Nibelung.* At Salzburg they heard Bruno Walter, Felix Weingartner and Arturo Toscanini conducting music of the great composers.

Museums and libraries provided an inexhaustible supply of books, manuscripts and musical instruments. Both Munich and Nuremberg were sites of research and examination of musical artifacts. Short stays in Bamberg, Jena, Weimar and Leipzig broadened the students' awareness of architecture and German university education, and focused attention on such personalities as Goethe, Schiller, Liszt, Wagner and Bach.

Berlin was a center of educational involvement for the group. It made a concentrated study of the German language and examined the German school system. In Bonn, Düsseldorf and Frankfurt am Main they visited teacher-training institutions and compared philosophy with American systems.

On November 5 the group left Germany for Paris. The Louvre and Cluny Museums, the Bibliothèque Nationale, the National Opera and the Opera Comique provided a wealth of musical and cultural environment. At Fontaine-bleau Mlle. Nadia Boulanger conducted a series of lectures and demonstrations on various aspects of musical art.

In London there was the British Museum, the Tate and National Galleries, music publishing houses, universities and other schools. Nearby were Oxford, Cambridge, Devon and Bedford and Charles Kennedy Scott gave an extended series of lectures on English music, with emphasis on madrigals. There were also many musical events such as Scott's own choral group in rehearsal and performance, the Oriana Society, the Royal Academy Symphony in rehearsal and performance, the BBC Symphony, the London Philharmonic Orchestra, the London Symphony and chorus with Nadia Boulanger as guest conductor, and many more.

Miss Hosmer's evaluation of the European tour was presented to the Crane department in a talk on December 9, 1937:

I should like to present to you a summary of the benefits of the trip as compiled by the 18 students and handed to me as a joint report. The first advantage in their minds is the great value of the access to libraries, museums, art centers, concerts, etc. There is a very practical application of the study of language. Real training is gained in adapting one's self to rapidly changing environment and to different groups of people. The personal contact with nationalities and with famous people is invaluable. To study music, many times in its natural setting, lends real significance. The learning process is so often a real experience, not a mere repetition of facts. "Learning through living" goes on by means of fusion and assimilation of geography, history, government, art and social customs. Through observation of how others live, there grows a greater appreciation of others' customs, as well as an increased appreciation of our own country from many points of view. A great personal responsibility is developed.

Study, as carried out during this trip, had the characteristic of being a concentrated effort, with a lack of distracting influences. Through the inspiration of the surroundings more work often can be covered in a shorter time. The group study habits meant 24 daily conscious and unconscious hours of education.

There is a decided development of an international view—social, religious, economic, political, educational and musical.

A feeling developed among the group, based on personal comparison, that each individual came away from this travel experience a more serious student.

Germany taught us real lessons in courtesy and discipline. England taught us a more leisurely evaluation and judgment of relations.

To conclude the benefits, the group offered the point that there is stimulated a greater interest in living.

The conclusions are endless. I think such an experience is one of the greatest motivators for learning that can be experienced. It stimulates to an untold degree a desirable intellectual curiosity and an interest in the total life. Living together develops a group morale which in turn strengthens the individual. Great independence in judgement is fostered and individual development is tremendous. There is a broadly enriched background. One learns budgeting of time, money and energy. We recognized and respected the value of humbleness and humility and learned that the greatest things in life are the simplest. We came back better Americans. And I believe we realized the aims of the trip and proved the value of future trips. I hope that foreign study may become a permanent feature for several reasons: first, because it developed each individual student, which in turn contributes to the school; second, it raises the entire cultural status of each individual, of the group and the school; third, it furnishes a desirable prestige for the department of the school.[28]

Miss Hosmer's final commentary on the project clearly identified the influence it had on education in Potsdam. "Any forward-looking project permeates other things. Its influence went on—goes on. The basic elements worked their way into the curriculum; the good was diffused into the general scheme." [29]

The bridge was erected. The Potsdam tradition was ready to meet the challenge of a new, modern era. Like Asa Brainerd, Dr. Hosmer worked on her objectives simultaneously so that the formal work of the Crane department occupied only part of her time.

Miss Hosmer was vitally concerned with promoting the musical heritage of the North Country. Two developments demanded a new program: the Adirondack Music Festival's program for public school groups had grown too large for the Lake Placid Club to handle, and Richard Tunnicliffe's local music festivals were discontinued in 1929. Another type of "May festival" was needed.

Mr. Tunnicliffe was director of the Potsdam High School chorus and other school musical activities. He had inaugurated a May festival as a culminating activity for the year's work. Students from the Crane Institute and Normal School had participated and Franklin H. Bishop of the Crane faculty had collaborated in providing the orchestra for festivals. In time, the high school became more and more state supervised, and eventually moved to its own building on LeRoy Street in 1929. The public school curriculum did not allow as much time for music as the high school had enjoyed as part of the Normal School; and as a result, the festivals were discontinued in 1929.

In May, 1930, the Crane department, under Mr. Bishop's direction, sponsored a festival on the college campus. His original plan called for an all-Northern New York Orchestra in a festival of rehearsal and performance. The Normal School Orchestra and Band presented the final concert. The festival was highly successful and area supervisors soon requested that vocal music be included in school programs.

The 1932 festival was an outstanding success. A stimulating two-day program featured a 600-voice chorus from 29 visiting choirs and a 300-piece orchestra from 17 schools. On the first day there were rehearsals and a performance for the choral group under the direction of Miss Hosmer and Miss Schuette. In the evening, a concert was presented by musical groups from the Crane department. A similar program was held for orchestras the next day.

The following year a third day of the festival was devoted to a "Band Day." In 1935 a clinic was held for music supervisors. Under the guidance of the festival directors, they examined music to be performed at the festival and helped plan details for the performances. At the same time, the Crane department began to assist at the festival and participated in many of the activities.

The Crane faculty performed the main tasks of conducting and adjudicating. Miss Hosmer, Miss Schuette, Mr. Bishop and Mr. Garfield made outstanding contributions. By 1939, additional conductors and adjudicators were selected from among the participating supervisors, and a concert by the Watertown South Junior High School Orchestra became a festival feature. Under Miss Hosmer's influence, the whole program became more and more a personal experience for the public school students and supervisors.

Dr. Samuel Spurbeck assumed leadership of the festival in 1940, and that year nearly 1,500 students participated in the three-day program. The following year the festival continued to grow:

Potsdam, April 26—More than 2,000 high school students and music supervisors are expected to attend the annual spring music festival sponsored by Potsdam state normal school for high schools of the area between Watertown and Chateaugay May 8, 9 and 10.

May 8 will be band day, May 9 will be choral day, and May 10 will be orchestra day.

Visiting bands will spend the morning playing for each other and in the afternoon the normal band will give a concert which will be followed by a parade. A program for massed bands will be given in the afternoon at the civic center and the last event on the day's program will be a concert by the normal band at 7:45 P.M.

Choral day will be given over to rehearsals of the various groups in the morning and at 2 P.M., the massed chorus will sing at the civic center. The first all-northern New York chorus will perform under the baton of Miss Helen M. Hosmer, head of the Crane music supervisors department of Potsdam normal. Afterwards normal musical groups will entertain.

The morning of orchestra day will be devoted to rehearsals untill 11:15, when concerts by high school orchestras will start. In the afternoon the normal orchestra will give a concert with Miss Betty Jane Cole of 1126 Academy Street, Watertown, a sophomore, playing Mendelssohn's "Capriccio Brilliant" on the piano with the orchestra. The concert of the massed orchestras will conclude the day.[29]

World War II interrupted the festival, but it was resumed in 1946. In 1948 the festival came under the control of the New York State School Music Association, an organization formed in 1932, but Crane faculty and students continued to play major roles in its success.

A strong strain of "Stowellism" ran through Miss Hosmer's efforts. She recognized, as he had also, that students with spirit became active learners and better teachers. Much of her work was spurred by efforts to make Crane students and alumni active in the work at Crane.

By 1931 Miss Hosmer sensed that the intimate spirit and atmosphere of the Crane department was being diminished by increased enrollment. So she inaugurated a weekly "Crane meeting" to create a unified spirit, and at the same time to allow time for discussions and lectures. It became a custom to close meetings with group singing of familiar songs, and from these songfests Miss Hosmer conceived the idea for the noted Crane Chorus, which has since received national recognition.

Memories of earlier festivals prompted her to pass her experiences along to Crane students. She had two objectives: a personal desire to work with the great choral masterpieces and the unifying effects of such performances on the Crane department.

Another long-awaited achievement for Miss Hosmer and the Crane department came in May, 1932:

Had you been in Potsdam in September 1931, I'm sure you would have been as thrilled as those of us who were here then, to have enough boys in the Crane Department to start a mixed chorus. We had to call on some good friends from among the townspeople, but combined with the Potsdam Civic Singers, there was a finely balanced choir and in May 1932, a performance of Coleridge-Taylor's "Hiawatha's Wedding Feast" ushered in what we now know as the Potsdam Spring Festival of the Arts. That was a milestone! [30]

A "Christmas Sing" had become a tradition of the Crane department. Originally these were informal get-togethers of students and townspeople before the holidays to sing favorite carols and other Christmas music. In December, 1932, the Crane Chorus prepared a few selections to present before the traditional "sing." This was the origin of the annual Christmas Concert of the Crane Chorus and Orchestra. Although formal choral works played a prominent role in these concerts, the informality remained with the chorus and audience joining an informal sing following the concert.

Soon the spring festival became the highlight of the academic year. The 1939 festival featured Mlle. Boulanger. Appropriately, she was the first guest conductor of the Crane Chorus and Orchestra, and the close friend of Helen Hosmer thrilled the audience, according to the following newspaper article:

Sunday, May 14th, 1939, was a red letter day in the history of the Crane Department of Music. On that day, Mlle. Nadia Boulanger, described as "The First Lady in Music," came to Potsdam and directed the Crane Chorus and Orchestra in a splendid performance of Brahms' Requiem.

The Chorus, well trained by Miss Helen Hosmer, the director of the School of Music, and the Orchestra, prepared by Dr. Kenneth Forbes, were ready for the finishing touches from the master hand of Mlle. Boulanger. Two days of intensive training under an inspiring leader resulted in an excellent performance of the Choral Masterpiece. . . .[31]

Doda Conrad, famous Polish singer, was baritone soloist at the first performance. He was the first professional soloist to perform at a Potsdam festival, and the artistic quality of the chorus made a lasting impression on him.

On February 16, 1940, Miss Hosmer added further enrichment to the Crane program by directing the chorus in a sight reading performance of Handel's *Messiah*. Highly successful, it became an annual event.

In February, 1941, the Crane Chorus was paid a singular honor in being invited to appear in a concert in New York City. The invitation was extended by Doda Conrad:

If I write all this to you, dear Miss Hosmer, it is because I think I need *your help!* We are planning for April 2nd in Town Hall, New York, an important benefit concert for Polish Relief, the

profit of which is to be added to the National Tribute offered to
Mr. Paderewski on the golden anniversary of his debut in this
country. Mr. Paderewski is turning the entire amount of this
Tribute to the Paderewski Fund For Polish Relief.

Nadia Boulanger has agreed to conduct the concert. The New
York Philharmonic Symphony is giving its services. . . . Amongst
the soloists there will be several members of the Metropolitan
Opera Company. I have kept present in my memory your admirable work, and your singers' work that night in the Brahms. The
musical and instrumental quality of your group greatly impressed
me. I don't know if you remember the fact—but I immediately had
thought that so excellent an achievement should not be solely
reserved to Potsdam music lovers!

I now have the idea (and Nadia agreed to it with enthusiasm)
to find out whether you think it would be possible to bring your
people down to New York to participate in the concert—singing
as beautifully as they did two years ago. . . .[32]

Miss Hosmer, Doda Conrad and Mlle. Boulanger met in
New York and worked out details for the event. Nadia Bou-
langer insisted on using the Crane Chorus and wrote to Miss
Hosmer of the importance of this performance:

When Doda Conrad thought of your possible coming for the
Polish concert to be given in New York, I dared not even consider the idea, fearing it could never come out from the world of
dream. Our concert in Potsdam May, 1939, remains as such a rare
achievement. But . . . I have now seen you, we have spoken of the
prospect, it has become a project, clearly settled, and I have to
say what it means to me, for so many serious, significant reasons.

First of all, be sure that everything, whatever the trouble might
be, will be done, to reach the finest possible quality of performance.
Secondly, demonstrate that patient, careful, intelligent work brings
invaluable results, permitting to progress, and to give a sense to
the real purpose of "doing" music. And these points bring light
on a question of vital significance in our shaken world. If men
realize that the only real reward is to do one's best, and that noth-

ing creates more real happiness than doing so, we may still hope in the future.

Great words, perhaps, to speak of a concert. But, it is when a civilization finds patrons for art, and artists to devote their life to serve it, that the greatest periods come to light.

Say to your singers that, having never forgotten the concert which made me appreciate their high standard, human as musical, it is with the most eagerness that I welcome the new occasion (and what a moving one!) to work with them, once more. For you, my dear, all the gratefulness and appreciation I have for your marvelous activity. You may not even think to what you have accomplished: your friends cannot forget it.

P.S. My regards to those who have remained in my memory, vividly.[33]

It was a benefit concert held in Carnegie Hall, and the Crane department earned expenses and raised an additional $220 for Polish relief.

The program consisted of the *History of the Resurrection of Jesus Christ* by Schütz; a Polish hymn of the fourteenth century, *Bogurodzica Dziewica; Stabat Mater* by Szymanowski and the *Requiem Mass* by Fauré.

The Crane Chorus performed magnificently under the inspired direction of Mlle. Boulanger. Charlotte Kellogg, chairman of the Paderewski Testimonial Fund, Inc., wrote the following letter to Dr. Lehman, president of the college:

That the concert of religious music presented at Carnegie Hall on April 4th was of such elevated beauty was due in large measure to the spirit with which the Potsdam State Crane Choir invested it.

Your devoted effort, and that of Miss Hosmer, which made possible the participation of these distinguished singers, lifted the whole presentation to a level of high moral, as well as artistic beauty.

The National Testimonial Committee deeply appreciates your action in re-arranging your college schedule, and the generosity of the members who financed their trip, and offered, in addition, a gift to relieve the suffering of the Polish people.

For these separate actions, and for the entire contribution of the Potsdam State College, the committee sends its heartfelt thanks.[34]

Each year saw a steady growth of the festival as an outstanding musical event. It assured perpetuation of the Potsdam tradition.

The interregnum was especially crucial for the Normal department. Normal schools had been established as professional schools to prepare teachers; and although Potsdam had made an enviable record, this period posed as its darkest hour. Dr. Stowell had clearly demonstrated that adaptation to change was more than receiving money from the outside—it required basic changes from the inside.

Potsdam had lost its lead in teacher education and the Potsdam tradition appeared to have lost its dynamism. There was an acute problem of inadequate curriculum.

The state prescribed the curriculum and made numerous rules. Albany appeared as a vague big brother who was running the Normal because there didn't appear to be anyone else to do the job. The curriculum was based on the idea that if you wanted to prepare an elementary teacher you taught that person everything possible about the elementary school. There was no concept of scholarship as a needed ingredient. Primary emphasis was placed on methodology.

The second basic cause for Potsdam's decline was the lack of bold, imaginative leadership. The times were demanding.

During the first phase of the interregnum the state lengthened the prescribed general elementary teacher curriculum to three years. Potsdam's reflection of this program was described in its catalogs of the period.

All students took the same fundamental subjects during the first year. During the second and third years they made special preparation to teach in the kindergarten and the first three grades, or in grades four, five and six, or in grades seven, eight and nine. The diploma was a life license to teach kindergarten or any grade of any elementary school in the state.[35]

The curriculum was reminiscent of the story about the French commissioner of education who took out his watch and said he could tell what was being taught in every elementary school of France at any moment.

The 1927–1928 catalog revealed few curriculum changes. However, some changes created a precedent for what some persons called revision. Organizational juggling became an occupational hazard for those who wanted genuine reform.

The principles underlying the curriculum were clearly stated in the catalogs of the period. They included:

The study of the principles of education, of methods in elementary school subjects and background courses designed to broaden the student's general knowledge of the subjects he is to teach; the observation of model teaching; and the application in the practice school of the principles studied in the Normal classrooms and observed in the model classes. The psychology taught in the first year is the nucleus of the work of the three years.

The effectiveness of the Normal training is measured by the efficiency shown in practice teaching. The practice teaching is second in importance to no other part of the course. In the practice school are tested the practical values of the principles and methods presented in the Normal classrooms. The work required of student teachers in the practice school embraces class instruction, supervision of study periods, class organization and discipline under the immediate oversight of skilled supervisors. This experience reveals the elements of strength and weakness in each student-teacher and makes possible the correction of faults and the establishment and strengthening of good qualities.[36]

The same description was in the 1927–1928 catalog.

Course outlines revealed the nature of the curriculum. It was subject-centered and placed a heavy emphasis on methods, and not in the tradition of Brainerd or MacVicar. They had placed an emphasis upon systematic bodies of knowledge. Courses in this curriculum were fragmented, and were largely a review of high school courses. To a great extent, proficiency in subject matter involved knowledge of a textbook and an accompanying teacher's manual.

The lack of unifying principles, and a lack of concern for the sweep of history, was clearly revealed in the description of the 1922–1923 course in European history:

Medieval types of life: castle, manor, monastery, town with the trade and exchange of ideas resulting from the Crusades and Renaissance as a basis for the study of modern European history; an analysis of Europe at the end of the French Revolution; the reaction of England and the continental nations to the extreme individualism of the revolution; the effect of the Napoleonic era; the readjustment by the Congress of Vienna; the final modification of the revolutionary principles in the expanding nationalism of Europe; the different political growths in the various nations after the revolution; the commercial and industrial conflicts coincident with the political development: the problems which have arisen as a result of the racial, linguistic and geographical differences of the European peoples. The present conditions have come about as an aftermath of the World War.[37]

Heavy emphasis was placed on the acquisition of facts, because this was what a teacher would have to pass on to her students. The introductory statement for the course in General Geography revealed:

A general course presented on a collegiate level to give prospective teachers a body of geographic facts so well organized in the mind of the teacher that these facts may be instantly available when needed.[38]

There were few course offerings, restricting any depth or specialization study. A sampling of course offerings in 1927–1928 revealed that there were two history courses, Modern European and American; two mathematics courses, Arithmetic and Junior High School Mathematics; two science courses, Nature Study and General Science.

There was heavy emphasis on methods, which indicated that teaching was something that could be learned. Teachers were trained, not developed. A training program provided the prospective teacher with the factual content to pass on to students and trained him in a method to dispense this knowledge:

Methods classes are shown that the purpose of nature study is to bring the pupil into a broad sympathy with the natural world, and to cultivate humaneness (Nature Study).[39]

Lesson plans and the most effective methods of presentation was one of the facets of the Arithmetic course.[40]

Language methods for grades one to six, including story-telling, reproduction, dramatization, picture-study, speech correction, language games, etc., are to be taken up in this course (Essentials of English I and II).[41]

A separate course in Geography Methods was taught in 1927–1928. This emphasized "a study of teaching practice (or method) in the presentation of this subject in the grades." [42] The college newspaper contained the following article:

Friday afternoon all members of the History Methods classes were invited by the committee on dramatization to attend a representation of an imaginary scene of medieval Europe. The play was written by members (of the class) and consisted of scenes from the life of a boy of the Middle Ages as he advanced from the station of a page to that of a squire, and from squirehood to knighthood. An intensive study of the past was necessary . . . to . . . portray the . . . correct language, customs, and appearance.[43]

Malcolm MacVicar and Miss Crane had both pointed out the dangers of an overemphasis on methods. First, a method could not do the work of a teacher. Second, reliance on method too frequently led to shallowness. Both MacVicar and Crane had acknowledged the need for a science of teaching, but had carefully attempted to combine it with systematic bodies of knowledge—knowledge of the child and knowledge of society. And, above all, they recognized the art of teaching. The problem of renewing the Potsdam tradition faced formidable obstacles in this type of training.

But there were stirrings in the field of curriculum. Steps were soon taken in the right direction. The 1927–1928 course in Educational Measurements reflected an adjustment to the measurement movement in education.

This course familiarized students with literature in the field and at the same time provided some practical experience in administering and evaluating tests. How to measure the results of teaching and how to improve classroom teaching were the main objectives.[44]

Brainerd had insisted that there was a body of knowledge to be included under the science of teaching. This would appear, on the surface, to be a continuation of his philosophy. But there were two inherent dangers in this course. It was difficult to determine how accurate it was and how would it be applied. Combined with the subject-centered curriculum and emphasis on methods, it was fraught with danger. Misapplied, it would be used to measure and classify students, and to set up limited expectations for them.

The course in sociology appeared to be a continuation of MacVicar's thesis of the impact of sociological forces on the educative process. Some of the topics covered in this course were origin and development of society, structure and function, social processes and the reciprocal relations between individuals. "The development of the social impulses of pupils should be studied with a view to point the way by which they may cooperate and live together. . . . The ethics of the teacher's position, and work, should have specific emphasis."[45]

But the course description was deceptive. There was no supporting evidence that would indicate a serious study of

The Interregnum

the sociological foundations of education. There was not a solid liberal arts background to permit such a course:

The present curriculum offered by the State Normal School is for the preparation of elementary school teachers is three years in length, one-half of the subject content professional-technical courses completed by the student in her first year of study are introduction to teaching, which includes some observation, and educational psychology. At the close of this year she must select the particular teaching level for which she wishes to prepare, e.g., the kindergarten-primary grades, the intermediate grades, or the grammar grades. Courses in educational measurements, history of education, and methods of teaching as applied to reading, writing, arithmetic, history, geography, music, art, physical and health activities take up four-fifths of the classroom time of a student specializing in either the intermediate or grammar grade fields during the second year of study. During that year, also, faculty members who give instruction in methods courses take their students to the school of practice occasionally to observe examples of good teaching. One entire semester of the third year's program is given over to student practice teaching while the other semester includes courses in the principles of education and specialized psychology whereby the professional technical phase of the student's preparation is completed.[46]

A rural education department was established at Potsdam in the spring of 1929.[47] Students would take the usual Normal courses the first year, but during the second year would take observation, practice teaching, methods and several special courses.

The new course got off to an auspicious beginning the following September, with twenty juniors and ten freshmen enrolled:

The State Department of Education has called this a three-year course, including two years of pre-service training and one year of inservice training. At the end of the first two years, students taking this work will be granted a Normal Limited Certificate with the specialization indicated on the certificate. This certificate qualfies one to teach for three years in any elementary school of the state. It may be extended two years more by satisfactory work in two summer sessions in the Normal School. After two or three summer sessions the regular Normal School diploma . . . may be obtained by one semester of the regular winter session at the Normal School.[48]

It was felt that teaching two to eight grades in one room successfully required special adjustment of the teacher's methods, an appropriate program, adequate school management, a reorganization of teaching materials and the like.

Special courses were added to the curriculum to support this new program. A course in rural sociology was provided "to develop a better understanding of the problems in country and village life with which rural teachers are associated." [49]

As late as 1938–1939 a course in the instructional problems of the rural school was offered. "The purpose of this course is to give teachers a command of acceptable principles of organization and procedures for effective work in schools of more than one grade. Some topics considered are the possibilities and limitations of the small group as a socializing agency, organization for instruction on the group rather than the grade basis, adaptation of reading techniques under such type of organization, and planning activities that include children of several grades." [50]

The professional aspect of teacher preparation also changed under state direction. A course in human growth and development replaced the old course in educational psychology. Method courses in specific subjects were replaced by a course on the child and the curriculum. As a result, the practice school became a laboratory course for all professional courses.

These developments represented a trend back to the fundamentals of teacher education that had developed at Potsdam —understanding of systematic bodies of knowledge, understanding of the child and understanding of society. But they were only a trend, and there was a long road ahead for a full-scale renewal of the tradition.

Second phase of the interregnum in the 1930's in the Normal School saw significant changes. Much of this was due to changes in state policy. In 1938 the Board of Regents extended the course of instruction for elementary teachers from three to four years. The new program mandated that 92 hours, or about three-fourths of the work required for graduation, should be in liberal-cultural areas. This was a step toward the Brainerd-MacVicar tradition.

In July, 1942, the Normal School was converted into a State Teachers College, with authority to award the bachelor of education degree. In 1945—1946, the pattern of distribution of courses was professional education, 36, general or academic, 92. Fifteen elective hours were included in the latter.

Real and permanent changes had to come from the inside and there were promising beginnings. In addition to new courses in education that followed basic ideas in the Potsdam tradition, there was a foundation established for a return to the ideal of scholarship. This was done through course offerings and new faculty.

New courses offered greater preparation in depth. In 1939 –1940 there were four courses in English. In 1945–1946, there were about fifteen courses in the English department, covering literature courses, drama, Shakespeare, modern novel, etc. In 1939–1940, there were four courses in social studies, and in 1945–1946 there were thirteen courses covering American and European history, sociology, regional and period courses and diplomatic history. The same was true of all departments in the college.

New courses offered by old teachers, with old ideas, do not necessarily mean an advance. Older teachers always have a tendency to view new ideas through an old framework of reference. This can nullify reforms. It is extremely difficult to evaluate how much of this went on at Potsdam. Some of it obviously did, but there was progress.

Much of this progress was due to new faculty who were added during the interregnum. By the end of this period the nucleus of a good faculty existed, and was waiting for an imaginative administrator who would lead them boldly into the modern era.

There were also indications in the interregnum that other phases of the Potsdam tradition were being carried on. Dr. Stowell had felt that there should be more student involvement in life at Potsdam.

The first student council, four girls chosen by the senior class and three from the junior class, was formed in 1926. Miss Draime, the dean, was faculty advisor. They concerned themselves with problems of entertainment, a school paper and freshman rules.[51]

The next year a faculty-student organization replaced the student council.[52] Dr. Surki, guest lecturer from New York University, suggested this type of organization.[53]

This new organization consisted of the faculty, student council, the principal of the Normal and a series of committees made up of teachers and students.

Committees worked on problems in their respective fields. The faculty and student council, composed of both men and women students, acted upon their recommendations. The principal had veto power. Each committee was composed of sixteen students and from six to eight faculty members.

Committees were created for scholarship, social activities and social training, athletics, public performances, welfare and housekeeping, publicity and publication and finance.

The Normal Racquette, school newspaper, made its appearance on April 2, 1927. Its policy:

Before this paper commences its weekly circulation it might be well to publish a frank and open statement in regard to the policies and standards which we hope to carry out. For many decades the newspaper has been the greatest single influence in the molding of public opinion and the focusing of man's thoughts upon the important matters of the day. *The Normal Racquette* hopes to be no exception to this rule.

This publication is to be made a medium through which the student body of the school may express . . . ideas as freely and fearlessly as in public debate. . . .[54]

Social organizations promoted social life on campus. There were four sororities by the end of the 1920's: Pi Delta Sigma, Phi Kappa Gamma, Zeta Gamma Upsilon (Ago) and Alpha:

These four organizations have regular meetings and carry out definite programs of study. Another, and fully as important, object is that of fostering pleasant social relations and friendships. The bringing together of groups and congenial individuals, engaged in the activities and living much the same lives, is bound to result in the formation of lasting friendships. . . .[55]

These sororities became an integral part of college life and were guided by an inter-sorority council formed in the spring of 1927. The council was responsible for seeing "that the strength, and therefore the good of the entire school, rests with its individual members, and not with any one group." [56]

Other campus organizations offered opportunities for a richer student life. The Dramatic Club, founded in 1917, continued to flourish. In addition to its dramatic productions, assisted by the "Franks," it provided social activities. Sleigh rides, dances, picnics and evenings at the homes of various club members provided outlets for the human spirit.[57]

The Camera Club and Art Club permitted students with specialized skills or hobbies to develop them further. Annual exhibits featured their work.

The Hikers Club was very popular. It conducted two hikes, or tramps, each week. Their "bacon-bats," "corn-roasts," "sugar parties," and afternoon tramps to a country hotel or farmhouse provided more student recreation. They purchased toboggans and skis for use on the hill behind the president's present residence on Pierrepont Avenue.[58]

Students danced to moaning saxophones in the 1920's and were aware of Prohibition runners in the area. Bobbed hair and other symbols of radicalism appeared on campus, but for the most part Victorian standards were dominant.

The Normal School had developed an enviable reputation in athletics, especially in basketball, before the interregnum. This was due to one of the great basketball coaches in the annals of the sport, Professor Ernest Blood.

The "Professor" had joined the Normal faculty in 1906. His basketball teams, fashioned from the few Normal school boys available, soon became famous, competing against some of the best college teams in the east. His 1912–1913 team trounced City College of New York 34–8.

"Most of the college teams we played didn't know we were high school kids until they took the floor," explained Rufus Sisson, one of Potsdam's great athletes.

City College, shocked by its loss to a high school team, immediately arranged a return game in New York City. This time Potsdam won, 26–21.

The "Professor's" Normal teams won 72 victories in 74 games.[59]

Normal athletes continued to hang up records during this period. "Normal Athletes Made Brilliant Showing in Sports This Year," proclaimed *The Racquette* in 1934:

> The Potsdam Normal's program of interscholastic sports came to a close recently when the Red and Gray wave ended a successful season on the diamond. The Maxcy-trained machine established a fair record in baseball, defeating the Clarkson yearlings in the annual classic to the tune of 8-1 and winning over the Madison Barracks nine, but dropping a game to the St. Lawrence Frosh.[60]

The article also commented on the records of the other

sports: basketball, won 10, lost 3, and the formation of a tennis team which lost to a "superior" Clarkson varsity, 5–2. Harmon Wade was an outstanding athlete of the period. During this period Potsdam Normal also produced some of the finest girls' basketball teams in the east.

The first winter carnival was held on Saturday, February 7, 1931. Eddie Crowley and Catherine Thoma announced the following events: grand parade, 7:30; prizes for best dressed man, best dressed woman, funniest or most original woman's costume; stunts for all who will "stunt"; men's speed race (20 laps); women's speed race (6 laps); backward race for men; potato race (any who will); couple race (old and young); broomball for men; dancing until 11:30." [61]

This joint Clarkson-Normal function was a success from its inception, and has grown since to one of the major social attractions of college life in Potsdam.

Dr. Stowell's ideal of the importance of student life on the campus is attested by the following pronouncement at the close of the interregnum:

"It is desirable that a teacher be a socially competent individual. The social program at this teachers college is built with this ideal in mind. First of all the life of the college is planned so that the individual may have numerous happy social experiences that, in the natural routine of the college, provide the maximum of pleasure that is consistent with and indeed are a help toward serious intellectual work." [62]

Traditional social events, such as the Halloween masquerade, were listed. Students were encouraged to join church organizations "where the townspeople are most cordial in their relations to the students." The catalog cited the cordial relations existing between the faculty and students.

The Student-Faculty Association gave the students a voice with the faculty and president in the social activities of the college and a general control of student affairs. There were three sororities, Agonian, Alpha Delta and Clionian. The one fraternity, Sigma Sigma Sigma, had been suspended during World War II. Other student organizations permitted an enrichment of college life, the Blackfriars, International Relations Club, En Femme, The Student Christian Movement, The Newman Club, and the various musical organizations. Honoraries, such as Kappa Delta Pi, Phi Sigma Nu and Alpha Sigma Omicron, rewarded outstanding achievement. *The Racquette* and *The Pioneer* afforded an outlet for students with journalistic abilities.

Student life was "unhitched" by the close of the interregnum. A full-scale renewal of the Potsdam tradition was in the offing as Dr. Frederick W. Crumb became the president of the State Teachers College at Potsdam in April, 1946.

Chapter Eight

HELEN HOSMER

Helen Hosmer had realized her four major objectives by 1945. By then the Crane department of music had gained national recognition as a result of programs such as the Spring Festival of the Arts. Curriculum development was centered on creating music specialists while performance and practice teaching gave it breadth. Total involvement in music was achieved through a variety of musical experiences. The continued expansion of the Spring Festival added much to the musical heritage of the North Country. Academic quality was achieved through extension of the music course to four years and its approval as a degree granting program.

The Crane department of music prospered under the presidency of Dr. Frederick W. Crumb. In this era there was developed an experience rich in the academic, professional and technical aspects of teacher preparation. The tradition of bringing students to a fuller realization of the arts, especially music, was expanded. The guidelines were focused upon developing a generally educated person who was skilled in his craft and sensitive to the arts as a meaningful way of life.

Dr. Crumb—a man who did not intend to stand still—sensed the college was undernourished in terms of equipment, salaries and building facilities, but had the nucleus of a very fine faculty, and took immediate action. Financing and building improvements were essential if promising new beginnings were to be continued. He made pleas to the Board of Regents and the State Budget Committee and obtained, almost immediately, an increase in equipment appropriation from $14,000 to $110,000.[1]

This was only the beginning. Dr. Crumb realized that a whole new campus was necessary to implement his plan and he worked tirelessly toward this objective. Few college administrators have accomplished so much in such a short time.

On September 26, 1950, Thomas E. Dewey laid the cornerstone for the first building to be constructed on the new campus. Construction of an administration and classroom building, a health and physical education building, and a music building followed in rapid succession.

Prior to 1956 the Crane department lacked adequate equipment and facilities. In 1952 Miss Hosmer was granted a four-month leave of absence to investigate music facilities in universities, colleges and high schools in eighteen states.

The new Crane building, a physical expression of her philosophy, is an outstanding facility. It includes two rehearsal rooms, administrative offices, classrooms, studios, instrument storage and repair complex, a recital hall seating 350 with a stage that will accommodate a symphony orchestra, a fine music library, a recording studio, and eighty private practice rooms.

The Spring Festival of the Arts became a dramatic expression of Helen Hosmer's philosophy and of the Potsdam tradition and spirit. A turning point in the Festival came when Miss Hosmer met with Robert Shaw at Tanglewood in the summer of 1946.

Norman Bell, a Crane student, was a member of Shaw's Collegiate Chorale in New York City. Bell received a Tanglewood scholarship that summer and invited Miss Hosmer to visit the music colony, where Shaw was conducting.

Helen Hosmer

Miss Hosmer and Shaw spent considerable time discussing music programs at the college. Shaw suggested that the Crane Chorus perform Hindemith's *An American Requiem* the following year.

Miss Hosmer agreed. "Good idea! Why don't you come and direct it?" Shaw replied, "That's what I've been waiting for." [2]

The 1947 festival program featured lectures on Hindemith's music by Julius Herford and Shaw, Saturday night. The concert Sunday afternoon consisted of three parts. Shaw conducted the Crane Chorus in *An American Requiem,* Miss Hosmer conducted Brahms' *Alto Rhapsody,* and an alumni chorus sang choruses from the *B Minor Mass.*

In 1948 and 1949 Herford and Shaw presented illustrated lectures on the festival music, and an alumni chorus prepared short compositions and the major work was performed by the Crane Chorus and orchestra. Beethoven's *Mass in C Major* was performed in 1948 and Verdi's *Manzoni Requiem* in 1949.

Intense rehearsals were held a week before the concert by the Crane staff and students. Shaw was impressed with the chorus:

In his dressing room after the concert, Mr. Shaw exulted over the spirit and abilities of his performers.

Gratefully fondling the handsome leather suitcase which they had given him in appreciation of his effort, he exclaimed, "A wonderful group! You don't often get a chance to work with people like that."

He had nothing but praise for the eagerness with which the singers and players approached their task, for the results which they achieved, and for the splendid coaching they had gotten. It was easy to see, from his remarks, why he was so willing to return to Potsdam. . . .[3]

Thornton Wilder wrote a letter of thanks to Miss Hosmer:

A big bread-and-butter letter is bursting out of me, for all the kind things you did for me, and which you carried so splendidly beside the burden of that complicated and finally triumphant Festival. Right from that first Monday rehearsal, I was your sworn admirer, not only had you everything well in hand, but you combined hard work with joy, and precision with exhilaration.

Wasn't it all wonderful?

All week, I went about in a cloud—not only of fragments of the Lacrymosa and the Sanctus, but of the Potsdam community and the trees and the streets and that mixture of kindness and goodwill and the sober dedication to teaching teachers thoroughly and well.

Don't take the trouble to answer this; I'll be back to tell it to you all over again. . . .⁴

The 1950 festival commemorated the two-hundredth anniversary of the death of Johann Sebastian Bach. There were three separate concerts. On May 14 a concert of selected works of Bach was presented by the Symphonette Orchestra, Collegiate Singers and Symphonic Band. A faculty recital featured solo and small ensemble pieces on Saturday, May 20, and the following day Shaw directed the Crane Chorus in Bach's *Mass in B Minor*.

A new element was introduced into the 1950 festival. Other programs at the college were generating a concern for unity among the arts. Through the efforts of Miss Hosmer, the college's art department and the festival committee, a group of oil paintings by American artists were exhibited from May 1 through May 21. The exhibition was continued the following year and Miss Hosmer obtained the services of Oliver O'Connor Barrett as visiting professor of sculpture and drawing.

The festival gained momentum. On May 19, 1951, the Crane Chorus and Orchestra presented the première of Norman Dello Joio's *Psalm of David,* commissioned by the college. The next night Shaw conducted a performance of Bach's

Passion According to Saint John, with Blake Stern as the Evangelist.

These performances drew national attention. *Newsweek* magazine carried the following account:

The chorus's high standard of performance is remarkable, for every Potsdam music student is a member—regardless of his caliber of voice.

Spirit and Sweat: This year's festival was a real challenge to Potsdam, for presented at the festival were such works as Bach's "Passion According to Saint John" and Norman Dello Joio's "A Psalm of David," commissioned for the occasion by the Crane Chorus. Said composer Dello Joio: "I accepted with the greatest of pleasure because I knew that here at Potsdam the spirit of faculty and students is one of dedication to music."

Robert Shaw, one of the country's finest choral directors, has been associated with the Potsdam Festival since 1947, and it was he who was in charge of the Bach "St. John Passion." "Two things hit you at Potsdam," said Shaw. "The first is the attitude that the arts are a reasonable and necessary part of anyone's and everyone's daily living . . . The second attitude . . . is that art is a matter of *doing.* It's an affair of sweat, sore throats, split lips, and bleeding hands—not a term paper title on a philosophic forum." [5]

The 1952 festival was massive. There were two days of concerts featuring Dello Joio's opera *The Triumphs of St. Joan,* Brahms' *Naenie,* Hindemith's *Apparebit Repentina Dies,* and Beethoven's *Missa Solemnis.*

Crane students thrived in this atmosphere. Music classes were canceled so that students could concentrate on festival preparations. They were able to learn under the direction of master musicians.

Dr. Crumb was concerned. Crane students comprised a small portion of the student body. He was "aware that the music students were tremendously excited, keyed up and thrilled with what was going on, [but] the rest of the students felt left out and disgruntled." Accordingly, the festival was expanded, exemplifying the College's concern to make the arts a part of every teacher's life.

The festival became an all-college event in 1953. Classes were replaced by cultural programs. Fourteen events were scheduled, ranging from a college drama production, *The Playboy of the Western World*, to a lecture by Gilbert Seldes.

Miss Hosmer conducted a performance of Mendelssohn's *Elijah* on Saturday evening and Robert Shaw conducted the group in a Bach cantata, the Schubert *Mass in C*, Stravinsky's *Symphony of Psalms* and the *Horn Concerto No. 3 in E flat* by Mozart with Mason Jones of the Philadelphia Orchestra as soloist. Part of the festival expenses were met by students assessing themselves.

Dr. Crumb obviously was pleased and wrote the following to Dr. Hosmer:

There was a theory that a sound once made never completely dies away. The sound waves get weaker and weaker and approach nothingness but never quite attain it. If this is true, and I were you, I would be happy to take the performance of "Elijah" and let it go around the world forever as my work. It was wonderful.[6]

The 1954 festival was unusual in that high school musicians were invited to participate. Nearly 300 student musicians from 44 high schools throughout the state participated with the Crane Chorus and Orchestra.

Robert Shaw summed up his personal feelings about the festival by writing:

In no sense can the Potsdam Spring Festival of the Arts be called a "local affair." Its influence is statewide; and it is rapidly gaining in national recognition. . . . When a State College will invite three hundred of the leading young high school musicians of New York State to a four day program of rehearsals, lectures and performances and can produce a performance of the Berlioz

"Requiem" of the finest technical calibre—this is an affair of national importance.[7]

Eleanor Roosevelt attended the 1955 festival at which Robert Shaw conducted a complete performance of Bach's *Passion According to Saint Matthew*. Mrs. Roosevelt reacted positively to the sweep of the festival's program in the following words:

My trip to Potsdam on Thursday was extremely interesting because I found that the state teachers college there, which has students from many parts of the state, is developing a very fine program in the arts. Their choral group, for example, has become well known in musical circles.

I had a feeling that real appreciation of the arts was going forward at the college. I think this is one of the most important things that can be done for our young people, and I was grateful for the opportunity to see what they were accomplishing.[8]

By 1958 the times had changed. The student body outgrew the college theater. Furthermore, there was a growing conviction that too many cultural events were being crowded into a short time. Also, Crane students were so occupied with rehearsals that they could not attend many events. Consequently the format, still in force, was changed in 1958.

Eleven events were scheduled between March 14 and the culminating conference on May 11. The schedule was: March 14–15, drama, *My Three Angels;* March 18, lecture, Ogden Nash; April 16, films, *Mr. Hulot's Holiday* and *The Bespoke Overcoat;* April 17, lecture, John Fischer, editor of *Harper's Magazine;* April 23, film, *Les Enfants du Paradis;* April 24, lecture, Dr. Saul Padover, Author; April 30, dance, The Sarah Lawrence Dance Group; May 1, lecture, Dr. Rudolph Arnheim; May 4–18, art exhibits; May 10, lecture, Nadia Boulanger; May 11, music, Crane Chorus and Orchestra with Nadia Boulanger conducting.[9]

Reflecting on the purposes and outcomes of a festival, Dr. Hosmer wrote:

Naturally the first aim was to celebrate in a festive manner the culmination of the year's work in the special field of music—the art to which the music majors of our Teachers College are dedicated. There is a core interest which propels through personal pride, professional growth and an inherent aesthetic reaction. The addition of allied arts to the music of the festival brings about a more total aesthetic realization, for each single art enhances and elicits the best in every other art. The fundamental relationship in all the arts rises to the surface, perhaps not at the moment, but it is there for cultural spending in the future. The more the spread through the allied arts, the greater heightening of the total effect. Scope permitting, every art adds depth to its sister arts. We feel that the musical offerings take on greater significance if supported by art exhibits, drama, dance and cinema. Since art is the residue of a culture, why not have available the expression in several media? Thus we may hope for a "Cultural snowball."

The student has lived these works and in a four-year period has personally experienced musical monuments brought to life. He has had these interpreted under the baton of his own regular directors as well as the refreshing and inspiring readings of guest conductors Nadia Boulanger, Thor Johnson, Robert Shaw, Jan Meyerowitz and Adnan Saygun.[10]

The success of the Spring Festival has never diminished. Robert Shaw conducted the *Mass in B Minor* in 1959 and Beethoven's *Missa Solemnis* in 1961. In 1960 Virgil Thomson conducted the chorus and orchestra in a première performance of the *Missa Pro Defunctus*.

Miss Hosmer completed forty years of dedicated service to the college in 1962. In recognition of her service the Crane Alumni Association designated the school year 1962–1963 as the "Fortieth Anniversary Year" in honor of Miss Hosmer.

President Crumb dedicated the 32nd Festival of the Arts to Dr. Hosmer and as a final tribute in the series of twenty-one events, Robert Shaw returned to repeat the same work he had conducted on his first appearance in Potsdam in 1947, Hindemith's *A Requiem.*

The Crane department's eminence in music was described by Lester Ingalls, following the 1964 concert of Verdi's *Requiem.* "The Crane department of music is incomparable in concerts and productions of this kind. These Spring Festivals are a great experience." [11]

The Crane Chorus, so vital in Miss Hosmer's philosophy, did not confine itself to the Festivals. Its annual Christmas concerts were another example of students' total involvement in music. Guest conductors such as Jan Meyerowitz and Adnan Saygun conducted their own works at these concerts. In 1961 Miss Hosmer conducted a première performance of Vaughan Williams' *This Day* (Hodie). In 1962 Arthur Frackenpohl's *Te Deum,* dedicated to Miss Hosmer, was presented under the direction of Carl Druba.

Miss Hosmer also continued the custom of "Sight Reading Performances"—another meaningful and total involvement in music.

The Crane Chorus was invited to sing in New York on two occasions. Robert Shaw promoted and conducted the Choral Masterwork Series in 1952, and on February 3 of that year he and Miss Hosmer shared the podium in conducting the Crane Chorus and Orchestra in the works of Hindemith, Brahms, Josquin and Dello Joio. The New York *Journal American* carried the following account of the performance:

Robert Shaw gave his choral Masterworks Series a new slant in Carnegie Hall last night. He imported the Crane Chorus and Orchestra of State University Teachers College at Potsdam, N. Y., to perform his third program and present the first New York performance of Dello Joio's "Psalm of David." [12]

In 1958 Seyfulalh Esin, Turkish Ambassador to the United Nations, invited Miss Hosmer and the Crane Chorus to participate in a concert sponsored by the Turkish government in honor of the United Nations and one of Turkey's own composers.

On November 25, 1958, the Crane Chorus joined with the Symphony of the Air in a performance of Adnan Saygun's *Yunus Emre,* under the direction of Leopold Stokowski.

In March 1964 Collegiate Singers, a mixed chorus of about forty voices, gave the American première of Stockhausen's "Momente" in Buffalo with The Buffalo Philharmonic Orchestra and in 1965 the American première of Kagel's "Phonophonie," also in Buffalo with The Buffalo Philharmonic Orchestra.

In a speech at Montreal, Quebec, in 1953 Miss Hosmer said:

> One of the strongest convictions I have after a 35 year period of teaching is that *travel,* added to a *vital campus or school room experience* . . . is one of the most contributing factors to the type of total personality we wish for teachers. . . .[13]

This was the basic reason behind her European study program in 1936. The summer European tours were revived in 1953 and repeated in 1954, 1956, 1959 and 1960. The first three were promoted by Potsdam and the other two were part of the State University's "Study-Live Abroad."

The first tour in 1953 set the pattern of Potsdam's tours and reflected Helen Hosmer and all the other molders of the Potsdam tradition. Advanced instructional plans, or pretrip preparation, called for reading of travel literature with a written report and research on two cities or places of interest through which the group would pass. Intra trip assignments included study, reports and attendance at a minimum number of concerts and other significant events. The itinerary included travels through Holland, Belgium, France, Italy, Austria, Germany, England and Scotland. The group attended music festivals, participated in the First International Music Educator's Conference in Brussels, saw dramatic productions, visited churches, museums, conservatories and universities.

The Potsdam educators stressed the value of personal contact with various national groups. Personal observations of the customs of these groups revealed that all people have many common characteristics and that human nature does have a common denominator.[14]

The Julia E. Crane Alumni Association has continued to play an active role in the modern era of the college.

Scholarship aid was continued with two significant additions. In 1947 an endowment fund of nearly $110,000 was established by the terms of the will of Mary Rowe McMenamin, class of 1917. Seven four-year scholarships of $200 each were established for music students. In 1957 two more scholarships, one of $400 and one of $600, were established with the income from this fund. In 1958 a $1,000 four-year scholarship was established as a result of an endowment by Mrs. Bertrand H. Snell, a Crane graduate of 1901.

The Crane Alumni Association was active in providing needed musical instruments for the department. A memorial fund was begun in 1954 by friends of Inafred Hoecker. This fund, plus an alumni drive, resulted in the purchase of a harpsichord in February, 1959. A portable Schlicker pipe organ was purchased in March, 1962, from alumni contributions.

One of the outstanding contributions of the Alumni Association was the establishment of a commissioning fund in honor of Dr. Hosmer:

For some time it has been Helen Hosmer's wish to commission works for performance by the Crane Chorus and Orchestra. As a fitting and tangible token of esteem and appreciation, the association is establishing the Crane Alumni Commissioning Fund in her honor, and alumni and friends are invited to contribute to this fund. . . . It is our hope that this fund will result in the commissioning of many important works in the future, and that . . . the fund may continue as a permanent activity of the association.[15]

Dr. Frederick W. Crumb, President of the college, said in a brochure in 1962:

It is with affection and gratitude that we at the State University College at Potsdam join the Crane Alumni Association in bringing to your attention some events planned in honor of Helen M. Hosmer.

For more than one-third of a century Miss Hosmer has endowed our college, and the state it serves, with vigorous, creative genius. Indeed, her talents have influenced music education everywhere. It is appropriate and important that the Crane Alumni Association has moved to fulfill one of Miss Hosmer's long-standing wishes, by establishing an Alumni Commissioning Fund. . . .[16]

Dr. Arthur Frackenpohl's *Te Deum* was the first work to be commissioned in 1962. Dr. Robert Washburn's *Quartet* was the second.

The activities of the Crane Alumni Association were a tribute to the ideals of Helen Hosmer. The dedicated and persistent efforts on the part of graduates to promote those ideals attested to the penetrating and lasting impressions which were made on their lives as students. Strength in unity, purpose and pride were reciprocal.

Beginning in 1948 the New York State School Music Association organized and sponsored festivals on the Potsdam campus, a fall meeting for bands, chorus or orchestra under guest conductors, and a spring festival for organizations and soloists. Crane students helped organize and direct the festivals.

Also, the Association often held annual reading sessions in Potsdam:

There has been music in the air in Potsdam during the past week! Three hundred school music directors and teachers from all corners of New York State have gathered for three full days to read through a large amount of music for use with their bands, orchestras, and choruses. These reading sessions under the sponsorship of the New York State School Music Association help the directors to choose at first hand much of the material that will be used with performing groups across the length and breadth of the state. During the autumn months at 18 centers throughout the state, some 5,200 students, carefully selected, will perform under expert guest conductors in bands, orchestras and choirs. And again in the spring, in 18 centers, another total of 53,000 children will appear before adjudicators as soloists or as members of small or large ensembles. During a weekend in May Potsdam residents see dozens of school buses parked throughout the town, transporting some 4,000 children to the Potsdam Spring Festival which is the largest one in the state, including about 60 schools.[17]

In 1964, construction on the college campus necessitated holding the school music festivals at Potsdam public schools.

Miss Hosmer and other leading musicians had long been concerned with the lack of opportunity for young composers to write. During the festival week of May, 1951, she and Mr. Dello Joio and Mr. Shaw discussed the problem. Miss Hosmer pointed out the needs of the public schools and suggested them as a means through which young talent might find expression. Two years later this idea was formally presented to the Ford Foundation by Dello Joio.

In 1959 the Ford Foundation announced grants for young composers to work in public schools throughout the country. Dr. Frackenpohl and Dr. Washburn, of the college faculty, were two of the first composers selected. Dr. Frackenpohl worked in Hempstead, Long Island, and Dr. Washburn in Elkhart, Indiana.[18]

Dr. Hosmer's life is full of rich experiences. She has excelled as teacher, musician, administrator and humanitarian by sharing the significant, positive elements of life.

She is fundamentally concerned with the democratic concept of education, with emphasis on the individual's total experience:

Music education is the contribution we make to help bring about a better life for our fellow men. In educating people through music, we travel one of the many ways of dynamic living and thus help to provide man's total experience.

Music education must add up to a broad and unifying perspective. At the same time, it results in the tolerant, understanding and well-adjusted individual. . . .[19]

It is interesting that in the last analysis the public demands that music be taught. Authoritative philosophers and psychologists urge that an active participation in the arts be extended to the mass population to the end that the lives of all the people may be permeated with a higher order of creative intelligence. We music educators feel strongly about what music means and wish to share this experience with others. We also feel that every child needs the kind of expressive experience which music so uniquely provides.[20]

Dr. Hosmer insists that faith of the American people in music must be the force behind the efforts of every good teacher of music. The justification for music must be based on what it does for the people, the impact it makes upon their lives and the understandings that result from universal meanings, sensitivity and beauty.

She has relied on three phases of curriculum development pioneered at Potsdam—understanding systematic bodies of knowledge, understanding the child and understanding society.

Her emphasis on content, the child and society is illustrated by the following excerpt:

It seems to me a broad knowledge of music is only one phase of the choral director's equipment. Practically considered, from the standpoint of the preparation of the choral directors of the future, if we in music are to meet the challenge of modern education, a thorough and well balanced musical training alone is not going to be sufficient to produce well integrated personalities who in their turn will make of their subjects well integrated personalities. We might state the problem in this manner: A broadening knowledge of music on the part of a choral director is an essential requirement, which by its breadth and scope carries along wide concomitant masteries in other fields. And the converse: An individual, well grounded and well-rounded in the fundamental generalizations of human knowledge will be turned in his specializations to a more successful execution of his specific task.

What a director knows of the real inner make-up of a human being, his reaction to his environment and his creative aspirations, all go to give more vitality and strength to the action of the conductor's baton.[21]

Dr. Hosmer believes that teaching is a science as well as an art, but she is very critical of relying heavily on any one method. Behind every method there must be an imaginative, flexible teacher. No method can do the work of the teacher:

Don't fall into the habit of doing and saying things in the same way all the time, or always as the other person says it. Be an individual, and be an interesting individual who can contribute something new and vital.[22]

She insists that certain tools must be mastered to understand and use music:

We believe our aim in promoting the ability to read music . . . is to make reading an integral part of the total process of making music. One justification for this point of view is the fact that upon examining music reading from the historical point of view, we find it arose as a means of facilitating the individual opportunities to *make* music. And is it too far out of line to think that in educating through music we *use* music's inherent tools rather than *neglect* them, hopefully wishing that mastery will come through the handling of rim or fringe factors? Let's not talk about *teaching music reading*. Let's *read music!* In other words, let's not skirt the edges and roost in the periphery of the mastery of the tools.[23]

The good conductor has mastered the fundamental techniques of conducting so that they have become automatic and habitual . . . if the work lives within him as an ideal, *undimmed by obstacles of mechanisms,* then he is worthy to bear the conductor's responsibility.[24]

A conductor must be flexible so that he can meet the unexpected but important needs of a group, and at the same time work through to the objectives previously established. . . .[25]

Dr. Hosmer has two guiding principles pertaining to the science of teaching: innovation and standards. In a speech in Montreal in 1953 she revealed:

I am an American and a modern educator who believes in experiencing, experimenting, and integrating experience. I believe in the importance of the arts in the life of all of us. Contained within the arts and the atoms, which are constant and complete around us, is the potential for the dynamic, creative, and rewardingly happy life. This is my background, philosophy, and design for practice.[26]

Central to her philosophy is an emphasis on standards:

The longer I teach and serve as an administrator, the more I am persuaded to subscribe to standards. Standards are the result of the considered requirements which have arisen through the best practice and organization of successful teachers.[27]

In the final analysis, she believes that teaching music is an art that depends fundamentally on being in love with music. Thus, teachers have the opportunity of bringing about a unique growth in students. She has proposed seven commandments for a choral conductor:

Helen Hosmer

1. *Be in love with the activity of conducting* if you wish to be successful.
2. *Forget yourself* entirely in what you are doing.
3. *Know your music* as only a real musician can.
4. *Employ every available bit of a sense of humor* that you can possibly corral for the use of the moment at hand.
5. *Untie or unlock your imagination* and play with ideas, words, effects.
6. In every bit of work I do, whether teaching, directing a chorus, working out a departmental policy or training my dog to shake hands, *I try to employ what I am pleased to term the affirmative approach.*
7. It seems to me that a choral director must have a pretty good idea of *the proper method of voice production.*

To repeat, I think the above suggestions are some of the most essential things in the effective production of good results. We have taken all rudimentary techniques for granted, and with them mastered, there is no limit to the possibilities for any one with a real love of the work.[28]

Chapter Nine

THE CRUMB ADMINISTRATION

THE history of the State University College at Potsdam from 1946 to 1965 witnessed two distinct periods of rapid and extensive changes, followed by periods of relative calm for evaluation of experimentation and consolidation of gains.

In 1946–1947, the college completed the preliminary steps in effecting a transition from a three-year normal school to a four-year, degree-granting college. However, its admissions and scholastic standards were relatively low; its program was limited; and its financial support was ridiculously inadequate. Moreover, its curricular programs were rigidly prescribed and tightly controlled by the Board of Regents and the State Education Department, with the result that local initiative had been stifled for years and there was serious danger that the institution would never be able to live up to its potential as a first-rate college.

A breakthrough came in the spring of 1947. Dr. Hermann Cooper, Assistant Commissioner for Teacher Education, held a curriculum conference in Syracuse. There was a good faculty representation from all eleven state colleges.

A turning point in the entire curriculum pattern for state colleges came when Dr. Crumb challenged the first committee report. The Potsdam president flatly refused to agree to any plan that would tell his faculty what to teach. He insisted that a good professor knows what to teach and that he should have freedom to do it:

> We met for a week on curriculum and I was in charge of the session in English and Fine Arts. We had a grand time and did a lot of creative work and came out with some fine ideas. . . . The first report in the group session was devoted to the sciences. The gentlemen presenting the report started out by reading the freshman biology curriculum, chapter and verse (just like a textbook index). Before he had gone on ten minutes I got up and said, "I'll have no part of this. No one is going to tell my biology professor what he is going to teach in his course. You question his competency the minute you tell him what to teach. He knows what to teach." [1]

Dr. Cooper gave Dr. Crumb's proposal strong support. This set the pattern for the future.

Under the leadership of Dr. Cooper, the State Education Department lifted its protective covering of uniform curricular patterns in all colleges and transferred to the individual units a high degree of autonomy in developing local curricular patterns. This transfer of authority, in combination with the establishment of State University of New York in 1948 and an accompanying increase in financial support, led to a period of institutional evaluation and institutional upgrading involving drastic changes which included significant curricular experimentation.

Once the "green light" was given to move ahead it became apparent that there existed a tremendous amount of interest in, enthusiasm for and excitement about institutional self-improvement.

The period 1947–1951 was characterized by the following significant changes:

Drastic raising of admissions and academic standards.
Increase in elective opportunities in both elementary and music programs.

Development of academic concentrations for all students majoring in elementary education.

Upgrading of faculty with emphasis upon "divisional organization."

Revision of professional sequence with greater emphasis upon practice teaching and accompanying seminar.

Expansion of foreign language offerings to include French, German, Spanish, Japanese, Russian.

Expansion of mathematics offerings beyond introductory courses; introduction of "meaning of arithmetic"—a forerunner of what is now labeled "modern mathematics."

Expansion of science offerings with more stress upon physics, chemistry, and geology in addition to the previous emphasis upon biology.

Introduction of master's degree programs for majors in elementary education and music education.

Emphasis upon total cultural development; the strengthening of the fine arts program and the expansion of the annual music festival to a Festival of the Arts, which has acquired an international reputation for excellence.

Establishment of a comprehensive student personnel program.

Expansion of extension and summer session programs.

Introduction of annual conferences, bringing to the campus participants from all sections of New York State and consultants recognized as national authorities: guidance, curriculum and social studies.

Curricular experimentation:

Foreign languages in the elementary school—beginning with kindergarten; preparation of teachers competent to teach. Comparative language courses in college.

Expression in arts—coordinated program for freshmen (art, English, music).

New York trip—week-long cultural program in New York City for all freshmen.

Introductory course in social science with emphasis upon sociology and anthropology.

White Pine Camp summer program with emphasis upon
fine arts.
Foreign study tours—music and comparative education.

The period 1951–1956 emphasized an evaluation of the
strengths and weaknesses of the various programs and experimental ventures which had been started back in 1946–1947.
Consolidation of the gains which had been made and concentration on refinement of new techniques and procedures characterized this five-year period during which the college paused
on a plateau and rested long enough to "catch its breath" in
preparation for another thrust upward. The pressure for continued self-improvement was overpowering and irresistible
and 1955 found the institution on the threshold of another
period of rapid and profound change—with the emphasis this
time upon the development of academic excellence and the
broadening of the mission of the college to include more than
just the preparation of elementary and music teachers.
Significant changes during 1956–1961 included:

The further strengthening of all academic areas and expansion of course offerings.
Transfer from "divisional" to "departmental" organization
of the faculty.
Establishment of separate departments of philosophy, psychology, geography and social sciences.
Strengthening of the faculty—with emphasis upon both
scholarly competence and teaching ability.
Introduction of programs for preparing secondary teachers
of English, French, mathematics, science and social studies.
Preparation of new programs for teachers of N-6 and N-9
levels with emphasis upon strong academic majors and B.A.
degrees.
Strengthening of the graduate program; addition of master's
degree for majors in secondary education.
Tremendous increase in library holdings.

Experimental program for freshman students of high academic ability.

Experimental program for freshman students with reading and communications deficiencies.

Introduction of advanced placement program and the use of "exemptions" whenever competence was demonstrated.

Seminar in humanities for upperclassmen.

Development of curricula for liberal arts students—looking forward to the time when authorization would be given to become a multipurpose institution.

Strengthening the instrumental program of the music department; emphasis upon performance and teaching; encouragement of composers.

History—emphasis upon a program of non-western studies.

Mathematics—development of a depth program and a respectable major.

Foreign language—development of depth programs in French, Spanish and German; preparation of teachers of Spanish.

Science—strengthening of all subdivisions with teachers of scholarly depth in biology, chemistry, geology or physics.

More extensive involvement in local and regional community programs; e.g., cooperative program with St. Lawrence County Mental Health Clinic.

Special Curricular Programs:

National Science Foundation Institutes for junior high teachers and also for high school students.

Summer session for highly talented high school students.

Reading and speech clinics for North Country students.

Music clinics for public schools.

Special programs for talented high school music students.

Discovery approach in the social studies.

Summer workshops for string and woodwind students.

The acquisition and development of a college camp for curricular and non-curricular activities.

Miss Julia E. Crane, founder of Crane Institute of Music

(Photo by Clarence E. Premo)

Dr. Helen M. Hosmer, director of the Crane department of music

(Photo by Clarence E. Premo)

Dr. Frederick W. Crumb, president of The State University College at Potsdam

Model of portion of The State University College at Potsdam campus as planned for 1970

These two periods of curricular change and experimentation represented a full-scale renewal of the Potsdam tradition. The test of a tradition is its ability to sustain an institution in the face of challenge and to inspire effective action through quality leadership.

Potsdam faced its greatest challenge in the 1940's—the college needed a builder, a maker, a developer. Dr. Frederick W. Crumb resolved the crisis by providing bold, imaginative leadership.

All the strands of the Potsdam tradition have reached a logical culmination in this man. He represents a passing parade—Asa Brainerd, Malcolm MacVicar, Thomas Stowell and other dynamic persons. Not only are their ideas a part of his administration, but he has imparted his own distinctive philosophy and personality to the traditions they established. By updating and projecting the Potsdam tradition he proved that it could cope with modern problems. But he frankly regarded this tradition as a point of departure.

Dr. Crumb accepted the central purpose of this tradition, teacher preparation, and set out to make Potsdam the best four-year teacher preparation college in the country. It has steadily moved closer to that goal because his thinking has kept pace with the changing times. But the purpose of the college had to be updated to meet the forces that were altering American society. Dr. Crumb early recognized that liberal arts was basic to the education of a teacher. Ten years before the State University designated Potsdam as a college of arts and sciences [1962] it had a strong liberal arts program.

State policy permitted local autonomy. The dynamism to achieve the purposes of the college was provided by the combined efforts of Dr. Crumb, faculty and students. The role that each played demonstrated the full potential of the ideas developed during Dr. Stowell's administration.

Dr. Crumb believes that "leadership and administration consist of finding ways to help able teachers do what they think they ought to be doing. He feels that this permits him to set the proper climate for the college but the tone has to be set by able teachers and scholars. An administrator should provide room for movement by professional teachers and to provide them with the things they need to do their job." [2]

To foster innovation and change he frequently used the resources of the Potsdam College Development Fund before the budget provided the necessary funds. "After you get a first-rate faculty member, you have to make the program fit in, even with such simple things as library acquisitions." [3]

The combined efforts of the administration and faculty permitted the college to make significant curricular adaptations to change. The work of the Curriculum Committee has been especially significant. Dr. Alfred Thatcher, Dean of the College and chairman of this committee which has both elective and appointed faculty members, recommended to the faculty and president of the College appropriate action on curriculum. Each department was given the responsibility and freedom to change the curriculum within the general guidelines and standards suggested by Dr. Crumb and faculty committees:

Early in the 1950's the curriculum committee at Potsdam decided that the traditional, but rather rigid, prescribed program of teacher preparation then in effect failed to provide future teachers with a strong liberal background and depth in an academic field which, combined with sound professional preparation, is needed by competent teachers for today's schools. The revision of the curriculum pattern for elementary teachers, which was adopted, provided for a required pattern of liberal studies of approximately two years' work, the equivalent of more than a year's work in elective academic courses and another year's credit for professional work. Under this program students were required to have a concentration of 15 hours in a division (humanities, science and mathematics, or the social studies) and at least two courses in two other divisions. This past year the curriculum committee modified this pattern to a concentration of 15 hours in a department rather than in a division and a minor concentration of nine hours in another department. This change in pattern by increasing the number and variety of elective offerings has strengthened all departments of the college and has enabled the college to move into the early secondary and high school teacher preparation program. In turn, this means the college is better able to meet its responsibilities as a multipurpose institution.[4]

In 1961–1962 Dr. Crumb inaugurated a self-study program by the faculty, and their statement of the college's philosophy reveals the spirit that was animating the college:

Our major premise is that the education of competent teachers demands the development of informed, creative, responsible men and women. To achieve this development there must be an integration of the student's professional and general education.

We believe in the intrinsic dignity and worth of each human being and in his potential for contribution to a better life for all people. We endeavor, therefore, to offer opportunities for each student to increase his

1. Alertness to relationships among concepts.
2. Ability to communicate ideas.
3. Mastery of basic principles underlying several academic disciplines, with depth in a special field.
4. Understanding of people.
5. Proficiency and enthusiasm for teachings.
6. Interest in developing a personal philosophy that will insure continued intellectual and professional growth.

To achieve these ends each member of the faculty must demand much of himself in competence in his field, in criticism of his own performance as a teacher, and in reflection on his responsibility.

The key to implementation of this philosophy in all college programs is found in three factors:

1. A sound program of selective admission to teacher education programs.
2. A strong liberal studies pattern which provides a reasonable acquaintance with a variety of areas of the liberal arts, coupled

with the opportunity for depth of study and competence in the specific teaching field.

3. A pattern of professional preparation which provides for theory and application to complement and supplement each other along with an understanding of the total education enterprise.[5]

Joint efforts of the faculty and administration produced the following curriculum that was registered by the State Education Department in 1963 for five years, the maximum period of registration in New York State:

1. Bachelor of arts (B.A.) with a liberal arts major in art history, English, French, mathematics, music history and literature, psychology, the sciences, history or the social sciences—120 credit hours.

2. Bachelor of arts (B.A.) with a liberal arts major in art history, English, foreign languages, mathematics, music history and literature, psychology, the sciences or history and the social sciences, and certification valid for teaching in the early childhood and upper elementary grades —128 credit hours.

3. Bachelor of arts (B.A.) with a liberal arts major in English, general science, mathematics or social studies certificate valid for teaching in the early childhood, upper elementary grades, and an academic subject in the early secondary grades—128 credit hours.

4. Bachelor of arts (B.A.) degree with a liberal arts major in English, French, social studies, biology, chemistry, earth science, physics, or mathematics and a certificate valid for teaching an academic subject in the secondary school—128 credit hours.

5. Bachelor of science (B.S.) with a major in music education and certification to teach music—128 credit hours.[6]

The firm belief in standards among the faculty and administration is reflected in the admission policy and academic standards of the college. This belief in standards is a flexible one and is strongly tinged by humanitarianism. Each application for admission gets individual attention.

The two-divisional level reflects a basic emphasis on scholastic standards. The freshman and sophomore years comprise the first level and the junior and senior years the second. A student must have a C average before he is permitted to go on to the second level. However, students are given a second chance to achieve this average.

Studies show that approximately 50 per cent of students offered this chance take advantage of it and approximately one-half of those who try again eventually are graduated.

The faculty flourished under the "climate" established by Dr. Crumb and set the tone for innovation and experimentation.

In 1947 a unique experiment in education was offered. Expression in the Arts was a logical course for Potsdam, because it placed an emphasis on the humanities and the interrelationships of the arts.

Members of the art, English and music departments of the State Teachers Colleges of New York met in Syracuse during February, 1947, to discuss the possibilities of an inter-departmental course in the humanities. The resulting proposal called for a course designated Expression in the Arts. The program, initiated at Potsdam in September, 1947, was directed toward seven objectives:

1. A clear realization of . . . communication. . . .
2. A "feeling" for an expressional medium as a means of communication.
3. Respect for an expressional medium—its potentialities, its unique characteristics, etc.
4. Sensitivity to the art point of view.
5. Alertness to the sensory impressions of one's environment.

6. Ability to interpret and enjoy non-literal, even symbolic, material in the arts.
7. A habit of reflecting on experiences and observations as being potential raw material for art expression.

An essential feature of the organization of the course was that of scheduling. In order to lend flexibility and make the most of available time block scheduling was employed. From eight to ten o'clock Monday mornings six sections of college freshmen met for two-hour classes. Two of the six met with music instructors, two with art instructors, two with teachers of written and oral expression. Tuesday mornings the six had two-hour sessions, but each section concentrated on an area; the two sections meeting for art on Monday had music on Tuesday, those studying music on Monday met as an English class on Tuesday, and those in English on Monday were in art on Tuesday. On Wednesday morning they shifted again, completing the cycle.

These two-hour periods accounted for about two-thirds of the weekly classroom time required for three semester hours of credit in each subject. Each section met for a one-hour session in music and for one hour in English on either Thursday or Friday. On one of those days each section also had a two-hour meeting in art.

Block scheduling was the key to the course and cleared the way for at least two serviceable procedures:

1. Combined meetings of two, three, or all six sections for periods of time up to two hours in length. Such large group meetings were practical for motion pictures, lectures, summarizing reports, or similar projects that are of interest to all students and instructors of the course.
2. Temporary regrouping of members of the two sections in any one area. In music, for example, students needing special training in some aspect of music fundamentals could be grouped for intensive work, during a whole period

or part of a period, with one instructor, while the remainder of the students, not deficient in that aspect of music, could devote the time to some profitable activity with the other instructor.

Under such a system each department kept its identity while the subject matter of all areas became fused.

In 1951 a major change in the schedule occurred. A weekly one-hour seminar was added to unify the course through "discussion of the nature of art and relationship between the arts, through shared experience of art forms."

During December, 1947, and January, 1948, joint meetings of all groups were held to plan a mid-year trip to New York City. Originally planned on a voluntary basis, the trip had become, by 1952, a required part of the course. The freshman class, as a whole, spent most of a week visiting art museums, attending concerts, musicals and dramatic productions, visiting the United Nations and other places of cultural and historic importance. Students were assigned work sheets which required written reports and evaluations of the art, music and dramatic presentations.

The New York Trip was so successful that it remained the sole feature of the Expression in the Arts to continue after the course itself was dissolved. After the course was abandoned, the New York trip was opened to all college students on a voluntary basis and approximately 400 have continued to participate annually. Purpose of the trip has remained as originally designed. Dr. Patience Haggard, one of the originators of the Expression in the Arts course, said in January, 1962:

The trip is designed as a learning experience in the arts of music, drama, painting and sculpture. . . .
The purpose we jealously cherish is that they [students] feel the wonder, awe and exaltation as they contemplate significant works of art—all in the effort to help them to become perceptive adults with enduring interests that will not fail them in offering them satisfaction.

Evaluation of students was made by instructors in individual departments and a separate grade recorded by the registrar for each course in the three areas. Some of the items considered in student evaluation indicate the content of the course:

Attitude: persistent effort to develop open-mindedness and an understanding of the intention of the artist; awareness of current reviews and criticism; attendance at dramatic productions, exhibits and concerts; initiative in calling attention to material in the press and periodicals concerning art and artists; sincere effort to become honest and discerning critics of art; willingness to experiment with new techniques in artistic expression.

Participation in class discussion: comments, questions, expressions of personal point of view with complete honesty and fairness. Readiness to admit change in point of view if a change comes about.

Interest: Class and seminar hours will be devoted to work of importance for which undivided attention is expected. A student's plan for the building of a personal library of literature, criticism, music, records and prints indicate his interest in the arts.

Improvement, growth, receptivity to new ideas, sensitivity to suggestion, eagerness to listen to a foreign language if a film happens to offer one, readiness to use imagination.

The course was very popular among students and faculty; it was "a delightfully effective way to open the student's mind to creative thinking and to aesthetic ideas." But its enemy was growth of the college. When the Expression in the Arts was initiated it was designed for a freshman class of not more than 200 students. This number could be accommodated in small classes or as a large seminar. As the student body grew and the size of the freshman class expanded in proportion, it became unmanageable. The faculty load, in terms of students to serve and time needed to collaborate and adequately plan an integrated course, became onerous, and, in addition, it became increasingly more difficult to find a solution to the problems of scheduling. Physical conditions brought about by dispersion of the college in vacating the old campus and occupying the new added to the confusion and problem of integrating three departments. As Dr. Crumb stated: "The idea couldn't withstand what you might call the academic bureaucracy of that large a departmental structure. We got too big." [7]

Teaching foreign language in the public elementary schools of the United States was pioneered at Potsdam by Dr. C. W. Snyder, former Chairman of the foreign language department and now Director of Liberal Studies. The program was inaugurated in 1948 in the Congdon Campus School with 60 children participating in the original project. By 1957, 750 children were engaged in learning a second language. A unique feature of the program was the emphasis placed on the teaching of a second language at the kindergarten level. This program was conducted with the following objectives in mind:

1. To show children and parents that learning to speak another language can be an interesting and enriching educational experience.
2. To familiarize the child with the culture of another people.
3. To stimulate an early interest in the communicative processes and to stimulate the thought processes.
4. To relate the work in the foreign language with the regular school work in English, art, music, etc.
5. To introduce a vocabulary of words and phrases related to daily activities in the home, school and community.

The procedure followed appears below:

1. Foreign languages introduced to all children in the kindergarten.

2. French and Spanish introduced in alternate years.
3. Children continue with same language through the eighth grade.
4. Emphasis on the oral-aural or conversational approach.
5. Children learn language through repetition of teacher's model.
6. Repetition varied through the use of games, songs, dialogues, simple skits, poems, etc.
7. Hearing and speaking stressed through fourth grade.
8. Reading introduced in fifth grade. Reading is based on simple stories already familiar to the children.
9. Grammar taught inductively without any explanation until seventh or eighth grades.
10. Records, tapes, language laboratory listening posts occasionally used to give students an opportunity to hear themselves and to hear another person speaking the language.[8]

Notable were workshops offered during 1949 and 1950 at White Pine Camp, located in the Adirondacks. Dr. Crumb and Dr. Hosmer developed the idea of a workship designed to provide elementary teachers an opportunity for direct personal experience in the arts and to develop, among music teachers, a better understanding of the interrelationship of the arts. The approach was to be through creativity and participation, rather than by studying methods and materials. The Summer Session Bulletin issued by the college for 1949 gave the following details of the proposed workshop:

[The college] through the cooperation of Paul Smith's College, Paul Smith's, New York, will conduct at the luxurious White Pine Camp estate a summer program of study in the arts. Varied workshop programs will meet the interests and needs of classroom teachers having a minimum of experience in the arts as well as those of advanced students. It will be recalled that White Pine Camp, a short distance from Paul Smith's College, was the summer White House for President Calvin Coolidge in 1926.

Students at White Pine Camp will live on the estate and participate in a workshop program of art, music, literature, and the dance. The workshop will be under the direction of the faculty of the Potsdam . . . College, assisted by visiting professors and special lecturers of proven expertness in the arts. Registration at White Pine Camp will be limited to one hundred students.

At its White Pine Camp division in the Adirondacks, the Potsdam . . . College summer session will concentrate on the types of study which the camp, because of its particular facilities and location, is uniquely fitted to accommodate. Courses there will be conducted as workshops in the arts, with special attention to music, art, literature, and the dance. They also will be planned to meet the needs and interest of the novice as well as of persons more skilled in the craftsmanship of an art.

Students at White Pine Camp will build their program around their preferences from activities such as:

Experimenting with original expression—composing instrumental music and songs; or writing stories, poems, plays, or essays; or painting, modeling, sketching, or producing some allied form of art.

Playing or singing in musical ensembles and working with dance groups.

Conferring with instructors or guest consultants who are skilled practitioners of a particular art.

Joining groups (large or small) in discussions on the products and the problems of craftsmanship in music, art, or literature.

Helping stage musical performances and plays.

Studying important examples of their chosen art as sources of inspiration and of standards for performance and evaluation and instruction.

Participating in forum discussions on the aesthetics of music, art, literature, and allied arts.

All the activities, in addition to providing a lasting satisfaction for the participants, will be designed to increase the greatest asset which a teacher working with any art can possess—confidence in handling the art, a confidence born only of personal experiences with the medium of that art.

The workshop in the arts will be useful to music and art teachers who want further experiences in performance and interpretation in their field; to elementary teachers who wish to gain greater facility in handling colors, lines, forms, tones, notes, words, or ideas; to teachers of English of any grade level, elementary or secondary; and to any other person who, however much a novice in art, wants six weeks of experience in the arts, in a location which is ideal for the summer months.[9]

The camp program furnished rich experiences in all types of special events. There were consultants, a choir presented several concerts, the play production class performed the last act of Wilder's *Our Town,* and programs were exchanged with the students on the campus at Potsdam. Enrollment for the first year totaled 45.

Under the direction of Miss Hosmer, the workshop had on its staff instructors from various fields and areas. Faculty for the 1950 White Pine Camp included Stanley Kunitz, poet and teacher in charge of creative writing, Stanley Glowski of Yale University directing the music workshop and general seminar in the integration of the arts, Bessie Schoenberg of Sarah Lawrence College conducting courses in the dance, and other members of the College faculty in music and drama. Emphasis was on learning by doing, and the integration of the arts was stressed:

The whole philosophy of the workshop is based on doing not talking about projects. One can experience and participate in the arts without being a professional artist. We treat the arts as essential parts of living—not as remote and untouchable media. Fundamentally, we strive to help the individual to be at home in all phases of the arts in our contemporary scene.

Could not the camaraderie of the arts and the predisposition of human beings towards the arts and toward creative participation be turned to good account in the profession of teaching? And could not that camaraderie be discovered and the direct experiences be obtained most effectively in a situation which enables students to live steadily and informally with one or more of the arts?[10]

Victor E. Minotti, administrative director of the camp, pointed out some of the more evident strengths of such an experiment. The latent creativity in almost every student was brought out and he began to realize for himself values and relationships to teaching. The student was made aware of the arts, and the community living brought about a deeper understanding of people. Through participation everyone became involved in the arts. Finally, the setting itself made possible an "arts" approach to learning the living which could not be duplicated on a campus.[11]

The experiment had been successful in almost every way, but the facilities of the camp were needed for the summer programs of Paul Smith's College. Also, the necessary expense involved in the venture was more than the college at Potsdam could maintain for a relatively small group. In order to include more students in the program, it was brought to the Potsdam campus in 1951.

The same purpose and philosophy, as well as faculty, were made a part of the campus workshop. Creativity and integration were the means used to accomplish the goals:

A unique feature of the Potsdam Workshop in the Arts is the Seminar, which focuses the program by coordinating all workshop activities. The view of integration is a belief in the wholeness of the person and in the possibility of achieving ths wholeness through work in the arts.

Problems arising out of workshop activities are gathered together for exploration and discussion of creative work. These center upon the faith that all persons have a creative potential which needs opportunities and critical guidance in order to attain full development.

The entire staff participates informally in the Seminar, placing emphasis on the fundamental concepts and techniques of each of the arts, and the relationships between the arts. This plan allows for great scope and frees the specific workshops for laboratory use.[12]

In addition to the regular instructors, many guest consultants were brought to the campus to enrich the regular session as well as the workshop. Following the summer session, letters received from some of the visitors confirmed the feeling of positive results. Lilla Belle Pitts of Teachers College, Columbia University, wrote:

What I sensed in this experiment seems to me to be of more than casual interest. In fact, I am more convinced then ever that the joy of creation in any art area is fundamental in helping others to use the expressive arts more effectively in everyday life. Certainly, teachers of all people should be given every opportunity to find new meaning in both their personal and professional lives through artistic expression of many kinds.

It was obvious that those young folks in the Potsdam Workshop were finding ways into large worlds of thought and feeling through words, pictures, song, dance and other art media. What they were doing, thinking, making and *expressing* was promise of bigger and richer personalities.[13]

After the summer of 1953 the workshop, as such, was discontinued but the basic ideas were incorporated into the regular courses on the campus. Although the experiment was ended, purposes and success provided the necessary groundwork for other ventures.

A series of workshops extending from 1954 to 1964 carried on the tradition, providing expression through experience with music and stressing creative participation. Planned with a view to variety and student needs, the workshops included sessions in choral and instrumental fields and opera. In 1960 an innovation in extending the geographical limits of the summer session established a precedent. Through cooperation with the public schools of Bay Shore, New York, an instrumental workshop was conducted by Prof. Willard Musser at Bay Shore. In succeeding years other workshops were held in Bay Shore, Schenectady, and Rome, New York.

The Summer Artist Series was inaugurated in 1961. Essentially the series resembled a festival. Recitals, concerts and other events of the summer session have been brought together with professional artists to form a varied program of the arts. Films, art exhibits, lectures and dramatic production have contributed to the total program. Approximately twenty events are scheduled each year.

The opening of Star Lake Camp in the fall of 1963 marked the culmination of a long-time desire of Dr. Crumb to provide a retreat for students and faculty.

Forty miles from Potsdam, the camp, purchased and developed by the Potsdam College Development Fund, Inc., provides a permanent facility for isolated study and recreation. The setting and purposes for which the camp was designed are reminiscent of the White Pine Camp.

During the summer of 1964 the college sponsored a unique string music workshop for high school students at Star Lake Camp. The New York State Chapter of the American String Teachers Association met at the camp in conjunction with the workshop. Prof. Maurice Baritaud of the Crane department of music was musical director. In addition to other members of the Crane faculty, the Lenox String Quartet, under sponsorship of the New York State Council on the Arts, was in residence, as was Frederick Zimmermann, principal double bass of the New York Philharmonic.

Enrollment in the youth string workshop was open to junior and senior high school pupils and college students. Mr. Baritaud, who referred to chamber music as a way of life, told the 100 young musicians: "Of all the achievements of man through the ages, none better epitomizes the civilizing influence, none better represents sophisticated democracy in action than chamber music. A successful exponent of this art must himself be superior in intelligence and musicianship. He must be aware and sensitive to musical as well as the human elements of cooperative performance. He must have

227

great personal integrity, high musical ideals, yet he must be a willing follower as well as an able leader. Above all he must cherish the ability to respect and be respected." [14]

In 1965 the college expanded the program to include two annual music workshops for talented high school students—string music and an orchestral winds under Prof. Harry Phillips.

The discovery method of teaching social studies was pioneered at Potsdam by Dr. Charles Lahey, professor of history. It was first used in 1953-1954 in a New York State history course. In 1958 the college offered a seminar in North Country Life, based on this method in its summer program. In the fall of 1958 Dr. Lahey and Prof. Robert Arnold of the education department used the discovery approach in grades 7-8-9 in the college's Congdon Campus School. Miss Laura Shufelt, curriculum bureau, New York State Education Department, made the following comments on this program:

My impressions of the purposes and techniques of the Potsdam program were highly favorable. It seemed to me that the pupils are being led, not so much to learn masses of facts, but to use facts to show relationships between man and his environment and to realize that these relationships change as man reaches different levels of civilization and as the environment itself is modified. Although school had been in session only a short time, the seventh graders had made excellent progress, judging from their responses in class and from the work in their notebooks.

I was impressed with the wealth and variety of materials that had been accumulated and the aids and devices that had been created for classroom use. I realize the effort required both in finding and making these materials and in inspiring pupils to find and make them.

I hope that the techniques observed at Potsdam may be more widely used. The right use of good textbooks is certainly to be encouraged; the practice of basing the whole year's work upon a single text, which is studied and parroted back in recitations and test answers is certainly not. Children will almost inevitably come out of their school experience more adequately equipped for life if they learn to find material, to evaluate it and to reach conclusions from it by using their own powers of reasoning. We have long given lip service to the aim of teaching pupils to think. It seems as though Dr. Lahey and Mr. Arnold are endeavoring to put this aim into practice. One of the major obstacles to the use of similar procedures is the heavy burden of work on the teacher and the real challenge to his inventiveness and ingenuity. . . .[15]

Dr. O. Ward Satterlee, Director of Education, recognized the possibilities of this new method of teaching and incorporated it into the college's education curriculum. Dr. Satterlee always has been receptive to tested innovations.

The spirit of innovation and experimentation, a key element in the Potsdam tradition, was illustrated by the work of Dr. Wilmer K. Trauger, retired Chairman of the English department. Dr. Trauger joined the faculty as an instructor in English in 1927 and was promoted to chairman of the department in 1930. He flourished under the spirit of the new administration in the 1940's and 1950's.

His favorite assignment was doing something that needed to be done. Genuinely concerned with the weaknesses of the preparation of English teachers, he did something about it. In August, 1950, he held a workshop in linguistics and cultural anthropology. He continued his pioneer work in linguistics until his retirement in 1964. Dr. Trauger is still active in the development of the "new" English which is bringing about necessary reform in public school English programs.

The updating of the Potsdam tradition to meet the challenge of education in the postwar period was demonstrated by the ability of the faculty and administration to develop entire new programs and expand existing ones.

A program of graduate studies was established at Potsdam in 1947. The program for a fifth year of study for elementary and music teachers was initiated and carried out through extension courses, workshop centers, and in the regular college summer session. Faculty committees for the control of matriculation, scholarship standards and guidance were appointed to administer the graduate program.

In 1948, the Intensive Teacher Training Program was inaugurated during the summer session. This was designed to give graduates with a baccalaureate degree from accredited colleges and universities the professional background and training necessary for certification to teach in the elementary schools of New York State. This program served a useful purpose of helping to alleviate a shortage of elementary classroom teachers but was deemed unnecessary after the 1963 summer session.

Another event of significance in the development of graduate studies at Potsdam occurred during the next three years with program offerings in secondary education with specializations in English, mathematics, social studies, French, physics, chemistry, biology and geology. This brought the number of specializations in master's degree programs to a peak total of 23 during 1963.

Certain organizational changes were instituted after 1962. Dr. Kenneth A. Gant was appointed Director of Graduate Studies in September, 1963. A graduate faculty was appointed with the direction of the graduate program as a major responsibility. Detailed administration of the program was delegated to the Committee on Graduate Affairs.

The continued expansion of the program requires more than adding courses and forming curricula. An atmosphere of professionalism and scholarship, of close and rewarding intellectual contact between graduate student and faculty—these intangibles, too, are of first importance. Graduate study also requires much in the way of research facilities and contact with people of varied background. The faculty and administration are now working on plans to satisfy these needs.[16]

The inauguration of a liberal arts program at Potsdam

resulted from two developments: the local faculty's and administration's pioneer work in the early 1950's and the decision of the Board of Regents on September 29, 1961, approving the State University's plan to establish such programs. Potsdam began enrolling freshmen in the liberal arts in September, 1964.

Under the direction of Dr. Charles Snyder, the liberal arts program provides breadth as well as depth. The curriculum provides for an integrated study of civilization as it is revealed in its history, philosophy, literature, science and fine and creative arts.

Students elect for concentrated study a major in one of the following areas, providing the beginnings of a specialization: art, English, French, mathematics, music history and literature, history, social sciences, psychology, biology or geology, chemistry or physics.

In 1964–1965, ten liberal arts students had their proposed curricular patterns evaluated by schools of dentistry, schools of medicine, schools of law and other professional graduate schools. In each case the proposed programs were acceptable to the graduate school in question. Potsdam is looking forward to becoming a preprofessional training center for northern New York.[17]

The science department, under the direction of Dr. William C. Hamilton, flourished under the climate of the present central and local administrations. This was reflected in an expansion of its curriculum and facilities. In September, 1964, Stowell Hall, a laboratory building serving biology, chemistry, geology and physics was opened.

Housing more than twenty diversified laboratories on three floors, it was planned to meet the requirements of Potsdam's expanding programs in the natural sciences. Added to several conventional laboratories for each field of science, there are specialized laboratories for each of these purposes: research in the physical sciences, research in the biological sciences, nuclear and radiation studies, electron microscopy, X-ray diffraction and spectrographic studies. Potsdam was awarded $28,-620 by the National Science Foundation toward the purchase of some of this specialized equipment. Collectively, these laboratories, together with equipment in conventional laboratories, will fulfill all anticipated needs in specialized undergraduate and graduate course work, and provide equipment for undergraduate, graduate and faculty research. Much of the new specialized equipment will be used for courses in instrumentation and instrumental analysis already being offered at the college.[18] But due to the rapid growth of the science department, a second science building was under planning by 1965.

Dr. Stowell pioneered a student policy that attempted to reconcile the academic discipline of the classroom with the social discipline of campus life. The present administration realizes that the forces that are altering American life are present on campus. It has made sure that the student personnel program at Potsdam has been broadened "to help the individual student develop to the fullest, intellectually, socially, physically and spiritually, in order that the public schools may be adequately supplied with highly competent teachers." [19]

Dr. Thomas Barrington, Dean of Students, has responsibility for the following student personnel services:

1. Recruitment
2. Admissions
3. Orientation
4. Counseling
5. Attendance
6. Academic Follow-up
7. Housing
8. Food Service
9. Medical Service
10. Financial Aid
11. Registration
12. Cumulative Records
13. Extra-class Activities
14. Social Program
15. Placement and Follow-up

This comprehensive program reflects Potsdam's concern

with the total educative process. "A sound student personnel program calls for a philosophy based upon the total needs of the individual student as well as the needs of the college, the teaching profession, and society at large. The student, however intelligent, frequently needs assistance in his understanding of personal and social relationships, financial matters, as well as in the areas of the educational program. Housing, study conditions, food services, all contribute to the success of the student in the classroom, and to his intellectual and social growth." [20]

The administration believes that college life should provide opportunities for students to benefit from responsible participation. Dr. Crumb has invited students to participate in many phases of the college, "planning, not necessarily authoritatively, but with a chance to contribute." But he insists that "the faculty and administration still must control the direction of the college and the direction of the curriculum. But that doesn't mean that you can't get a lot of first-rate thinking out of students." [21]

The administration not only talks about participation but tries to live by that philosophy. The college's plans for the next ten years were first discussed with 300 interested students.

The student government program at Potsdam emphasizes student participation in different phases of college life. It is made up of the entire student body, has a responsibility for most of the the extra-class program of the college. Through its several parts, a large portion of the program is determined, financed and executed. A variety of student activities (clubs, sororities and fraternities, service groups, dormitory groups, etc.) related to the student association, but which operate independently, add to the total social, recreational and educational program of the college.

In the 1960's increased emphasis has been placed upon the fact that student government makes its largest contribution when it joins the faculty and administration in "helping to operate the total program of the college" instead of concentrating solely upon the function of protecting the student from "unreasonable encroachment" upon students' rights on the part of the professional staff.

Some of the first advice Dean Barrington gave to the freshmen in 1965 was "this year concentrate on proving yourself as a student and a person; next year you can help us write better rules and regulations." [22]

In 1946 a student-inspired movement for the return of varsity athletics got under way. Dr. Crumb gave his full support, qualified only by the understanding that the resulting program would be compatible with the academic mission of the college. An Athletic Committee was chartered and became the direct governing arm of the sports program. Students dominated the committee, with some faculty representation.

The sports program continued to expand in the 1950's and 1960's. By 1965 Potsdam was represented by teams in soccer, cross country, basketball, wrestling, baseball, golf, tennis. Athletic programs enjoy student and faculty support and the administration recognizes them as an integral part of college life. Potsdam maintains membership in the Eastern College Athletic Conference, the National Collegiate Athletic Association and the State University of New York Athletic Conference.

The challenge of the last twenty years was met by the combined efforts of the administration, faculty and students. These efforts are now part of the Potsdam tradition, because the college is molded by the tests it meets and conquers, and the record of these conquests becomes its living tradition.

Chapter Ten

THE FUTURE

DR. Samuel B. Gould, inaugurated as president of the State University of New York on May 13, 1965, extended the horizon for all fifty-eight units of the State University. In his inaugural address Dr. Gould said:

The environment of the twentieth century is not designed for the static, the stagnant, the complacent, or the smug. It is designed for men who dare greatly and dream greatly and let their work catch up with their dreams.[1]

The faculty, administration and students at Potsdam welcomed such a challenge. Said Dr. Crumb:

President Gould has placed on each college the joy and responsibility for self evaluation and increased striving for excellence, and the development of a 10-year plan for the future of Potsdam as a college of the arts and sciences. The leadership of Dr. Gould is now apparent on every campus of the university.[2]

Potsdam's future plans were first discussed with 300 interested students and each department was invited to submit its recommendations to the Curriculum Committee, which in turn submitted a proposed outline to President Crumb and the College Council.

Because of prior developmental programs in the period 1946–1965, the college has little need for curricular changes as such. Instead, emphasis will be placed on improved excellence in teaching, expansion and modernization of facilities for increased effectiveness, and the establishment of new courses, institutes and degree programs designed to meet the needs of students, faculty and the region.

Future plans reflect what is believed to be unique to Potsdam, and are an attempt to convert particular characteristics into particular strengths. The rural area in which the college is located challenges the college to expand its cultural, educational and service functions. Seldom can a small college become a cultural center for an entire area. It is equally unlikely that a college of this size can, through well-conceived and executed programs of remediation and research, improve an entire area or offer significant assistance in solving different problems. Its geographical location, however, makes it possible for the college to be very effective in advancing some improvement in some areas and in solving some problems. In addition to offering opportunities for service in projects like the North Country Learning Center, Potsdam's geographical position makes the college a natural source for such projects as a Canadian-American Studies Center. So, too, the traditional excellence and sophistication of the Crane department of music make it possible for Potsdam to offer an unusually broad program of specialties and degrees in this field, ranging from an instrument repair workshop to doctoral work.

All future programs are designed to help the college reach one or more of the following basic goals:

To provide adequate undergraduate and graduate education for qualified students.

To provide expanded community services.
To provide leadership through research.
To provide the leadership in the conservation and wise utilization of human resources.

Potsdam's immediate response to Dr. Gould's challenge has been in the best spirit of the Potsdam tradition. This challenge and response represent a fitting climax to the first 150 years of the Potsdam tradition. In 1816 the St. Lawrence Academy was founded in answer to a major challenge in American life. Initial response established a tradition emphasizing quality leadership, innovation, experimentation, and a multipurpose institution to answer the needs of an expanding democratic society.

Footnotes

CHAPTER I

[1] *St. Lawrence Academy Records* (Potsdam: Potsdam Museum), I, 9–10. Hereafter cited as *Academy Records.*

[2] George F. Miller, "The Academy System of the State of New York," *The State Department of Education, Annual Report, 1919* (Albany: The University of the State of New York, 1922), II, 91. Hereafter cited as Miller, *Academy System.*

[3] *Academy Records,* I, 9.

[4] *Ibid.,* I, 9.

[5] *Ibid.,* I, 10.

[6] *Ibid.,* I, 10.

[7] *Ibid.,* I, 11–13.

[8] Miller, *Academy System,* p. 91.

[9] *Academy Records,* I, 9, 15, 22, *passim.*

[10] *Ibid.,* I, 15.

[11] *Remarks on the Settlement of New Lands in General Compared with the Measures Adopted for this Purpose in the County of St. Lawrence* (New York: Printed by Day and Turner, 1818), p. 1. Hereafter cited as *Remarks on Settlement.*

[12] *Ibid.,* p. 3.

[13] Frank B. Hough, *A History of St. Lawrence and Franklin Counties* (Albany: Little & Co., 1853), pp. 433–434.

[14] *Cursory Remarks on the Settlement of the County of St. Lawrence* (New York: Printed by Day and Turner, 1818), p. 2.

[15] Luther H. Gulick, Jr., Charles Lahey and Carleton Mabie, *The St. Lawrence Valley—Avenue of History* (Gouverneur: Printed by Mason Rossiter Smith, Inc., 1964), pp. 18–19. Cited hereafter as *Avenue of History.*

[16] Horatio Gates Spafford, *A Gazetteer of the State of New York* (Albany: H. C. Southwick, 1813), p. 276.

[17] *Academy Records,* I, 5, 15.

[18] Jessie J. McNall. *Sesquicentennial History of the First Presbyterian Church of Potsdam, New York,* pp. 1–3. Cited hereafter as McNall, *A History.*

[19] *Lands in the County of St. Lawrence, State of New York.* A brochure describing lands in St. Lawrence County. This was produced in 1818 at a meeting of Federalist landlords in New York City. A copy of this may be found in the County Historian's Office, Canton, St. Lawrence County.

20 *Avenue of History*, pp. 9, 19–20.
21 Carlton E. Sanford, *Early History of the Town of Hopkinton* (Boston: The Barlett Press, 1903), pp. 270–271.
22 *Academy Records*, I, 3.
23 *Ibid.*, I, 4–5.
24 *Ibid.*, I, 6. The original charter is in the Potsdam Museum, Potsdam, New York.
25 *Ibid*, I, 15–56, *passim*.
26 *Ibid.*, I, 22–29, *passim*.
27 *Ibid.*, I, 19, 23.
28 Horatio Gates Spafford, *A Gazetteer of the State of New York* (Albany: B. O. Packard, 1824), pp. 424–425.
29 *Ibid.*, p. 425.
30 *Ibid.*, p. 424.
31 *Academy Records*, I, 27.
32 *Ibid.*, I, 23, 68.
33 *Ibid.*, I, 15, 38, 45.
34 *Ibid.*, I, 27.
35 *Ibid.*, I, 64. Actually there were two appropriations of $2,500. On April 9, 1825, the state granted the trustees $2,500 out of the proceeds of the sale of "certain" lands. On April 1, 1826, the state granted another $2,500 out of the state treasury.
36 *Ibid.*, I, 62.
37 *Ibid.*, I, 49.
38 This is a copy of the actual plaque now located on Union Street, Potsdam, New York.
39 *Academy Records*, I, 15–72, *passim*.
40 Miller, *Academy System*, pp. 169–170
41 *Academy Records*, I, 67–72.
42 *Ibid.*, I, 68–69.
43 *Ibid.*, I, 68–69.

CHAPTER II

1 *Academy Records*, I, 85–86.
2 *Annual Report of the Regents of the University of the State of New York*, 1845, pp. 144–145. Cited hereafter as *Regents Report*.
3 Miller, *Academy System*, p. 202.
4 *Academy Records*, I, 103.
5 *Ibid.*, p. 110.
6 *Ibid.*, p. 114.
7 *Regents Report*, 1834, p. 61.
8 *Ibid.*, p. 7.
9 *Academy Records*, I, 118.
10 *Ibid.*, p. 129.
11 *Ibid.*, p. 129. Eventually this lecture and demonstration met for one hour per day.
12 Miller, *Academy System*, p. 202.
13 Thomas E. Finegan, *Teacher Training Agencies* (Albany: The University of the State of New York, 1917), p. 26.

Footnotes

14 *Ibid.*, pp. 29–30.
15 *Regents Report*, 1935, p. 4.
16 Finegan, *Teacher Training Agencies*, p. 31.
17 *Catalogue of the Trustees, Officers and Students of St. Lawrence Academy, 1935*, pp. 13–15.
18 *Regents Report*, 1835, p. 102.
19 *Academy Records*, I, 161.
20 *Ibid.*, I, 157, 179.
21 *Ibid.*, I, 121.
22 *Ibid.*, I, 165, 184.
23 *Ibid.*, I, 212.
24 Finegan, *Teacher Training Agencies*, p. 37.
25 *Ibid.*, p. 40.
26 *Ibid.*, p. 41.
27 Miller, *Academy System*, p. 213.
28 *Regents Report*, 1838–1839, p. 121.
29 George H. Sweet, *St. Lawrence Academy, 1816–1869* (Potsdam: August 3, 1916), pp. 9–10.
30 See p. 2, Chapter I.
31 See *Historical Statistics of the United States, Colonial Times to 1957.*
32 *Census of the State of New York for 1845* (Albany: Carroll and Cook, 1846), No. 48–1.
33 *Ibid.*, No. 48–2.
34 *Ibid.*, No. 48–5.
35 *Ibid.*, No. 48–5.
36 McNall, *A History*, pp. 3–4.
37 Miller, *Academy System*, p. 170.
38 *Ibid.*, p. 171.
39 *Regents Reports*, 1831, pp. 7–8.
40 *Academy Records*, I, 146.
41 *Ibid.*, 123, 128–129.
42 *Academy Records*, I, 156.
43 *Regents Reports*, 1831–1836, *passim.*
44 *Academy Records*, I, 170.
45 *Regents Reports*, 1831–1836, *passim.*
46 *Regents Report*, 1835, p. 94.
47 *Regents Report*, 1844, p. 145.
48 *Catalogue of the Trustees, Officers and Students of St. Lawrence Academy, 1935*, pp. 12–13.
49 *Academy Records*, I, 161.
50 *Ibid.*, p. 277.
51 Oliver Goldsmith, *The Deserted Village.*
52 *Regents Report*, 1834, p. 61.
53 *Regents Report*, 1835, pp. 93–95.
54 *Ibid.*, pp. 91, 93.
55 *Ibid.*, p. 93.
56 *Ibid.*, p. 101.
57 *Ibid.*, pp. 101–102.
58 *Ibid.*, p. 103.
59 *Academy Records*, I, 52–56, *passim.*

CHAPTER III

1 Finegan, *Teacher Training Agencies,* p. 38.
2 Miller, *Academy System,* pp. 207–208.
3 *Ibid.,* p. 208.
4 *Ibid.,* p. 208.
5 *Ibid.,* pp. 208–209.
6 *Ibid.,* p. 209.
7 *Ibid.,* p. 210.
8 *Ibid.,* p. 210.
9 *Memorial of the Trustees of St. Lawrence Academy to the State Legislature.*
10 Miller, *Academy System,* p. 212.
11 *Memorial of the Trustees.*
12 *Ibid.*
13 *Ibid.*
14 *Ibid.*
15 *Ibid.*
16 *Ibid.*
17 *Ibid.*
18 Miller, *Academy System,* p. 220.
19 George H. Sweet, *St. Lawrence Academy, 1816–1869,* p. 9.
20 Miller, *Academy System,* pp. 220–221.
21 *Ibid.,* p. 223.
22 *Ibid.,* p. 225.
23 *Ibid.,* p. 225.
24 *Ibid.,* p. 226.
25 Finegan, *Teacher Training Agencies,* p. 54.
26 *Ibid.,* pp. 81–84.
27 *Ibid.,* p. 87.
28 *Ibid.,* pp. 88–90.
29 *Ibid.,* pp. 91–92.
30 *Ibid.,* p. 92.
31 *Ibid.,* p. 104.
32 *Ibid.,* pp. 105–106.
33 George H. Sweet, *State Normal and Training School, Potsdam, New York,* p. 2.
34 *Ibid.,* p. 2.
35 *Ibid.,* p. 3.
36 *The Normal Magazine,* XXIII (April, 1917), 36–37.
37 Sweet, *State Normal and Training School,* p. 3.
38 *Ibid.,* p. 4.
39 *Potsdam Courier Freeman,* July 2, 1868.
40 *Ibid.,* April 8, 1869.
41 *Records of the Local Board of the Normal and Training School at Potsdam, Book A,* p. 1.
42 Sweet, *State Normal and Training School,* p. 5.
43 Helen M. Hosmer, *The Musical Heritage of the North Country,* December 21, 1933, pp. 1–6.
44 William Dolan Claudson, *The History of the Crane Department of Music, The State University of New York College at Potsdam* (Evanston, Illinois: Northwestern University, August, 1965), p. 52. This is an unpublished doctoral dissertation. Cited hereafter as Claudson, *Crane Department.*
45 *Academy Records,* I, 107.
46 *Ibid.,* I, 268.

Footnotes

CHAPTER IV

1 Hamilton Child, *Gazetteer and Business Directory of St. Lawrence County, N. Y. for 1873-4* (Syracuse: Printed at the Journal Office, 1873), pp. 315-325.
2 *Census of the State of New York, 1865* (Albany: Charles vanBenthuysen, 1867), pp. 354-361; 416-417; 498-511.
3 *Census of the State of New York, 1875* (Albany: Weed, Parsons and Company, 1877), pp. 374-379; 418; 435.
4 Child, *Gazetteer and Business Directory*, pp. 315-325.
5 *The Normal Magazine*, XIII (May, 1909), 45.
6 *Ibid.*, p. 49.
7 *Ibid.*, p. 48.
8 *Ibid.*, p. 45.
9 *Ibid.*, p. 45.
10 *New York State Normal Schools, Entrance Examination, February, 1893.*
11 Dorothy Rogers, *Oswego: Fountainhead of Teacher Education* (New York: Appleton-Century-Crofts, Inc., 1961), pp. 5-6.
12 *Ibid.*, p. 7.
13 *Ibid.*, pp. 7-8.
14 *First Quarto-Centennial History, Normal School, Potsdam, N. Y., 1869-1894*, p. 34.
15 *Ibid.*, p. 34.
16 *Ibid.*, p. 36.
17 *Ibid.*, p. 36; *Records of the Local Board of the Normal and Training School*, p. 30.
18 *Circular of the State Normal and Training School at Potsdam, New York, 1870.*
19 *First Quarto-Centennial History*, pp. 40-41.
20 *Ibid.*, p. 41.
21 *Ibid.*, p. 44.
22 *Ibid.*, p. 44.
23 *Ibid.*, p. 44.
24 *Ibid.*, pp. 40-41.
25 *Ibid.*, p. 41.
26 *Ibid.*, pp. 41-42.
27 *Ibid.*, pp. 39-40.
28 *Ibid.*, p. 44.
29 *Ibid.*, p. 45.
30 *Ibid.*, p. 42.
31 *Courier-Freeman*, July 4, 1894.
32 *The Normal Magazine*, XIII (May, 1909), 46.
33 *Ibid.*, XXIII (May, 1927), 23.
34 *Ibid.*, p. 23.
35 *Ibid.*, XIII (May, 1909), 47.
36 *The Normal Magazine*, VIII (June, 1904), 24.
37 *Ibid.*, p. 9.
38 *Ibid.*, p. 11.
39 *Ibid.*, p. 14.
40 *Ibid.*, pp. 14-15.
41 *Ibid.*, p. 17.
42 *Ibid.*, p. 18.
43 *Circular of the State Normal and Training School at Potsdam, New York, 1870.*

44 Finegan, *Teacher Training Agencies,* p. 126.
45 *Ibid.,* p. 127.
46 *Ibid.,* p. 127.
47 *Ibid.,* p. 128.

CHAPTER V

1 *The Normal Magazine,* XIII (May, 1909), 35–36.
2 *Ibid.,* XIII (July, 1909), 22.
3 *Ibid.,* pp. 21–22.
4 *Ibid.,* pp. 22–23.
5 *Secretary's Book of the Alumni Association, State Normal School,* 1873, p. 6.
6 *The Normal Magazine,* XIII (July, 1909), 24.
7 *First Quarto-Centennial History of the State Normal and Training School, Potsdam, N. Y.,* 1869–1894 (Potsdam: Elliott Fay & Sons, Printers, 1895), p. 53.
8 *Ibid.,* p. 53.
9 *Circular of the State Normal and Training School at Potsdam,* 1890.
10 *The Normal Magazine,* I (May, 1897), 23.
11 *Ibid.,* p. 24.
12 *Ibid.,* p 24.
13 *The Normal Magazine,* XIII (July, 1909), 22.
14 *Ibid.,* p. 20.
15 *Ibid.,* pp. 22–23.
16 Edward W. Flagg, "Reading—A Class Room Study," *The Normal Magazine,* I (June, 1897), 8.
17 *Ibid.,* p 8.
18 *Ibid.,* p. 9.
19 *The Normal Magazine,* II (Nov., 1897), 15–16.
20 Alice A. Bristol, "The Kindergarten," *The Normal Magazine,* II (January, 1898), 6–7.
21 *Ibid.,* p. 8.
22 *Ibid.,* p. 7.
23 *Ibid.,* p. 10.
24 *Ibid.,* p. 11.
25 *The Normal Magazine,* I (April, 1897), 18.
26 *Ibid.,* p. 18.
27 *The Normal Magazine,* I (May, 1897), 24–25.
28 *The Normal Magazine,* II (January, 1898), 1.
29 *Circular of the State Normal and Training School,* 1893.
30 *The Normal Magazine,* I (June, 1897), 10.
31 *Ibid.,* pp. 10–11.
32 *Ibid.,* p. 11.
33 *Circular of the State Normal and Training School, Potsdam, New York,* 1901.
34 *The Normal Magazine,* XII (October, 1907), 29.
35 *Ibid.,* XII (December, 1907), 35.
36 *Ibid.,* p. 35.
37 *Ibid.,* XII (January, 1908), 31.
38 Louis H. Pink and Rutherford E. Delmage, *Candle in the Wilderness* (New York: Appleton-Century-Crofts, Inc., 1957), p. 170.

39 *Ibid.,* p. 170.
40 *The Normal Magazine,* XIII (July, 1909), 23.
41 *Circular of the State Normal School at Potsdam, New York, 1893.*
42 *Ibid.,* p. 13.
43 *Ibid.,* p. 14.
44 *The Normal Magazine,* XIII (July, 1909), 19.
45 *Ibid.,* p. 20.
46 *Ibid.,* p. 20.
47 *Ibid.,* p. 20.
48 *Ibid.,* (April, 1909), p. 61.
49 *Ibid.,* (January, 1909), p. 35.
50 *Ibid.,* p. 36.
51 *Ibid.,* XII (March, 1908), p. 34.
52 *Ibid.,* p. 35.
53 *Ibid.,* pp. 35–36.
54 *Ibid.,* I (March, 1897), 25.
55 *Ibid.,* XXXIII (May, 1927), 7.
56 *Ibid.,* X (November, 1905), 22.
57 *Ibid.,* XIII (July, 1909), 23–24.
58 *The Normal Magazine,* I (April, 1897), 14–15.
59 *The Normal Magazine,* XIII (July, 1909), 23.
60 *Ibid.,* p. 24.

CHAPTER VI

1 Julia E. Crane, "History of the Institute," *The Yearbook,* Potsdam Normal School, 1918, p. 17.
2 *Ibid.,* p. 17.
3 *Ibid.,* p. 17.
4 *Ibid.,* p. 18.
5 *Circular of the State Normal School, Potsdam, New York, 1903.*
6 *New York Press,* Aug. 5, 1901.
7 Crane, *The Yearbook,* 1918, p. 19.
8 *Ibid.,* p. 19.
9 *Ibid.,* p. 20.
10 Julia E. Crane, "The Relation of the Professional Musician to School Music," *Papers and Proceedings of the Music Teachers National Association* (Poughkeepsie, New York, 1912), p. 108.
11 Julia E. Crane, "The Training of the Music Supervisor," *Journal of Proceedings of the Twelfth Annual Meeting of the Music Supervisors National Conference* (St. Louis, Missouri, 1929), p. 84.
12 Julia E. Crane, "The Ultimate Ends of School Music," *The Music Bulletin,* I (June, 1915), 12–13.
13 Julia E. Crane, "A Talk," *Official Report of the Nineteenth Annual Meeting of the Music Teachers National Association* (New York, 1897), p. 124.
14 Julia E. Crane, "A Standard Course as Outlined by the Educational Council," *Journal of Proceedings of Fifteenth Annual Meeting of the Music Supervisors National Conference* (Nashville, Tennessee, 1922), pp. 49–50.

15 Julia E. Crane, "The Value of Music in Education," *Herald Recorder* (Potsdam, New York), January 18, 1899.
16 Julia E. Crane, "Is Correlation a Fad?", *The Normal Magazine*, II (May, 1898), 5.
17 Julia E. Crane, "Training in Sight Singing and Song Interpretation Which Normal School Students Should Receive," *National Education Association*, XLI (Boston, 1903), 691–692.
18 Crane, "Is Correlation a Fad?", pp. 5–6.
19 Crane, "Training in Sight Singing," pp. 692–693.
20 Interview with Dr. Helen M. Hosmer, July 23, 1964.
21 Julia E. Crane, *Music Teachers Manual* (Potsdam: Herald Recorder Press, 1923), p. 7.
22 *Tribute to Julia Etta Crane* (Potsdam: State University Teachers College, 1952), p. 3.
23 Crane, *Music Teachers Manual*, pp. 44–45.
24 *Utica Press*, July 7, 1899.
25 Crane, *Music Teachers Manual*, pp. 59–60.
26 Julia E. Crane, "The Ultimate Ends of School Music," *The Music Bulletin*, I (June, 1915), 14.
27 Interview with Dr. Helen M. Hosmer, July 23, 1964.
28 Julia E. Crane, "Report of Public School Conference," *Papers and Proceedings of Music Teachers National Association* (New York, 1907), pp. 102–103.
29 Julia E. Crane, "Some Mistakes of the Music Teacher Which the Viewpoint of the Child Would Correct," *National Education Association*, XLIX (San Francisco, 1911), 794–795.
30 Julia E. Crane, "The Relation of the Professional Musician to School Music," *Papers and Proceedings of the Music Teachers National Association* (Poughkeepsie, New York, 1912), pp. 104–105.
31 Crane, "The Training of the Music Supervisor," p. 84.
32 Julia E. Crane, "Crane Normal Institute of Music," *The Normal Magazine*, XVI (March, 1912), 21–23.
33 *Ibid.*, p. 21.
34 Julia E. Crane, "Crane Normal Institute of Music," *The Normal Magazine*, XVIII (December, 1913), 17–18.
35 *Circular of the State Normal School at Potsdam*, 1912.
36 *Ibid.*, 1903.
37 *Ibid.*, 1911.
38 *Ibid.*, 1916.
39 *Ibid.*
40 *Ibid.*
41 Interview with Dr. Helen M. Hosmer, July 23, 1964.
42 *Circulars of the State Normal School at Potsdam*.
43 *Courier-Freeman*, October 9, 1907.

CHAPTER VII

1 See Irving Kustol, "The 20th Century Began in 1945," *The New York Times Magazine*, May 2, 1965.
2 Potsdam *Herald Recorder*, January 26, 1923.

Footnotes

3 Frank L. Cubley to Frank Graves, Commissioner of Education.

4 Lewis D. Dewey to stock subscribers, September 3, 1924.

5 Claudson, *Crane Department*, p. 161.

6 Frank L. Cubley to Harry Ingram, January 12, 1925.

7 Claudson, *Crane Department*, p. 164.

8 *The Normal Magazine*, XXVII (January, 1921), 6.

9 Rosabel Parker, "The Modern School Life at Normal," *Normal Magazine*, XXVI (October, 1919), 25–26.

10 *The Normal Magazine*, XXVIII (October, 1921), 7.

11 *Ibid.*, p. 7.

12 *Ibid.*, p. 9.

13 Dorothy Klein, *A Brief History of Potsdam State Teachers College*, p. 6.

14 *Ibid.*, pp. 6–7.

15 Claudson, *Crane Department*, p. 174.

16 *Ibid.*, p. 174.

17 *Ibid.*, p. 175.

18 Marie Schuette to Randolph T. Congdon, January 10, 1929.

19 Joan Foster, "When Music Spells Play," *Musical Digest*, XIII (August, 1928), 46.

20 *Ibid.*, pp. 46–47.

21 Potsdam *Herald Recorder*, October 16, 1925.

22 *Adirondack Musical Festival Bulletin*, August 1, 1927.

23 Claudson, *Crane Department*, p. 194.

24 *Ibid.*, pp. 194–195.

25 *Minutes of the Experimental Group*, October 24, 1933.

26 Helen M. Hosmer to Dr. Hermann Cooper, February, 1931.

27 *The New York Times*, December 16, 1936.

28 Helen M. Hosmer, talk before the Crane Department, December 9, 1937.

29 Potsdam *Herald Recorder*, April 26, 1941.

30 Helen M. Hosmer, "Spring Festival," *The Review* (Potsdam: Student publication, May, 1954), p. 8.

31 Potsdam *Herald Recorder*, May 16, 1939.

32 Doda Conrad to Helen Hosmer, February 1, 1941.

33 Nadia Boulanger to Helen Hosmer, February 18, 1941.

34 Charlotte Kellogg to Dr. Lehman, April 14, 1941.

35 *Catalog of the Potsdam State Normal School*, 1922–1923.

36 *Ibid.*, pp. 17–18.

37 *Ibid.*, p. 23.

38 *Catalog of the Potsdam State Normal School*, 1927–1928.

39 *Ibid.*, pp. 35–36.

40 *Ibid.*, p. 35.

41 *Ibid.*, p. 32.

42 *Ibid.*, p. 40.

43 *The Normal Racquette*, December 12, 1929.

44 *Catalog of the Potsdam State Normal School*, 1927–1928.

45 *Ibid.*, p. 30.

46 Hermann Cooper, "Education of Tomorrow's Teachers," *New York State Education*, October, 1934, pp. 7–10, quoted in *The Professional Preparation of Elementary Teachers in State University of New York*, p. 2.

47 *The Normal Racquette*, May 23, 1929. The State Education Department applied the term rural to any school under the supervision of a district superintendent.

48 *Ibid.*
49 *Ibid.*
50 *Catalog of State Normal School, Potsdam, New York,* 1938–1939.
51 *The Normal Racquette,* June 7, 1934.
52 *Ibid.,* September 24, 1927.
53 Interview with Dr. Wilmer Trauger, May, 1965.
54 *The Normal Racquette,* April 2, 1927.
55 *Catalog of Potsdam State Normal School,* 1927–1928.
56 *The Normal Racquette,* April 2, 1927.
57 *Ibid.,* June 7, 1934.
58 *Ibid.,* June 7, 1934.
59 Thomas P. North, "Hall of Fame for an Amazing Coach," *Clarkson Tech Alumnus,* April, 1961, pp. 44–45.
60 *The Normal Racquette,* June 7, 1934.
61 *Ibid.,* February 5, 1931.
62 *Catalog of the State Teachers College, Potsdam, New York,* 1945–1946.

CHAPTER VIII

1 Claudson, *Crane Department,* p. 264.
2 *Ibid.,* p. 318.
3 *Watertown Daily Times,* May 31, 1949.
4 Thorton Wilder to Helen Hosmer, June 1, 1949.
5 "Potsdam's Festival," *Newsweek,* XXXVII (May 28, 1951), 85.
6 Dr. Frederick W. Crumb to Helen Hosmer, May 29, 1953.
7 Claudson, *Crane Department,* p. 329.
8 Eleanor Roosevelt, "My Day," distributed by the United Feature Syndicate, *Watertown Daily Times,* May 9, 1955.
9 Claudson, *Crane Department,* p. 332.
10 *Ibid.,* pp. 332–333.
11 *Ibid.,* p. 337.
12 *Ibid.,* p. 339.
13 *Ibid.,* p. 311.
14 *Ibid.,* p. 312.
15 *Ibid.,* pp. 346–347.
16 *Ibid.,* p. 347.
17 *Ibid.,* pp. 349–350.
18 *Ibid.,* p. 352.
19 *Ibid.,* pp. 354–355.
20 *Ibid.,* p. 363.
21 *Ibid.,* pp. 369–370.
22 *Ibid.,* p. 361.
23 *Ibid.,* p. 366.
24 *Ibid.,* p. 367.
25 *Ibid.,* p. 370.
26 *Ibid.,* p. 353.
27 *Ibid.,* p. 358.
28 *Ibid.,* pp. 372–373.

Footnotes

CHAPTER IX

1 Interview with Dr. Frederick W. Crumb, July 21, 1965.
2 *Ibid.*
3 *Ibid.*
4 *Report Prepared for Commission on Institutions of Higher Education Middle States Association of Colleges and Secondary Schools and the National Council for Accreditation of Teacher Education and the National Association of Schools of Music* by the State University College at Potsdam, New York, December 15, 1961. Hereafter cited as *Accreditation Report, 1961*, p. 125.
5 *Ibid.*, pp. 118–119.
6 *1963–1964 Report Prepared for Commission on Institution of Higher Education Middle States Association of Colleges and Secondary Schools*, pp. 1–2.
7 Claudson, *Crane Department*, pp. 276–282.
8 C. W. Snyder, "Experiment in Teaching Russian in Grade 3," *School and Society*, Vol. 86 (October 11, 1958), pp. 353–354.
9 Claudson, *Crane Department*, pp. 304–305; *Potsdam State Teachers College, Summer, 1949*.
10 *Ibid*, p. 306.
11 *Ibid.*, p. 306.
12 *Ibid.*, pp. 307–308.
13 *Ibid.*, pp. 308–309.
14 *Ibid.*, pp. 315–316.
15 Charles Lahey and Robert L. Arnold, *A Proposal for the Development of the Discovery Approach to the Teaching of Social Studies, First Edition* (Potsdam, 1962), p. 39.
16 Dr. Kenneth A. Gant, "Graduate Studies at Potsdam," *Alumni Bulletin, State University College at Potsdam* (March, 1965), p. 11.
17 Dr. Charles Snyder, "Liberal Arts at Potsdam," *Ibid.*, p. 14.
18 Dr. W. G. Hamilton, "The Sciences at Potsdam," *Ibid.*, p. 6.
19 *The Student Personnel Program in the Teachers Colleges of the State University of New York*, December, 1958, p. 4.
20 *Ibid.*
21 Interview with Dr. Frederick W. Crumb, July 21, 1965.
22 An address to the Class of 1969, September 30, 1965.

CHAPTER X

1 Dr. Samuel B. Gould, "A Fine Steel Wire of Truthfulness," *State University Newsletter*, XIII Sp 2 (May 28, 1965).
2 Interview with Dr. Frederick W. Crumb, October 5, 1965.

Index

Index

Industrial patterns, 7, 9, 15, 16, 37, 38, 74, 75–76
Ingram, Harry, 154
Intensive Teacher Training Program, 230
Inter-sorority council, 187

Jacksonian democracy, 5, 20, 21, 23–24, 37, 39
Johnson, Rev. James, 10, 19
Jones, Margaret E., 81

Kindergarten, 109–111

Lahey, W. Charles, 228–229
Lewis, Mylon, 68
Liberal studies, 214–215, 230–231
Literary societies, 94, 118–119
Literature lots, 2, 12, 14, 15, 17
Little, D. H., 62

MacVicar, Malcolm, 77, 78, 80, 81–82; qualities of a teacher, 86–89; program, 89; method courses, 89–90; student regulations, 91–92; student life, 92–93; student organizations, 94; discipline, 92–93, 94–96
Manual training, 105–106
Marcy, Governor William, 55, 62
Master's Program. *See* Graduate Studies
Mathematics, 41, 210
Maxcy, John, 161, 187–188
May Festival, 171–173. *See also* Spring Festival of the Arts
McIntyre, Catherine, 73
Merritt, General Edwin A., 65–66, 123
Method courses, 25–26, 46–50, 86, 87–88, 89–90, 90, 124, 133–135, 145, 146–147, 181–182, 184, 204–206
Methodist Church, 15, 39, 67

Minotti, Victor E., 225
Music building, 192
Musical heritage of North Country, 68–73
Musser, Willard, 226

New Normal Building, 66–67, 155–156
New York Concerts, Carnegie Hall, 175–178, 199–200
New York State School Music Association, 202–203
New York Trip, 219–220
Nixon, Nahum, 4, 14
Normal School movement, 54–55, 59–60, 61–65
Norse, Stanbury, 111–112
North Academy, 17–18
Northern New York Musical Association, 70–73

Object teaching, 81, 83, 85, 89, 90, 107
Oswego Normal School, 80, 89

Parish, David, 1, 13, 16
Partridge, Samuel, 18, 73
Petition to Board of Regents, 12
Phillips, Harry, 228
Physical education, 61, 93–94, 112–113
Pitts, Lilla Belle, 226
Potsdam, N.Y., Town of, 6, 9, 16, 18, 38; Village of, 7, 9, 15, 38
Potsdam Normal School Board of Trustees, 67–68, 124–125
Potsdam spirit, 119–120
Potsdam tradition, 22, 25, 52–53, 77, 99–100, 102, 121–122, 123, 129, 130, 143, 150, 151, 153, 159, 162, 165, 171, 173–174, 178, 179–180, 182, 185, 186, 190, 213, 214, 217, 229, 232–233, 234, 237